AF482523

CREATIVE FINANCING

HOW TO WRITE

1001

PURCHASE OFFERS SELLERS CAN'T RESIST

BY DAVE DEL DOTTO

© Copyright 1989 by Dave Del Dotto
Published by Stanford Pubublishing

stanfordpub.com

TABLE OF CONTENTS

ABOUT THE AUTHOR

Dave Del Dotto entered construction work after attending the University of Arizona. Eight years later, he found himself dreaming of a better life than hanging drywall for long hours, coming home exhausted, and never having the time or money to do what he really wanted for himself and his family.

In pursuit of his dreams, he sought fresh challenges and greater opportunities in real estate. He began his new career in 1979—only a few weeks before interest rates began to skyrocket toward 21 percent, and the real estate market went into a prolonged slide. Many people were unable to buy homes, and many agents and brokers went out of business.

As a new agent, Dave had an advantage over those with more experience. Before rising interest forced massive changes on the industry, everything had remained unchanged for years: low interest, and conventional lending practices. Real estate brokerages and banks were nice, conservative money trees for their owners. Those who worked in the field weren't interested in doing deals any way except the "way it's always been done."

This obsolete thinking didn't hold Dave back. Instead, he was able to analyze the problems of buying and selling in a totally changed market with a fresh and open mind. Far from being discouraged, he went to work looking for "the way it *can* be done."

He succeeded. Dave became widely known for his innovative, creative techniques.

In 1982, responding to popular demand, he wrote his first book, the classic *Creative Financing: 101 Purchase Offers Sellers Can't Resist*. He has his own TV show, has been a guest on numerous national radio and TV programs, and has given countless seminars all across the nation. He has continued to write books, and has produced a series of educational tapes, all available from the International Corporation for Financial Security, Inc.

Today, Dave lives in a million-plus dollar house on the beach in Hawaii, owns property in many states, has established the Dave Del Dotto Real Estate Executive Club for advanced investors, and is involved in a number of multi-million dollar projects.

He went for his dreams, and made them come true.

CHAPTER 1

HOW REAL ESTATE MAKES MONEY

S ometimes people come up to me at seminar intermissions and ask, "Say Dave, how to do you make money buying and selling real estate?" Well, it would be easy to say that I've just been telling them exactly that for the last few hours—but what they're really saying is that they don't understand some or, occasionally, *all* of the ways that owning real estate creates wealth. I've been doing it so long it all seems obvious to me; as basic as, there's air, so I breathe, and there's real estate, so I make money. But it isn't that obvious to everyone.

Now, chances are you have a good idea of some of the ways real estate can make you rich, but I'll bet there are some you haven't thought of. So I'll begin with a few pages about the basic principles of real estate wealth creation.

We normally talk about "buying" property, but what we are really doing is buying with a loan, so the bank "owns" that part of the property covered by the loan. What we actually do is *control* the title to the property, so that when the property is sold we make the profits, not the bank.

I use "buying" and "controlling" pretty much interchangeably. But it may help you to think of "controlling" the property rather than "buying," because we don't "buy," in the sense of paying the full price in cash out of our own pockets, as we would when buying a pair of shoes. In real estate investment, controlling property with the least amount of our own money is the name of the game.

There's more than one way to play the game.

GAME STRATEGIES

You can buy a property and hold it for a number of years, and then sell it.

When you do this, you expect the property to increase in value, because property has, historically, always increased in value, and so it should be worth more in five years, or ten or twenty, than it was when you bought it. You also expect to take income tax deductions for your loan interest and property taxes.

This is the simple, basic way of making money, and it is what we all do when we buy our own home. It's the good old American Dream.

For an investor, this is a slow way to make money, and it requires spending money for payments and maintenance. And where will the money for maintenance and payments come from? If it comes out of the investor's pocket, he or she has a problem.

If an investor feels that a property will gain enough value to be worth holding on to, he or she needs a way to control the title to the property with no money out of pocket and preferably money coming in. That's where buying with no money down, or as little as possible down, is important.

The simplest way to cover ongoing expenses is to rent or lease the property for more than the cost of payments, taxes, expenses, and maintenance. That means you make money while you own the property and make more money when you sell it.

It isn't always so simple.

What about a property you can buy, but can't rent for enough to cover the expenses of owning?

There are two ways to deal with that. One is the lease option, the other is equity sharing. (My book *Equity Sharing* is part of the Cash Flow package.) Both methods are ways to cover the expense of controlling real estate that costs more than you could charge in rent.

NINE KEY CONCEPTS

Now, stop and think about what I've just said. You have, in the preceding few paragraphs, the key concepts of making money in real estate. I talked about buying with the bank's money, buying with no money down (or as little as possible) and paying the bank and every other expense with payments from renters, lease optioners, or equity sharers. So:

1. Control the title to property.

2. Do it using other people's money, not your own. (This is called "leverage.") Use as little of your own money as possible.

3. Let other people's money make the payments and pay the bills.

4. Sell at a profit.

Now, is that complicated? Not at all.

That's the simplest, basic way to wealth.

Suppose you want to make money faster.

Okay.

The basic principles still apply.

Instead of buying a property which you plan on holding for a number of years, buy one you can sell at once, for a profit.

I call this "buying wholesale and selling retail."

Where do you find such properties? You can do it simply by careful selection of the properties you buy, by buying with favorable financing, by buying foreclosures and tax sale property, or by buying properties which will be worth much more than their purchase price if you fix them up. I'll talk about those methods in coming chapters, too.

Two more basic principles:

5. Buy property at less than market value (wholesale).

6. Sell at retail, and do whatever is needed to make the property saleable at its true (retail) value.

You may buy property for its rental income. (Income property.) In this case, you buy on the basis that normal occupancy and rental rates will give you a profit. But *don't* buy income property if you don't expect it to be worth more than its purchase price whenever you chose to sell it.

As a beginning investor, you might use income property creatively by buying a duplex and living in one unit while the rent from the other half pays more than half the costs of the property. What you'd be doing is "making" money by reducing the cost of your own housing, while you make money in the usual way through the normal increase in value of the property and any improvements you can make.

Suppose, for example, you bought a duplex which needed repair. You live in one side, even if it amounts to "camping out," while you fix the other. Then you move into the fixed- up unit and fix the second unit. You'll be able to charge a higher rent, which will pay more of your expenses—you've got a *nice* building, now—and you've increased the value of the entire building, so you'll make more when you sell it. This works if you buy a three-, four-, or more unit building, too.

More principles:

7. If you buy property for income purposes, be sure it will produce the income you expect.

8. Always be ready to combine any of the ways you can make money. (In the duplex example, I assumed that you bought it with nothing or little down, at a "wholesale" price because it needed work; that you did as much of the repair work as possible yourself;

that by fixing it up you made it worth retail; and you used its income to reduce your own cost of housing.) Assume that most deals will be that kind of "combination of ingredients," and go into any negotiation with your creative mind wide open.

Finally, let me point out that buying raw land can do two things for you. The principles of buying improved property apply, but if you buy raw land you will pay less for it—*much* less if you follow my advice and buy it at tax sales—and it will have little or no maintenance cost and low tax expense. *How to Buy and Use Tax Sale Property* is part of the Cash Flow package. If you pick up raw land in many parts of the country, you can afford to just let it sit until its value goes up.

The other thing raw land can do is improve your financial statement.

9. Don't ignore the value of raw land.

Now, let me review the nine basic principles of creating wealth with real estate:

1. Control the title to property.

2. Do it using other people's money, not your own. (This is called "leverage.") Use as little of your own money as possible.

3. Let other people's money make the payments and pay the bills.

4. Sell at a profit.

5. Buy property at less than market value (wholesale).

6. Sell at retail, and do whatever is needed to make the property saleable at its true (retail) value.

7. If you buy property for income purposes, be sure it will produce the income you expect.

8. Always be ready to combine any of the ways you can make money. Assume that most deals will be a "combination of ingredients," so go into any negotiation with your creative mind wide open.

9. Don't ignore the value of raw land.

In the chapters to come, you'll see these principles used over and over, in various combinations, to show you how to be creative, flexible, and able to give your sellers, buyers, renters, lease optioners, and equity sharers what they want while creating what *you* want—the wealth to bring you financial freedom and make your dreams come true.

CHAPTER 2

Ways To Buy Real Estate With Little or No Money Down

Y ou're sure to meet people, probably many people, who will tell you that you can't buy a house for nothing down. You used to be able to do it when people couldn't sell their homes any other way, they'll say, but now that interest has come down, you just can't do it. No way!

Those people are wrong. There are plenty of ways to buy a house with no cash, or very little cash, which for our purposes is about the same thing. We want to control as much property as we can with as little of our own cash as possible. In this chapter I'll list the ways to buy with little or no cash, talk about the types of financing available to us, and show several kinds of buyer qualifying sheets which you can use to determine what you, or a buyer of your property, can afford.

You'll find details on government loan programs available in 1988 in *A Treasury of Government Loans*. Stay alert for new government programs, and pay attention when you read in your newspaper or are told by a loan agent that old programs are being dropped or have run out of funding.

On any given deal, you may combine two or more financing methods. Real estate deal-making is flexible. That's what I mean when I talk about being creative—being able to see which buying tools you can combine to make a deal work.

Easy No-Down Financing

- The easiest way to buy with little or no cash is to take over an assumable mortgage. There are millions of such loans in existence and available. Ask an owner or real estate agent about assumability.

- Ask the seller to help finance the sale. This was a basic tool in creative financing when interest was 18 percent, and is still a basic tool of the "nothing down" deal. It can take many forms, but is usually a second or third loan, interest only, at lower than current bank rates, for a period of years, with a balloon payment due at the end.

- You can borrow the down payment. Lenders and real estate agents will tell you that they don't like down payments to be borrowed money, but if you show up with the amount required, they are not usually going to ask where it came from. You have more places to borrow than you think. The equity in your existing home is one easy place, and it is much easier now, with banks falling all over themselves to offer home equity loans and home equity lines-of-credit. If you borrow from friends or relatives, the lender won't even see the loan on your credit report. If you own an expensive car or RV, you may be able to borrow on that.

- Some of my students have simply applied for every Visa or

MasterCard offer that came to them in the mail, and borrowed the limit on each one! If you do that, be sure you have a deal on a house you can sell quickly—credit card interest is expensive, and the total monthly payments do add up!

If you borrow a down payment, do it *before* you make an offer. That way the money is in your bank, in your name, before the lender checks your credit, and you know how much you have to work with.

* Trade something to the buyer instead of a cash down payment. Maybe you'd rather get rid of your RV and buy a new and better one with the profit from your deal. My students have traded almost everything you could think of for a down payment, or part of a down payment.

* If you are an armed forces veteran, you can usually get a new VA-insured loan up to $110,000 without a down payment. This is a wonderful way for many people to get started in investing, without needing to try more complex financing on their first deal. The VA requires that you *intend* to occupy the home as a primary residence. Once you have complied with that requirement, you can sell. Under current law, the loan becomes assumable in two years. You could live in the house yourself for two years, sell, and use the profits to buy two houses, one to live in and one to resell. For loans over the limit, a down payment of 25 percent of the amount over $110,000 is usually required—and that's still a low dollar amount unless you're buying something way over the limit. Each lender sets his own rules on VA loan limits, so you'll find some who will loan less, or who don't like to do VA loans at all, and some who are even more flexible.

* Buy with an FHA loan. FHA loan limits vary according to the average home prices in an area, usually between $69,500 and $90,000 for single-family residences, or up to $110,000 to $142,600 for a four-unit building. They normally require a 5 percent down payment ($4,500 on a $90,000 loan) but sometimes are available for less. Ask.

FHA loans have strict building inspection requirements. They require the seller to pay the buyer's loan points, which may make the seller hold out for a higher price, but that's fair enough if it helps you to get the loan and low down payment you need.

- Many lenders offer loans for 90 to 95 percent of the property value. They'll require Private Mortgage Insurance (PMI) and usually will look for a good credit rating and reliable income.

- You can buy a foreclosed property. Banks don't want to be in the business of selling real estate. When they foreclose, they're stuck with property. These are called "REOs," which means "Real Estate Owned." Often, this property has been allowed to deteriorate, because owners who can't make payments can't afford maintenance, either. Banks are *highly motivated* to unload these properties, so you may be able to buy at fire-sale prices and on exceptionally good terms.

  When you buy from a bank, you're dealing with a motivated seller who has the power to approve your loan. Down payment requirements are rarely over 10 percent, and can be much lower. If you combine this purchase method with the ability to do routine home fix-up—painting, cleaning, lawn and garden care—you can buy below market and increase value considerably with relatively little effort or expense. I've written *How to Make a Fortune in Foreclosures,* included in the Cash Flow package, because the opportunities are so great.

- Buy a home through a lease option or by equity sharing. These are methods I normally recommend that you, as an investor, use to make money on your properties when your monthly payments exceed the rent you could charge. You lease option or equity share with a potential buyer of your property, rather than using either technique to buy property. These are not the best methods for buying your first investment property, not by a lot, but they could be used if all else fails. After all, you begin an investment career by buying one property, and if the only way you can manage it is by taking several years to buy the first one, then do it. But I think the methods in this book will show you plenty of easier ways.

  This gives you an idea of how many ways and how easily you can buy for little or nothing down.

In this listing, I'll review the methods discussed above, and cover other kinds of financing.

Conventional loans Loans that are not insured or guaranteed by the government. The term is often used to mean "fixed rate, 20 percent down" financing, but covers all non-government insured bank or S&L loans. When "conventional" lenders make 95 percent loans, they usually require PMI, or Private Mortgage Insurance, which serves the same insurance function as the government insurance in an FHA or VA loan. The buyer pays for such insurance.

Fixed rate loans The interest rate is set at the time the loan is made, and does not change for the life of the loan. The payment (principal and interest) will not change. A variation on fixed rate loans, being tried by a few banks as of early 1988, offers the borrower a one-time opportunity to refinance at a lower rate, free of the usual refinance charges, if the rate at the time of refinance is at least two percentage points below the initial fixed rate. Rates on such loans are currently slightly higher than those on loans without the "free refinance" feature. These loans could be a good thing to suggest to a buyer of your properties in times of high interest.

Adjustable Rate Mortgages (ARM, VRM, AML) The interest rate is raised or lowered according to a selected economic index. The monthly payments (principal and interest) are changed periodically, usually every six months or every year. The rate calculation *may* be adjusted every month, with the cumulative change reflected in the annual or semi-annual adjustment. There are many ways to write these loans, so if you use one, be sure you understand how it is written.

Convertible ARM An adjustable rate mortgage with a clause which permits the borrower to convert to a fixed rate loan at or within some fixed time or period of time, usually between the second and fifth year. These can be useful for a property you buy to lease option or equity share. It gives you an ARM's low initial rate, with the choice to convert to fixed interest if your tenant does not complete the lease option or equity sharing deal.

Graduated Payment Mortgage (GPM) A loan in which the payments in the first years are less than the true principal and interest payment, sometimes with negative amortization (the full interest charge is not paid, so the unpaid interest is added to the remaining principal and the amount of the loan *rises* for a time). Monthly payments increase, usually every year, until a given time, when the payments reach a fixed level which remains constant for the remainder of the life of the loan. This kind of loan is useful for a buyer whose income will rise and who wants to buy more house than he or she could qualify for with a conventional loan. It isn't a good tool for buying investment property you expect to keep— you have rising payments and negative amortization—but can be a useful thing to suggest to someone who can't quite afford to buy a property you're selling, or for a property you *know* you will sell within the first year or so.

Graduated Equity Mortgage (GEM) Basically, this is a GPM without negative amortization. Payments increase according to an agreed schedule, with the increase applying entirely to principal.

Government loans Any loan which is insured, guaranteed, or originated by any government, federal, state, or local.

FHA loans Loans for which the federal government insures a private lender against loss. The FHA *does not* make the loans; it merely insures them. The borrower pays for the insurance, called "Mutual Mortgage Insurance" (MMI).
All parties must abide by FHA rules in the transaction, among them a requirement that the seller pay loan points, which will make some sellers insist on a higher price for an FHA transaction. The buyer gets the advantages: a 95 percent loan, often with more flexible qualifying criteria, sometimes on property a conventional lender would not consider for a 95 percent loan. There are limits on the size of an FHA loan, which vary according to the average housing price in an area.

FHA loans granted before Jan. 1, 1987, are assumable without need for the buyer to qualify. On FHA loans made after that date a buyer must qualify to assume the loan within the first two years of the loan's life.

VA loans Available only to qualifying veterans (anyone who has served in the armed forces, not just those who served in time of war) and guaranteed by the Veteran's Administration. Like FHA loans, VA loans made before Jan. 1, 1987, are assumable without qualification; after that date a buyer must qualify during the first two years of the life of the loan, but after two years need not qualify.

Cal-Vet loans A California loan program for veterans of that state. The requirements are strict, and there is not always money available in the program, but the rates are low. This is often a tool for selling a property. If your state has a similar program, learn how it works and how you can use it.

FmHA loans The Farmers Home Administration makes loans directly for purchase or improvement of rural property in towns of less than 10,000 population, and some with populations between 10,000 and 20,000. Usually, this money is available only when loans cannot be obtained from normal sources.

Creative financing A loosely-used term which means almost all financing other than conventional, government-insured, or government lending. I use it in this book to also mean creative use of any kind of financing, including the above. Some examples follow:

AITD (All-Inclusive Deed of Trust) or "Wraparound" Mortgage Combining new financing with an old loan into a single package with one monthly payment, which lowers the total effective interest rate and makes paying the loan simpler for the borrower while requiring less paperwork for the lender. You will find this used often in times of high interest when there is a wide gap between current rates and the rate of the old loan.

Zero Interest Plan (ZIP) Sometimes offered on new construction, usually as a device to sell houses in a slow or highly competitive market. The builder will allow the buyer to pay principal only for a period of time, perhaps even for the entire loan period, in order to sell. The builder must either be desperate to sell, or increase the price of the house to cover his interest costs. A variation on this idea is:

Reduced Interest Plan   A selling device in which a builder has arranged with a lender for loans, usually ARMs, in which the rate for the first six months or year is below that offered by the bank to other customers. These low rates are usually "teasers," or a device to enable financially marginal buyers to qualify for the loans. The builder either has built houses or condos for which there is a weak market, or has built the low initial rate into the price of the house or into the eventual cost of the loan.

As a creative investor, you might use either of these devices in seller-carried financing if you found yourself with a "mistake" property and wanted to move it fast. (I hope you never find yourself in such need.) Or, you might ask it of a seller who has had his house on the market for a long time. If you are contemplating buying a new house for investment, avoid developers who offer unusually attractive financing—it will usually mean they can't sell any other way, or have overpriced the property, or both, and the property will increase in value slowly, or may even drop in value.

Seller Carry; Taking Back Paper; Carrying the Financing   All terms meaning the same thing: You ask the seller to give you a loan, usually a second or third mortgage, and usually at lower than bank rates, but higher than the seller could get from CDs or other "safe" bank investments. The seller partially finances the sale of his or her property by extending a loan to the buyer in the form of a promissory note secured by the property instead of taking cash. Occasionally (very rarely) you may find a seller who owns a property free and clear, who needs income more than cash, and will offer a seller-carried first loan for the entire price.

We use this form of financing as part of our creative deal-making strategy. It is also used when a buyer is unable to come up with enough cash for a down payment, or cannot qualify for regular new financing.

Purchase Money Second   Another term for a second mortgage. It means a second loan which is part of the purchase price of a house, making up the difference between an existing first loan and the cash available to the buyer. We might use a seller-carried second in addition to a new first loan.

Secondary markets You will have no direct dealings with these unless you have the cash to invest in mortgage-backed securities, but because they have an effect on your borrowing ability and interest rates, you should know what they are. You'll read about them on the business pages or in the real estate section of your local newspaper. A bank or S&L, having made a loan to you, will often sell your loan to one of these markets, usually retaining the servicing of the loan (accepting your payments and keeping records) in order to get cash for more loans.

Federal National Mortgage Association (FNMA, or "Fannie Mae") Formerly a federal agency, it is now a part-public, part- private corporation. Fannie Mae buys and sells mortgage loans, conventional, FHA, and VA. Like all secondary lenders, is does not loan to the public directly. FNMA funding comes from its corporate stock and the sale of FNMA notes and bonds. It also sells loans it has purchased to insurance companies, savings associations, pension funds, and other mortgage investors. Thus, the loan you got from Friendly Local Savings & Loan may be sold several times during its lifetime without you ever knowing it.

Federal Home Loan Mortgage Corporation (FHLMC, "Freddie Mac") A federal agency established in 1970 to provide a market for the Federal Home Loan Bank system. Buys and sells conventional, FHA, and VA loans, does mortgage participations, and offers its own mortgage investment certificates. Financed by selling stock to the twelve Federal Home Loan Banks and by sales of notes and bonds.

Government National Mortgage Association (GNMA, "Ginnie Mae") Primarily purchases pools of FHA and VA loans. Ginnie Mae was split off from Fannie Mae in 1968 and made part of HUD (the U.S. Department of Housing and Urban Development).

Qualifying For A Conventional Loan

Lenders and loan programs have qualifying criteria based on varying factors. The method and percentages shown here are an *example only*, but show a typical and approximate method. If you, or someone qualifying to buy a property you are selling, meet these criteria, you should be able to find a lender who will fund the loan, assuming other factors, such as job stability and credit record, are satisfactory.

Gross income of family $__________________________

(This means income before *any* deductions are taken for taxes, insurance, retirement, Social Security, etc.)

First ratio: 29% of Gross Income = $_____________________

Second Ratio: 36% of Gross Income = $____________________

The total housing cost should not exceed the first ratio of 29 percent. This includes principal, interest, insurance, taxes, and any assessments. Thus, a family with a gross income of $30,000 could afford payments of $8,700 a year, or $725 a month. If property taxes and insurance cost $125 a month (that might be a little low many places) the family could afford $600 a month payments for principal and interest.

A $63,000 loan will cost $599.97 in monthly payments at 11 percent interest. Thirteen percent interest would reduce the amount they could borrow by about $9,000, while 9 percent interest would raise the loan amount by about $12,000. With 5 percent down, such a family could afford a bit over $66,000 for a house at 11 percent. They'd need $3,316 down, plus their share of closing costs.

If the family had a large down payment, some lenders might loan at a higher ratio, probably assuming that the large down payment demonstrates good financial planning and fiscal responsibility.

The second ratio, 36 percent, is the total long-term indebtedness the family can have. That means all housing costs plus all monthly debt which will take more than 9 months to repay. Thus if there was a car payment, a Visa or MasterCard bill, a large department store charge, and a monthly payment plan to pay the orthodontist, the total could not exceed $10,800 a year, or $900 a month. All those other payments would have to cost less than $175 a month, or the excess would reduce the size of the allowable house payment.

Now suppose the family that wants to buy your house has a hundred bucks in charge card minimum payments, but their car payment is $200? Okay, their 29 percent ratio doesn't work; the most they can afford is $600 in housing costs, not $725. Now, if we subtract $125 in taxes, insurance, etc, they can only afford a house payment of $475. At that figure, they could only afford a $50,000 loan.

Does that mean they can't buy a more expensive house? Not at all! With just a little bit of creativity, you can see that if they sell their car and get rid of that payment they can qualify for the full 29 percent ratio. The family has to decide which is more important, the nice car or a nice house. You can point out that auto lenders tend to be less stringent than housing lenders, so if they sell their car and buy something that's cheap transportation, they can drive it for the time it takes to apply for a loan and close escrow, and then buy a better car again, after they're sure they are comfortable with their house payments.

All of this assumes that their other expenses are normal, and they are comfortable with those payments.

As I said at the beginning, this is an example which should be fairly typical, but you will find many variations among lenders and in the individual financial situations of buyers.

VA LOAN QUALIFYING WORKSHEET

The conventional loan qualifying ratios above are very simple. You could even say they oversimplify because they only look at a few factors. A worksheet for a VA loan is more detailed and gives a clearer picture of a family's financial condition.

I'd suggest that any family buying a home use this or a similar worksheet for their own information before beginning the house-hunting process. It can tell a lot about where the money is going and how to control where it goes. It might give a family which cannot qualify now the information needed to clean up their debts and expenditures so they can afford the house they want in the future. For your own private use, you could make this sheet even more detailed. I'll talk about that later in the chapter.

Note that the worksheet assumes two incomes. If there is only one income, ignore the "borrower 2" column.

Gross monthly income	Borrower 1	Borrower 2
Salary		
Overtime pay		
Part time job		
Alimony/child support		
Commissions and bonuses		
Interest and dividends		
Net rental income		
SS or retirement income		
Net taxable income (if self-employed)		

Note: Income other than salary should be included only if it can be verified and is long-term (two to five years or more). This can make it hard on people who are self-employed, who get income from tips, who work a part-time job which is paid in cash, or whose part-time income is variable. I'd suggest that if you, or people buying your property, are in doubt about whether to include a source of income, put it in. If the bank rejects it from consideration, you're no worse off than if you had not put it there at all.

TOTAL GROSS INCOME

Borrowers 1 & 2 $_________________
Less state and federal income tax $_________________
Net effective income $_________________

EXPENDITURES

Monthly payments (all bills with six months or more to pay)
                                         $_________________
Social Security or retirement payment $_________________
Child support/alimony $_________________
Child care expense $_________________
Utilities $_________________
Property maintenance $_________________
Minimum required family support $_________________
Should be no less than:
    Loans up to $65,000: $250 per person up to a family of 4
    Loans up to $80,000: $275 per person up to a family of 4
    Loans up to $100,000: $300 per person up to a family of 4
    Add $75 per person for each additional family member

TOTAL EXPENDITURES $_________________
Subtract total expenditures from net effective income
Net effective income $_________________
Less total expenditures $_________________
Remainder available for housing cost $_________________

Housing cost includes:
    Principal
    Interest
    Taxes and insurance
    Condo homeowner's assessment, if any

You can see that this is a careful analysis of a potential borrower. Since VA loans are intended for borrowers who might have trouble affording a home through conventional sources, both the lender and the VA want to be sure the borrower isn't getting into more than he or she can handle.

I've found many people who don't understand how VA loans work, and many misconceptions about what you can do with them and the amount that can be loaned. The following should answer most questions. For more detailed information, and any changes in the law or regulations, talk to your real estate agent or call the nearest VA office.

1. The VA guarantees loans for eligible veterans. They don't guarantee the entire loan, just the high-risk part.

2. The VA does not lend money. They guarantee loans. They will, in rare, special circumstances, make the loan if the veteran can't find a lender who will accept him or her.

3. There is no maximum allowable loan. There is a maximum which the VA will *insure*, however. The lenders decide how much they will actually lend. The general rule is that they will lend four times the amount shown on the veteran's certificate of eligibility.

4. One hundred percent financing is allowed. This is one way to make a nothing down deal.

5. You can use your VA eligibility over and over. There is a lot of confusion about this. The key is that your previous VA loan must be *paid off*, and you cannot still own the property you bought with the loan. Since VA loans are easily assumable, what happens in most cases is that a veteran buys a first home with a VA loan and when he sells it, the new owner assumes the loan. That loan is *not* paid off, so the veteran is not eligible for a new loan. If, however, the buyer is also a veteran, with entitlement to a VA loan, the buyer's entitlement can be substituted for the original buyer's entitlement, leaving the original buyer free of liability and able to seek another VA loan.

6. If the veteran has paid off some but not all of the loan, he or she

has a partial entitlement, based on how much has been paid off.

7. You can refinance with a VA loan.

8. You must *intend* to occupy the property as your primary residence. This would appear to make a VA loan a bad way to begin an investment career. However, if you buy and occupy the house for a short period of time, nothing in the regulations says you cannot sell, rent, or lease option the property. If you now own a house which has equity, and was not purchased with a VA loan, you could buy with VA financing, move into the new house, and sell the old one to get investment capital.

9. You can buy with another veteran as co-borrower, but you must both live in the property.

10. The VA limits the fees and interest which can be charged to a veteran. This means that if the lender charges more than the allowable fees or interest, the seller pays. If you are the seller, this means you must hold out for a higher price when selling with VA financing if you are to make the same profit you would from a conventional loan or all-cash sale.

BUYING POWER
ANALYSIS

For your first investment, you'll want to know how much you can afford; and every time you sell a property, you'll find potential buyers who wonder if they can afford it, how much they can "really" afford, and how much down payment they can put together.

This is a quick checklist for estimating expenses and sources of cash to meet them.

(1) How Much Cash Will You Need?

Estimated buying and closing costs	$__________________
Moving costs	$__________________
Estimated renovation costs, if any	$__________________

Reserve fund (for unexpected expenses) $_______________
Total cash needs $_______________

(2) How Much Cash Can You Raise?
Sale of your present home $_______________
Savings $_______________
Gift (or private loan) from family $_______________
Investments $_______________

Total cash $_______________

Subtract total cash needs (1) from
cash you can raise (2): total cash needs: $_______________

(3) Balance $_______________

The balance is how much you have left for a down payment

FIGURING FAMILY EXPENSES

You may find that for your own use, or for the use of a family buying
your property, you want a more detailed analysis of family expenses. This would be particularly true of someone who thinks they
really ought to be able to afford a house, but "just can't imagine
where the money goes," or where anything could be saved. Sound
familiar? Most of us wonder this, in private or out loud, at some
point in our lives. In that case, we'd like to find out as exactly as
possible where the money really does go.

The VA form lists most of the sources of income, but is general
about expenses. If you were to analyze expenditures, these are some
of the headings you might list. If you find that they are not detailed
enough for you or a potential buyer, you can always add categories
to fit any individual situation.

1. **Rent or mortgage**

                                    DAVE DEL DOTTO

2. Property taxes

3. Property insurance or renter's insurance

4. Any other property assessments or condo association fees

5. **Utilities** (list each utility separately so you can see what each costs)

6. **Installment payments** (this includes *every* bill, other than utilities or housing costs, which you do not pay off in full each month. For the purposes of this analysis, you're trying to find out how much money goes where, on a regular basis)

7. **Regular payments** (This is one you won't find in most expense analysis forms. These are payments that don't show up as "installment" debt, because you either pay cash or pay off the charge each month. If you have an American Express card, you pay it every month, but you might well have a balance to pay every month. The same is true if you use a charge card to shop at your favorite department store, but pay the bill every month.

    Take a year's worth of bills, add up what you spent, and divide by 12, and you know what your average monthly expense for that card was. If you regularly pay by cash or check for a lot of your purchases, keep the sales slips or write down what you bought and how much it cost, each time you come home. Doing this will find "hidden" expenditures that don't show up on most forms.)

8. **Savings** (if you don't have a savings plan, you should, and whatever you save should be on your list as a regular monthly expense)

9. **Insurance** (Take a good look at your insurance, both to see whether you are paying too much for it, and to see whether you have enough. The true meaning of "insurance poor" is the discovery, after you have a loss, that you thought you were covered and were not. You may want to list some insurance in the category it affects. There is already a listing for homeowners insurance; auto insurance could be under transportation, and health insurance could be under medical.)

10. Support or alimony payments

11. **Transportation** (includes all costs of owning a car or cars, or taking public transportation)

12. **Food** (If you buy a lot of fast food, snack food, treats, or drinks, you might want to make a separate category for that kind of expense. It is possible to spend a lot for convenience and never realize how much it's costing.)

13. **Clothing**

14. **Household supplies** (Chances are you buy most supplies—soap, light bulbs etc.—with the groceries, so you might include them in that category, and make this one "Home maintenance" so you don't forget to keep track of the new towel rack in the bathroom, the new curtains in the living room, or the new sheets for the kids' beds. Or, you could make "Home Maintenance" an additional category.)

15. **Medical and dental** (Don't forget to include health insurance in this category, since it is a health expense, unless you included it under the general "insurance" heading.)

16. **Recreation**

17. **Entertainment**

18. **Miscellaneous** (or any other categories you wish to list)

As you see, we spend our money in a lot of places. It's no wonder we have a hard time keeping track of where it all goes. You can make an expense analysis as detailed or as general as you wish. The important thing is to do enough for you or your buyer to feel comfortable in adding the expense of a new home mortgage.

Your Credit includes a chapter on financial planning which will help you figure out where your money goes and how you can live more economically.

CHAPTER 3

THE BEST WAYS TO BUY

I wish I could tell you one "best way" to buy property. It might make your first deals easier—but if it were that simple, everyone would be doing it, and it would get awfully dull after a while. That's why this chapter is about the best *ways* to buy property. It's up to you to decide which method or methods feel most comfortable to you, which will work best in your local market, and how you go about using them.

I'll tell you about some things that almost always apply, and then talk about the effects of low interest rates (which at this writing means anything under 10 percent), moderate interest (anything around 12-14 percent), and high interest (when rates head toward 18 percent).

There is one basic principal to remember at all times: *You are buying to make money!*

Now, that seems obvious, right? I mean, you wouldn't be reading this book if you didn't plan to make money, would you? Of course not.

But—

You would be *amazed* how many beginning investors go out and want to buy a piece of property because it is such a nice house.

Well, shouldn't you? Wouldn't a nice house be easier to sell and bring more money? *No*, my friends, the odds are it won't. These investors make the mistake of shopping for investment property as if *they* were going to live there. That's very understandable, but it has nothing to do with investment.

Investment means buying property for less than you can sell it for: buying wholesale and selling retail. If you were running a grocery store, you wouldn't buy your stock from the nearest 7-Eleven at retail and expect to add your profit to that price and sell much.

It's the same with real estate. If you buy at market value, the only way you will make money is to hold the property until its value increases through normal appreciation. There are ways to do this, but you can see that even if you plan to hold a piece of property while its value appreciates, you'll make more if you buy below market.

So—when you look at a potential investment property, you don't think, "Three bedrooms, two baths, nice kitchen, big yard (etc.)." You think, "Market value $100,000, it needs some work, and the seller has been transferred; if I can get it for $85,000 and put $5,000 into it, I can make money."

In other words, the financial numbers are important. If it happens to have a nice kitchen and pretty green shutters on the windows, great, but the numbers are all that matter.

FINDING WHOLESALE HOUSES

But, you ask, where can I find wholesale houses? It's easy, if you know where to look. What you look for, first, are *motivated sellers*. That's a term real estate agents use to try to get people interested in making offers on a house. As they use it, it may mean nothing at all. As I use it, it means any seller who has a pressing need to sell his or her property *now*.

Motivation can take many forms, and I'll talk more about it in Chapter 11. The sellers you're looking for are those who *must* sell. These include sellers who have already bought another house, those who have been transferred, and those facing foreclosure.

Also included are sellers who didn't want to own the property in the first place—banks, S&Ls, and government agencies which have foreclosed on loans and taken possession of property, or governments that have taken property for unpaid taxes.

Where can you find foreclosures and tax sale property? There are several sources.

First, it's obvious that if you can reach a seller facing foreclosure *before* the foreclosure takes place, you can usually work out a better deal for yourself and for the seller.

It takes less work to find such properties after foreclosure, but the deal may not be as good, and you will not be able to do anything for the poor person who has lost his or her home *and* had a credit record ruined.

This doesn't mean you shouldn't pursue those post- foreclosure sources. You'll find these in notices of tax sales, in VA and FHA foreclosure lists (available through those agencies), and in bank's lists of "REOs." (Real Estate Owned.) You'll find some advantages you can use in these sources.

Tax sale property may go very cheaply, but you are usually required to have funds available at the time of the sale in the form of cash or a certified check. (That eliminates you if you are beginning and have little cash to work with, but can be very good once you've established yourself and either have cash or have found a partner with cash who will back you.)

The FHA and VA are often stuck with properties which have not been maintained, or which have been torn up by disgruntled owners. They don't expect market price for properties which need work. You have to determine whether you can do the work yourself or hire it done cheaply enough to make money.

Bank REOs can be very attractive, depending on the bank. Some banks will hang on and try to get their money out; others will work hard and listen to creative deals in order to be rid of REOs. Remember, when you are dealing with a bank or S&L for a REO, that you are dealing with an institution which has the power to approve your loan for its own benefit as well as yours. You may have to talk to several banks and S&Ls to find the right one, but it can be worth the effort.

One of my students tells of making an utterly ridiculous offer on a failed condo development, with half the clauses in the bank's contract crossed out and marked "void," and the bank accepted it. That bank was *real* anxious to move those units, and my student was the first person to come along and say, "Hey, be realistic and I can take these off your hands." He got a deal even I wouldn't believe if he hadn't done it.

REOs may need work, but tend to be in better shape that FHA-VA foreclosures.

All of these sources will usually show up in the MLS (Multiple Listing Service) of the local Board of Realtors.

But now let's get aggressive and creative.

Let's find those properties *before* they are foreclosed. This takes some work, but not a lot of work.

UNDERSTANDING THE FORECLOSURE PROCESS

The key thing is that foreclosures don't "just happen." It's not like the last century when the Simon Legrees of real estate could and would knock on someone's door and say, "Pay the whole loan now, or I'll take your farm, heh heh!" The lender *does not* want to foreclose, and will usually do everything possible to keep the loan good and paying off, and to help the person stay in the house.

When that can't be done, the lender files a *notice of default* at the county courthouse, in the County Recorder's office. The notice gives the borrower a certain period of time to bring the loan current or be foreclosed.

By law, all notices of default must be published in a "newspaper of general circulation." This may not be the largest paper in the county, but more likely will be the cheapest which fulfills the legal circulation requirements. If there is a legal newspaper in your county, notices may be published there. If you go to the courthouse and ask, they are required to give you the list of properties in default, since notices of default are public record, open to anyone who wants to look. They'll also tell you where they publish notices.

Once you have the list, you can call the owners who are about to lose their homes, sympathize with their problem, find out what their needs are and what the financial numbers on the house are, and determine whether you may be able to help them, and in so doing help yourself. You may find they don't like your offer and think they can get more for their house. Then you decide whether you can give it to them and make money, or not.

If you decide not, you can say you *may* call back a week before the foreclosure deadline and see whether they've been successful in selling at the price they want. If they haven't sold by then, they are very likely to listen to any offer that will keep the foreclosure off their credit record.

A word of caution: *Do not* take unfair advantage of a distressed seller. This is illegal in California and many other states, and should be in any state where it is not. Make a fair offer. You can do that and make money.

TAILOR OFFERS TO YOUR MARKET

So far, I've been talking in general. All that I've said applies in any market. Now let's look at how different markets affect the way these things work. I'm tying "markets" to interest rate levels, but other factors can have an effect. A market may be locally "hot" or "cold" regardless of interest rates, depending on the local economy.

In general, a cold market will act like high interest, regardless of the actual rate, and a hot market will act like low interest. What's important is demand and the average prosperity of the population—if employment is high, there will be fewer foreclosures, and if there is high demand, more homes will sell for closer to market value.

In Times of High Interest

I wrote *101 Purchase Offers* when interest rates were 18 percent and published figures claimed only about 8 percent of the population could afford a new home. (Such figures can be misleading; they usually assume buying a first home with minimum down payment, which is not the way most homes are sold.)

Most of us remember those days with a shudder and hope for the lowest interest possible. But, for investors, there were advantages: There were more foreclosures to choose from; homes sat on the market for months, creating motivated sellers; and those sellers were often willing to listen to and accept very creative offers.

The negative side was that when we sold the properties we purchased, *we* had to sell in the same tough market and had to be able to hold on until a qualified buyer came along. Because the market was "cold," real estate did not appreciate nearly as fast as it had in the previous five or ten years. There were and are creative ways around those negatives.

At that time, many loans were assumable, usually without the buyer having to go through the qualifying process needed for a new loan, which made deals a little easier. You could work deals like this "classic" nothing-down purchase and resale:

(I'm going to use a $100,000 house in all my examples, partly because the numbers are easy to figure and understand, and because, if all the deals use a property of the same value, you can more easily compare them and see how they differ.)

$100,000 house

$ 50,000 existing first loan, assumable.

Seller wants $20,000 for his cash needs and expenses of sale.

Offer the seller full price. Ask the seller to obtain a new, assumable second loan for $30,000, and to carry an assumable loan, low interest, interest-only payments, with a balloon payment due in five years, for the $20,000 balance.

You get title to the house, the seller gets the cash he or she needs, plus interest income for five years, and you have a property you can move.

How can you move such a property in a market where property is not appreciating in value?

You put an ad in the paper offering to let a purchaser get into the house by paying you a couple of thousand, plus expenses of sale, and assuming all the loans. You've made your couple of thousand for the effort of signing a bunch of papers. Such houses often sold very rapidly because they made it possible for people to get into the house they wanted and otherwise could not qualify to buy.

Neat. Lots of investors made money. If they could get the house for less than the asking price, they made even more money.

Today, many loans are not assumable, and many that are assumable require the buyer to qualify, so if 18 percent interest returns (I hope it doesn't; it's too hard on too many good people, and investing is really easier at lower rates) this method will be harder to use—but not impossible.

FHA and VA loans made before January of 1987 remain assumable, and there are still older conventional assumable loans out there, just fewer and fewer of them as years pass. After January of 1987, new FHA and VA loans remain assumable, but for the first two years of the loan, the buyer who assumes the loan must qualify to do so. After January of 1989, there will begin to be a new pool of assumable FHA and VA loan for which buyers don't have to qualify. Pre-1987 FHA and VA remain assumable without qualifying.

Some adjustable rate mortgages are assumable. Exact terms and conditions vary. Always check.

Seller-carried financing is assumable if you write it that way, because such financing is not regulated or insured by the federal government.

So you see, a deal such as I described above would still be possible, though not as easy as it once was.

The trick is to get the assumable adjustable second. Banks are not about to make such a loan to someone facing foreclosure, but they might make it to you, if you offered enough down payment to satisfy them. You probably could not work a nothing-down deal, with the seller carrying the entire balance, on a pre-foreclosure property.

However, in times of high interest, you may well be working with motivated sellers who are *not* facing foreclosure, and who have the credit to get that second. Because the tax law of 1986 encouraged home equity loans, it might well be easy (assuming Congress doesn't get around to plugging that great little loophole) to get the assumable second you need.

Two selling tools which are especially useful under high interest are the lease option and equity sharing. These are good any time, of course, but in high interest years can make the difference between profit and loss for you, and between being able to buy a home or not for a buyer.

IN TIMES OF
MODERATE INTEREST

This may the ideal market for an investor, if there is such a thing as an "ideal" market. There are still a large number of foreclosures to work with. Homes can sit on the market for six months, increasing the motivation of sellers, and home sales are slow enough that sellers are willing to consider creative deals. Enough buyers are priced out of the home they really want to provide a ready pool of people who will buy creatively, through the methods described under high interest. Property you hold for a time instead of selling at once will appreciate at a reasonable rate in most markets.

It is a time in which almost anything that will work at either extreme will work—you have access to every tool of investment and deal-making there is.

You have some advantages which, if you are the nervous type, will help you sleep better at night: The interest *you* pay on the loans which control your property is at a lower rate, you'll sell property more easily and usually for a better price, and your buyers, lease-option tenants, or equity sharers are more likely to be able to come through on their deals.

In short, this is as close to an ideal investment market as you can get.

In Times of
Low Interest

This may be the toughest market, but anyone who tells you it's impossible has given up before trying. Two recent *Cash Flow Report* (my monthly newsletter) Investors of the Month are working in the northeast, where the market is supposed to be so hot some properties get five offers the first day on the market and sell above the asking price, and in Texas, where everyone says *nobody* can make any money. They're both doing fine, thank you.

What's the secret?

No secret. The deals are *always* out there. What changes is how many you have to choose from, the pressures on sellers and buyers, and the amount of effort you have to put in to find the deals that work.

When interest is low, it's even more important to seek out foreclosures or other distress property. They are there, in the most prosperous of times, in the most prosperous of areas and hottest of markets. Unfortunately, we have not yet figured out how to run a society in which everything goes perfectly for everybody.

I've talked about the importance of meeting people's needs, and being able to do a real service to many people, while making a profit. This may be even more true in times of prosperity. I mean, how would you feel if you were the person who suffered financial misfortune while everyone around you was buying new houses and BMWs? If a real estate investor came along with a deal that would help you work your way out of your problems, would you be grateful? You bet! Or you sure should. So when you make your deals, never forget that you're helping people.

In Conclusion

In this chapter, you've seen that no matter what the market may be, you can find a way to make deals and make money. I've also discussed the importance of motivation and a few techniques. In the next two chapters, I'll tell you what makes a deal good, and how to manage your cash flow to turn what others might consider a bad deal into a good one.

CHAPTER 4

WHAT MAKES A DEAL "GOOD"? (AND HOW TO TELL GOOD DEALS FROM BAD)

I n simplest terms, a good deal is one in which you make money.
That isn't quite all that's important.

You have to make enough money to make it worth your time and effort, and to justify keeping that much of your wealth tied up in that piece of property for that length of time.

Then, you have to consider your goal. The same property could be a good deal for one goal and a bad deal for another.

In all investment, and real estate is no exception, risk is involved in spending money to make money. Usually, but not always, the higher the potential profit, the higher the risk.

The stock market is a classic example of risk—guess right and you make bundles of money; guess wrong and you lose your shirt—as many did the fall of '87. In real estate, the fact that you control something physical and real, not just a piece of paper, is a powerful hedge against losing even a collar button from your shirt. Still, losses can happen.

In any deal, you should estimate the risk as well as the profit potential. If you choose to be a conservative investor, plan your deals so that even if you don't make the money you expect, you at least won't lose. If you choose to take greater risks, do enough deals that if one of them turns sour the profits from others will let you walk away and not worry. A working crystal ball would help, but since such things don't exist, the knowledge you gain as you study and continue to make deals will provide a much more reliable substitute. You'll learn to judge how much money you can expect to make, and the degree of risk, in each deal.

SOME GOOD DEALS

Let's look at a house which is on the market for $100,000, firm price.

If similar houses are selling for that amount or less, it is not a good deal. There's no room for profit.

However, if you intend to hold the house for a time, and property is appreciating at 10 percent per year, it would be a good deal unless it gives you a negative cash flow. Remember, when you figure your return on investment, this would not be 10 percent per year on $100,000, as you might get from a bank CD at that rate, but would be $10,000 (10 percent of the value of the house) for the first year, and more thereafter, on *whatever amount of money it cost you to control title to that house!*

If you paid a few hundred dollars to assume a VA loan, and rented the property for enough to cover payments, insurance, and taxes, you'd be making ten grand in one year off your few hundred bucks! Let's look at the other extreme: Say you controlled title to the house with a conventional 20 percent down payment ($20,000) and sold it after a year for $10,000 profit. That's a 50 percent annual return on your investment. Where else can you get that?

Most of your deals, if you follow my advice, will control title with far less than 20 percent.

Now let's look at a real example. One of my students has four years to go before retiring from the army. He's stationed in Texas, where everyone tells you the market is terrible. He controls title by assuming VA mortgages. Because of the large military population, there are plenty of VA loan properties, plenty of motivated sellers (when they are transferred, they need to dispose of their houses in 30 days), and plenty of buyers who are delighted to lease option for two years.

He's buying in an area where prices are not rising (yet), getting properties at anywhere from several thousand to ten thousand dollars below appraised value, lease optioning for a small positive cash flow, and he does not need to sell right now. If his tenants pick up their options, he makes money. If they don't, he holds the property.

He plans to acquire a property a month. He has, I assume, been reading the same estimates I've seen, which predict that the Texas economy, even without oil, will recover sometime in the early to mid-90s. He'll retire in 1992. At that time he can either sell his holdings, or find someone to manage them until the time to sell is right. So far, he hasn't paid more than a VA assumption fee for any house—less than $1,000 each! Is he going to make a profit? Is he going to have a high return on his investment?

Now, what would make a good deal like that bad? In his case, the worst thing that could happen would be that Congress would shut down the army base. That's hardly likely. The next risk is that other factors in the local economy would go sour and drag down values. Again, that's not likely. The Texas economy has already taken its hits. The only other risk is the one we all take: that he makes some poor decisions on his purchases. In his case that is also not likely, since he's buying homes which, on the current market, appraise well over the amount of the loans he's assuming.

Does this mean that anything that's a VA (or FHA) assumption, anywhere, is automatically a good deal? Not at all. Suppose a house appraised for $100,000, but had a $110,000 loan against it? That happens. Such houses usually don't sell until the lender discounts the loan. (One of my students bought a property which was encumbered with loans and liens to over twice its appraised value! He got everything discounted and bought for well below appraised value!)

Suppose the house had a loan of $90,000 against it, but the military base or major industry of the area closed down. Such a house might lose more than $10,000 in value, or be impossible to sell, rent, or lease, which for us would be the same thing as losing value.

We don't want to own a property on which the loans have to be discounted!

This is what I mean when I say it is vitally important for you to study and be aware of the market forces at work in your area.

KNOW YOUR MARKET

Don't get the idea that you should study your market only for the negative purpose of avoiding disaster. The real reason for studying your market is to know where and how you can make the most money, most easily. Knowing where *not* to invest is a byproduct of knowing where *to* invest.

Let's look at some kinds of good deals.

1. Anywhere the market is appreciating rapidly. "Rapidly" usually means around 10 percent per year, or more. Almost anyone in California can tell you a story about someone, perhaps themselves, who bought a house in the San Francisco or LA areas back about 1975, for maybe $40,000 or $50,000, and now the place is worth over a quarter million (or more!) and currently going up at 10 to 20 percent a year! If property values are rising rapidly and seem likely to continue to do so, then all you need do is control the title for as little cash as possible, avoid a negative cash flow while you hold the property, and take your profit when you sell.

2. *Some* properties which have become run down and sell below market because of their condition. I say "some," because property can deteriorate past the point where economical repairs can bring it back to the value it should have. In most cases, property which has been let go can be brought back for much less cost than the increase in value a little fix-up can provide—especially if you can do most of it yourself.

    One of my students describes her investment selection method as driving up and down streets, looking for the property "that would gross anyone else out." It takes a lot of looking time, she says, but her positive cash flow from such properties has already bought her a new Pontiac Fiero—which has made driving up and down streets much more fun.

She uses the condition of the properties as her lever for negotiating the price down. Then, with her husband and in-laws, she cleans, paints, fixes plumbing and wiring, and even put on a new roof once. She adds some inexpensive "luxury" touches like ceiling fans and mini-blinds, buys good second-hand appliances, and gets tenants who appreciate a nice house and are willing to pay a little more for it—and who take better than average care of her houses.

Note that neat little trick—a nice house, at a slightly *higher* than average rent, attracts people who take better care of the property! It's a self-selecting process for good tenants—if it's worth extra money to them to be in a nice house, they're more likely to keep it that way.

3. Property you can buy via assuming loans and assumable seller-carried financing, at market price or less. You want to buy this property at or below market, preferably below, of course, and you want to be certain you have a positive cash flow. A nothing-down, fully assumable deal with a negative cash flow is *not* a good deal!

4. Foreclosed property. If I were to say that there is one "best" way to invest, I'd say this is it. (The reason I don't pick a "best" way is that any way can be best for any individual investor or particular market.) I talked about foreclosed property earlier, in Chapter 3. Also, see my book *How to Make a Fortune in Foreclosures* in the Cash Flow package.

    Sheriff's sales, tax auctions, and IRS auctions are other sources of foreclosed property. See my books *How to Buy and Use Tax Sale Land* and *Government Auctions*.

To sum up, a good deal is one which:

1. Meets the needs of your investment strategy

2. Can be sold at a reasonable profit either at once or after being held for a time

3. Will produce a positive cash flow

4. Is usually a property which can be purchased below market value

5. May need repair (the fixer-upper)

6. Will often be a property which is "distressed" due to financial problems of the owner, or, as above, the need for repair.

A bad deal is one which:

1. Will not increase in value sufficiently to make the profit you seek

2. Cannot, through renovation, be made worth a sufficient price

3. Cannot be purchased on favorable terms

4. Cannot be purchased at a price which will provide a positive cash flow

5. Is a kind of property which, even if purchased on favorable terms, will be difficult to resell or rent because of location or other factors

6. For any reason does not serve the goals and methods of your personal investment plan

It is possible to turn some "bad" deals into "good" workable deals. This can be particularly important in times of high interest or in "hot" markets where it is difficult to find below-market property. The next chapter tells how.

CHAPTER 5

WAYS TO MAKE A "BAD" DEAL "GOOD" —HOW TO MANAGE YOUR CASH FLOW

What makes a deal "bad"?

Anything that prevents you from making money, anything that leaves you with a negative cash flow, and (on a slightly lower level of badness) anything which reduces your profits.

When you buy a property, you buy it in the expectation that it will make money. If you don't know *how* it will make money, you haven't studied my books or bought wisely.

Let's suppose we're dealing with a hot market where you can't buy anything much below appraised value. In that case, you'd buy and figure on holding the property for a year or two, or more. Usually, in such markets, values are rising, and usually, you can rent for enough to cover your payments while the property increases in value.

But you may find deals, otherwise good, which you can't make without creating a negative cash flow. Maybe it's a fine property in a rapidly-appreciating part of town, but you can't structure a deal which brings your payments down to the rent you can charge.

In such a market, you can often manage your cash flow through a lease option or equity-sharing contract. Both these are methods by which you can charge a higher rent in return for offering your tenant an opportunity to buy a home he or she could not have afforded otherwise.

But what if it is a market, like that faced by my student in Texas, where you can buy below appraised value, but if you try to sell for the appraised value today, your property may sit on the market for months while you make payments and pay taxes? Again, a lease option or equity sharing is the answer. You see, a good technique is not limited to just one kind of market. These two methods can even work *when you pay market price or higher in a poor market!*

HOW LEASE OPTIONS WORK WONDERS

This is how a lease option works:

You want to buy a $100,000 house. You add up your payments, insurance, and taxes, and discover you can't rent it for enough to cover the total. You suddenly get a case of the nervous shakes. If you buy it, you've bought a negative cash flow money-loser and, with the costs of sale, you may not be able to sell it for as much as you paid! You can see that it will take a year or two for appreciation to make it worthwhile, and you can't afford the negative for that long. This is a *bad* deal, and you want out!

Ah, but don't worry. There's a way to make it work, if the negative is not prohibitive. You advertise it as lease with option to buy. You set the lease rent high enough to cover your expenses. You promise that a certain part of the rental payment will go toward the purchase price. You set either a specific date or a time period in which your tenant can exercise the purchase option, and, most important, you set the sale price high enough to make money, and make it part of the contract. Be sure to have lease-option contracts checked by a real estate attorney to be certain you have complied with the laws of your state.

Don't think that a lease option can cure *every* bad-deal problem. If you have to charge a rent too much higher than the going rate, or if a buyer can get a better deal with an FHA loan, your lease option won't solve his problem. In that case, use one of your escape clauses (I'll talk about them later) if you've gone far enough to sign a contract.

Your ad might look like this:

LEASE WITH OPTION TO BUY!
3br, 2ba ranch, yard, family room,
close to transportation. $950 mo, $250
credited to purchase. Call Dave, 000-0000

Don't run this ad under "Homes For Sale." You're looking for people who can't afford a house, but wish they could.

Run it under "Homes For Rent." Who'll respond? People who don't have a down payment, those who can make higher payments than the banks will let them qualify for, and those who need more house than their down payment and income will buy. And, this is important, people will call who can afford the price you put in the ad. If you don't give the monthly payment price, you'll waste hours answering the phone to tell people they can't afford the lease payment.

But shouldn't you worry that someone the banks have turned down is a poor risk?

No.

You're not taking a risk. One of two things will happen: Your tenants will meet the terms of the option and buy the house, and you'll make money; or they'll come to you, regretfully, and say they just can't do it, for any of many reasons. They may be getting divorced, not have made the money they expected, been poor savers, spent money on luxuries, like a new car, or even—spent their money fixing up *your* house, because they thought of it as their own, and now they don't have money to exercise the option.

What do you do if your tenants can't complete their lease-option purchase? You can extend the lease if you wish, with the eventual purchase price raised accordingly; lease option to someone else; or sell, depending on your needs and the market. You may also be able to do a straight rental, if rental prices have risen to cover your costs.

The best possible lease option would be one in which all your loans are assumable. All your tenant has to do is come up with a down payment that is the difference between your loans and the agreed price, and part of that has already been paid as part of their rent.

This is where owner financing can be handy. Say you assumed an $80,000 FHA loan and the owner carried an assumable $20,000 second. You set a purchase price of $119,500, after a two-year lease. The tenant has built up $6,000 in credit from the monthly lease payments, and need only come up with $13,500 additional cash. The tenant is not going to want to lose six grand, so he'll come up with the money if there's any way he can. You've made your property easy to buy and given the tenant a $6,000 incentive to come up with the balance.

Notice that I used a two-year option in the example. Why? Under the new FHA and VA assumption rules, loans are assumable without qualifying after two years! The lease option provides a perfect way to work within those restrictions if you bought the property with a new FHA or VA loan.

Equity Share to Turn Bad Deals Good

What about equity sharing?

I like it even better than a lease option for some difficult markets. This is a technique that works especially well if you are dealing with high interest or a depressed market, when everyone else is crying about how hard it is to sell a home, much less make any money at it.

In equity sharing, you take the lease-option idea one step farther.

You offer your tenant half ownership of the house!

Now, I can just hear you asking, "Hey Dave, I just bought this house! Why should I give away half of it for nothing?"

Good question.

First, you don't "give away" half ownership for nothing. You get paid for it.

The key is that your tenant becomes a partner, with a *right* to half ownership when certain conditions are met, and a right to buy your half at a set time or within a set time period, for a predetermined price. Technically, the occupant of an equity-shared house is a "partner." I use "tenant" often in this discussion because the partner really is a tenant, occupying my house, until he or she meets the conditions of the contract.

As with a lease option, the tenant's name does not go on title until the conditions are met—that is, until you get paid. Be sure your equity sharing contracts are written that way. Some are not, and carry the risk that you'll find yourself with an irresponsible partner whom you can't evict because his name is on the title. If in doubt, consult an attorney.

As with a lease option, but even more so, you are likely to find tenants who will improve the property. If they don't meet the conditions of the contract, you get the benefit of those improvements.

Some people might find it easy to take the money and the improvements and run, but I advise against this. If you have a partner who has put money into your property, and then can't complete the deal, do everything in your power to help them find a way to make it work. Even if you have to take a slightly lower price, you'll feel good about having helped someone. While you can't spend "feeling good," there's not much point in having cash to spend if you don't feel good, is there?

With equity sharing you have some hidden advantages over a rental or most lease options, in addition to the possibility that your tenants may improve your property. In a rental, if the plumbing breaks on New Year's Eve, *you* are the one who has to go fix it or find plumber willing (for a holiday premium price) to come do the job. An equity-sharing partner should be responsible for normal minor maintenance. (Be sure it is written into the contract.)

If major repairs are needed, say a new roof, you should agree to split the cost above a set figure. I usually write these contracts to read that the tenant pays anything up to $1,000, and over that amount I'll split the cost. That protects me from constant nickel-and-dime expenses and assures that if the tenant wants to replace the roof, the roof really does need to be replaced.

I like to put some of that language in lease-option contracts, too, but a lease-option tenant is usually less willing to take on major repairs. You may be able to ask the tenant to take care of routine maintenance and split the total cost of major repairs.

The advantages of equity sharing are that you can ask more than the house would rent for (but not too much more, or you'll find no takers), the tenant will save you the maintenance time and expense you'd have with a rental, and you can get a buyer into a house who will make you a profit more easily.

LET NUMBERS BE YOUR GUIDE

Let me re-emphasize that when doing deals like this, you *must* think numbers. If you've bought a house at 20 percent under market, when others are selling at market value, you shouldn't need to lease option or equity share. The numbers should be good enough that you can turn around and sell for a profit or rent with a positive cash flow. When you buy at nearer market value, or in a slow market, under high interest, or any other condition which makes immediate resale or positive cash flow rental difficult, *then* is when these techniques shine.

Before using them (or buying any property), you should know as exactly as possible:

1. How much the property will cost you in
    a. monthly payments
    b. taxes
    c. insurance
    d. upkeep

2. How much you can get for rent (what other similar houses are being rented for)

3. Whether a prospective lease option or equity sharing buyer could get a better deal with an FHA or VA purchase (that is, is

there a market for your kind of deal?)

4. How much you can expect the property to appreciate in value over the period of the lease option or equity sharing contract

5. How much you will have to sell it for to make a profit

6. How long it will take for the property to reach that value (how rapidly are values rising in your area?)

7. Any local economic factors which might affect your profits; for example, if my student in the army were stationed at a base which Congress was telling the Pentagon it ought to close, investing in property near that base would suddenly become a high-risk venture

If you know these things, you can put the numbers together and *know* whether a deal will work or not. If the deal looks borderline, my advice, normally, is to avoid it. There should be better deals out there if you go looking for them. Should you find yourself in a market in which all deals come up with borderline numbers, my suggestion is that you look very hard at them, pick the best, and go for it; but it is up to you to determine whether such deals are worth your time and risk.

CHAPTER 6

THE BASIC ELEMENTS OF A PURCHASE OFFER

This is one of the most important chapters in the book. You could even say that for this chapter alone, the book is worth its price.

The simple fact is that you can't make a purchase offer if you don't know how to write one, and one of the main reasons many people don't or won't get started investing in real estate is because *they don't know how to write a simple, basic, ordinary real estate contract!*

How can you be creative if you don't even know how to be ordinary? You guessed it—you can't!

On the next pages I'll discuss two examples of standard California real estate purchase contracts, produced by the California Association of Realtors. Forms and requirements differ between states and within states, but *they all contain similar basic elements and use similar basic agreements.* In all states, forms are legally worded to comply with the real estate law of that state. It is your responsibility, wherever you buy and sell real estate, to know the laws of the state in which you deal, just as it is your responsibility to know the state's traffic laws when you drive there.

Real estate law is determined by state governments, not the federal government. Some of the laws governing the *financial* aspect of real estate—loans—is regulated or influenced by the federal government, through its regulation of the banking industry and its control of FHA and VA loans. But basic real estate law—how you buy, sell and own property—is a state function.

The first example is a two-page California form. The second, longer form, though more complex, makes it easier for an agent to be certain all legal requirements have been met. It looks lengthy and complex, and while it is long—four pages—it is simple if you look at it one step at a time, as I will here.

The short form will be more like those you'll encounter in most states. I show the longer form too, because its printed clauses cover so much of what can be part of real estate deals everywhere. You probably won't find *all* of these clauses used in most deals. The main difference is that the short form leaves you to write out financing details and other conditions which are dealt with in clauses written into the longer form.

Understanding these contracts will help you fill out the forms used in your state, or in your area. Remember that wherever you buy real estate, you have the responsibility for understanding and complying with state and local real estate law.

STANDARD OFFERS WON'T MEET OUR NEEDS

The way a contract is *filled in* can make it favor either sellers or buyers, particularly in the matter of who pays which fees. Who pays the fees is an important place to watch if you are dealing with a contract written out by someone else, especially by a real estate agent. In any area, there will be "customary practice," and real estate agents will automatically write it that way. There's nothing wrong with that—it makes life *much* easier for agents and ordinary buyers—but it can work to your disadvantage if "customary practice" favors the other party.

Unless your state law mandates otherwise, *everything* is negotiable between buyer and seller. You want the seller to pay for everything—or as much as possible, so you write it that way. (If you are the seller, you want the buyer to pay, of course.) You'll rarely get everything you ask for, but if you ask, you'll get more, more often.

If there is a printed clause in a contract that you don't like, you can strike it out or write "void" across it, initial the change, and have the other party do likewise (unless the clause is mandated by state law). You may get some argument but, as I say, everything is negotiable. You'll win some and lose some, but you'll probably win more than you'll lose and *for sure* you won't win if you don't try.

Anything typed into the blank spaces takes legal precedence over the preprinted sections, and anything handwritten takes precedence over everything. If you make a change after an agreement is signed, the change *must* be initialed by all parties who signed, on all copies of the form. (For example, a handwritten change on a form that has been typed and signed would not be valid unless initialed, on all copies.)

If you have questions about *any* details, either preprinted or written in, you should consult a real estate broker or your attorney. When you consult an attorney, find one who specializes in real estate law.

READING OUR EXAMPLES

In our example contracts, most sections and clauses of the contract are numbered or lettered, and will be referred to by number or letter.

Both forms are the same down to (1).

At the head of the form (above [1]), the blanks establish basic information about buyer, seller, property, and where the deal will take place.

The top line is for the city, date (day and month), and year in which the contract is made.

"Received from" is the buyer's name. (Yours, if you are the buyer.) Use your full name as you normally sign it. If more than one person is buying the property and will be on the title, all names should be given. (I include the phrase "and/or nominee" after my name here if I think I may sell my rights to the property before the deal closes.)

"The sum of" is the amount of the deposit in written form, such as "Five hundred dollars," followed by the amount of the deposit in numerical form. (Just as you would write a check, but with the amount written out first instead of second).

"Evidenced by" shows the form of the deposit (cash, check, collateral, promissory note, etc.). Note that there is a box which is not labeled, which you would check and fill in if you used a promissory note, put up a piece of property, or used anything but standard means—cash or a check—for your deposit.

"Payable to" gives the name of the person to whom the deposit is payable, normally the seller. As with your name, if more that one person is on the title, you should list them all. You may encounter cases where the deposit is payable to an agent of the seller.

"Purchase price of" is the offered purchase price in written form, followed by the offered purchase price in numerical form.

"Purchase of property, situated in" gives the city and county in which the property is located. Note that this need not be the same as the city and county in which the offer is made, which is the information on the top line.

"Described as follows" gives the address of the property, number and street. Be sure you include whether it is "St." or "Ave." or whatever; most cities have more than one street name that exists in several forms, such as Elm St., Elm Ave., Elm Rd., Elm Blvd. Elm Ct., Elm Pkwy., and so on and on. If there is a possibility of confusion, use additional description, such as, "between Oak and Pine Streets," or whatever is needed. On rare—very rare—occasions, it may be necessary to use the full legal description, as it appears on the title. Usually, a simple street address is enough, if it is complete.

Beginning with (1), the forms differ. I'll describe the short form first, and then go on to a complete discussion of the longer form.

(1) After "buyer will deposit in escrow with," which names the title company which will handle the paperwork, this clause gives the general terms and conditions of the offer.

This is the most important single part of the purchase offer. This is where you write out the details of your offer, how you will finance, what conditions you put on your acceptance, and everything important to the kind of creative purchasing I'm talking about. Most of this book is about how to do things that you will write out under this heading. This is where you get creative. If there is not enough room in the space provided, you can continue on an addendum. I expect that in most states, a form will look something like this.

(2) Whether or not there will be a deposit increase, how much if so, and within how many days. It is customary to increase the deposit after acceptance, but not *required*. Don't do it unless the seller demands it.

(3) This clause tells whether you will or will not occupy the house as a primary residence. This is important to some kinds of financing.

(4) A list of supplements to the agreement. Most sales include additional forms and agreements, which become part of the total offer. Because the purchase offer form is the primary document, all other documents are listed on it.

(5) California is an escrow state, in which a title company normally handles all the paperwork involved in the transaction. In mortgage states, the paperwork is usually handled by attorneys. This clause sets the number of days within which buyer and seller shall deliver signed instructions to the escrow holder, sets the closing date, and specifies how the escrow fees are to be paid. If you are the buyer, you want the seller to pay; if you are the seller, you want the buyer to pay. This is a negotiable point, so always write it in your favor.

(6) This form comes as two separate NCR multi-copy sets, not one sheet of paper printed on both sides. Every separate sheet in a purchase offer must be signed, or initialed, so there is space for the signatures of the buyer and seller. This is not a signature to the *contract* but only acknowledges that both sides to the transaction have received a copy of this *page*. Because this is the first page of the contract, it also has a blank for the total number of pages in the contract, so both parties agree on how many pages are part of the agreement.

The second page of this form provides for title insurance, and that the title be free and clear, who pays what fees, proration of rents, interest, taxes, and such, how title will vest, and what happens if the buyer defaults. It also includes the date of possession by buyer, followed by signatures for the buyer and his or her broker, and a section for acceptance, which designates the fees (commission) to be paid the broker, with space for signatures.

There is a lot of legally important language here, and if you don't understand the significance of similar language on the contracts you use, ask your agent to explain, or consult a real estate attorney. The exact wording and legal significance will differ from state to state.

You'll also note that there are many blanks in which you can write in who will pay what fees or costs. Ask the other party to pay, regardless of local "custom."

Also note that (10) on this page shows how title will vest, and cautions that the way title is taken may have significant legal and tax consequences. Be certain you understand how the various ways to take title affect the deal you are making.

You'll see that (16) sets the time the offer remains open for acceptance by the seller. This is usually a short time, often one day, and rarely more than three. The buyer does not wish to give the seller the option of delaying acceptance in the hope that a better offer will be made.

The final section of this page, headed "Acceptance," sets the commission to be paid the agent and provides spaces for the seller to accept the offer by signing, and for the brokers of both parties to agree.

In the new, longer form, (1) contains letter-designated lines (A) through (L), which cover most financing possibilities. It covers *only* financing. On the other form, the space could be used to list many other terms and conditions, such as the pest control report contingency or personal property to be included in the deal, which are covered elsewhere on this form.

It begins with a most important line which is *not* part of the other form and would have to be written in by the buyer or his agent. This line states that the entire agreement is contingent upon buyer obtaining financing. Can you imagine the problems that might result if someone, through ignorance or carelessness, wrote an offer which *did not* make the deal contingent on obtaining financing, and the buyer couldn't get credit approval? Yes, this is a line to *be sure* you include in any contract which does not have it printed on the form.

(A) Gives the amount of the deposit and the title company into which it shall be deposited on acceptance of the offer.

(B) Shows whether the deposit will be increased, how much, and by when.

(C) States when the balance of the down payment shall be deposited, and where. The deposit is normally less than the down payment, so in almost all deals there is a need to state how much remains, and when and how it will be paid.

(D) Covers the details of a new first loan. On the other form, you'd have to write all this out. That's true for all the financing clauses provided here. Note that you'd have to write out not just the amount of the loan, but the interest rate, whether variable or fixed-rate interest, due date, loan fee, and, if an FHA or VA deal, how many points the seller is paying, and any additional terms.

When you write in a loan as part of a deal, be sure you specify everything that is important. When the form is not as detailed as this one, double check to be sure you wrote it all in.

With this form, remember that what is listed is not *all* the creative things you can do. (There is a line, (K), for "additional terms.")

(E) Covers the details of assuming an existing first loan.

(F) For seller financing, a tool we use often.

(G) For assumption of an existing second loan.

(H) For buyer obtaining a new second loan.

(I) Provides that if buyer assumes a loan or loans, seller must provide buyer with copies of the notes and deeds, with buyer having a set number of calender days to approve or disapprove. An important note: if buyer is to disapprove, he or she must do so in writing, within the days allowed.

This is one of several clauses in this contract which contain the line *"Failure to notify seller shall conclusively be considered approval."* That's important. It means that you don't have to do anything to approve such a contingency, but you *must* take action, in writing, to disapprove.

If you find reason to disapprove—to get out of the deal or to demand changes, if possible—then you *must* do it in writing and within the time allowed. This puts the burden of disapproval on you, the buyer.

(J) A "good faith" clause, which means you promise to work hard to obtain the financing in the offer.

(K) For additional financing terms—anything else you want to put in goes here.

(L) The total purchase price—the total of all the loans and the down payment.

These clauses offer a very comprehensive set of financing options for creative investors.

(2) is the same as the occupancy clause, (3), in the other form.

(3) is supplements ([4] in the other form), but only has space for six supplements. Three are listed. Some agreements listed as supplements in the short form are part of this version. The short form had signature spaces on each page, but this one provides for initials, with signatures on the final page. Page 2, and each following page, begins with a line for the

property address. That way, should the pages get sepa-
rated or mixed up in handling, there can be no doubt which
page was part of which agreement.

(4)   Sets a deadline by which time buyer and seller must send
signed instructions to the escrow office. It also sets the
closing time allowed. This clause is worded "within" so
many days. If you encounter a form which does not have
either that language, or "on or before" the closing date,
write in one of those terms so that you can close early if
everything is in order and you find it beneficial to do so.
Finally, it specifies how escrow fees are to be paid.

There is no set time in which a deal must be closed. The
practical limit on the short end is ten days to two weeks—
which requires that *everything* happen as fast as possible,
there is no new bank financing unless pre-approved, and
no problems at all. That's rare, but it can happen with some
kinds of assumptions plus seller financing.

Normally, thirty days is the "short" limit, and thirty to
ninety is the normal range. You may find some variation
from state to state depending on laws and procedures. If
you want an early closing, write it for thirty days. You can
always agree to extend if you must. If you see no need to
rush, write it for sixty days. That's plenty of time for all
financing arrangements, inspections, repairs, and even a
few normal or abnormal delays.

But—would you believe me if I told you there was a
way to make money on a house you *don't even own?* You
can, if property values are rising. For example, in the past
year, values have risen at an annual rate of 10 to 20 percent
in much of California and many other parts of the country.
Look what happens if property is increasing in value at a
rate of 12 percent per year, and we write a closing date of
120 days.

```
    $100,000  house
x      12%  appreciation
    ─────────────────────
    $ 12,000  appreciation per year, divided by 12 months
```

= $ 1,000 appreciation per month

x   4 months, the 120-day escrow period

= $ 4,000 amount made during escrow period

If, on the other hand, we have money coming to us in the deal, or have the house resold before we take title to it, we might want the shortest possible escrow. In that case, ask the seller to cooperate in closing escrow within ten days, or whatever period is the shortest realistic closing time we could request.

So you see, closing time is not something to be taken lightly. It can be very important to us. Either a short or long closing can make a difference in our ability to profit. Every deal is different, so take the time to think whether you will benefit most from a short, normal, or long closing time.

(5) This is the title insurance clause. It provides that the title is clear of any liens or other encumbrances other that those of record and is not restricted from continuing in its present use. It gives the buyer the right of "reasonable" disapproval within a specified number of days, specifies that seller shall furnish buyer a title insurance policy, and names the title company, with a blank for who pays the expense. Always ask the seller to pay.

Note that a *preliminary* title report is what is to be approved or disapproved, and then the title insurance policy, showing title vested in the buyer, is issued. If seller fails to do so, buyer may terminate the contract.

(6) Prorations. These are expenses which are normally divided between buyer and seller according to the time each has title to the house (prorated). They include taxes, insurance premiums, interest, and rents.

If the seller has paid any of these items in advance, and many of them are customarily so paid, he will want to be reimbursed for the portion of the payment period which goes into your ownership. As a buyer, you want to take over these funds without reimbursing the seller. If you reimburse, you have to come up with money out of your own pocket. If you can't convince the seller to pay your share of prorations, you may be able to cover the expense as part of the loan, so you pay no money out of pocket.

Never pay the seller's share of prorations.

On most 90 and 95 percent conventional loans and FHA or VA loans, the lender requires an impound account to pay taxes and insurance when they come due. This means the owner has paid in advance. Always ask to be credited with impounds!

If you're buying a rental property, the owner will normally have collected rents in advance and (if he or she is a smart landlord) will have a security deposit for each tenant. Ask for rents to be prorated to the closing day. And *always* ask to be credited for the tenants' deposits! If you don't, you're still required to pay back those deposits when the tenant leaves the unit in good condition, or for the repairs the deposit would have covered if the tenant does not. You can see how a collection of small things could add up to a lot of expense for you, and make the difference between being able to buy a property for nothing down and making a profit or not.

This form has an important addition to the version used in the short form. It notes that property will be reassessed upon change of ownership, and a supplemental tax bill issued. It provides who will pay what part of the bill, and that bills issued after close of escrow will be handled by the buyer and seller. This is a result of the change in property taxes brought about by Proposition 13 in California, which has inspired changes in property tax methods in other states as well. If your state reassesses on sale, you should learn what the consequences are, and who pays what.

(7) Establishes the date buyer takes possession. I've talked about the potential importance of this earlier. In most cases you'll take possession on closing, but there are circumstances which make a different time advantageous. If you know for sure the deal will close, but there is a long escrow period, ask for *possession* of the property as soon as possible. Then you can rent the property and collect money during escrow (when little or none of your money is tied up and you don't have to worry about cash flow or payments).

One example of a situation where this would benefit both you and the seller is when the sellers have to or want to move now, but don't want to close escrow until one of them turns fifty-five. After that age, they can claim a one-time capital gains exclusion on their income tax, and pay no taxes on the first $125,000 of equity increase in their property.

This is more common than you might think. The middle fifties is a time when many couples no longer have children at home and want to sell that big old place and move to a smaller house, condo, or apartment. That "big old place" will often be worth a lot more than the new dwelling, so they need to shelter its equity.

(8)   The names which shall appear on the title, and how the title shall be vested. This is important. Find out the meanings of the ways you can take title in your state (any Realtor will know) and use the one which best suits your purposes.

(9)   Authorizes a broker to report the transaction to the MLS. This is important to real estate people; it provides them with their source of information on how much houses are actually selling for (not what the asking price in the listing was) and enables them to accurately price comparable homes they list.

(10)   Initials of buyer and seller on the liquidated damages clause. This is a California clause which may appear in some form in your state, or may not. It is intended to provide damages if the deal does not go through due to a fault on the part of the buyer, and to eliminate lawsuits over such matters.

(11)   and (12) are clauses providing how controversy shall be legally settled, and who pays, if there is litigation.

(13)   Requires the seller to provide keys to all locks and alarms. You might think that was obvious, but this makes it a requirement of the deal.

(14)   Personal property included with the sale would be listed under (1) on the other form. Here, there is a separate clause for the purpose.

(15) Fixtures are anything permanently attached to real property. The basic definition is that land and buildings are
"real property" and everything else is "personal property," but there are gray areas. This clause spells out things
that are normally "attached" to real property, and leaves
spaces to add or remove items from such a definition.

(16) Covers legal requirements for smoke detectors and who
pays for installation if there are none in the building.
Smoke detectors are not legally required everywhere, but
I feel they are so important that you should insist they be
part of any property you buy, and, certainly, any property
you rent, lease, or sell. How would you feel if someone
died in a fire in a building you owned or sold which didn't
have smoke detectors? They're very cheap now, so there's
no reason not to have them. I feel the seller should pay for
them, but if he or she refuses, you should do it.

(17) Covers legal requirements for a Real Estate Transfer Disclosure statement, required by California state law.

(18) Covers federal requirements for withholding tax if a property is purchased by a foreign buyer. You may not see this
clause in a contract form; this does not, however, mean the
deal is exempt from meeting its requirements.

(19) A "legal language" clause, which states that what is written and signed is the entire contract and that no other
written or verbal agreements are or can be considered part
of the agreement. It also includes the line "time is of the
essence," which requires all parties to the transaction to
respond and perform without delay.

(End of page 2, with space for initials; beginning of page 3
with property address.)

(20) states that the captions (the bold print at the beginning of
each section) are not part of the legal language of the
agreement, but are to be used only to refer to the legal
language, which is in regular type.

(21) Additional terms and conditions are clauses which in the
older, shorter form would have been covered in adden-

dums or supplements to the basic contract, or would have been written in the "terms and conditions" (1) section. Here they are written out, with space to fill in where needed, and become part of the contract only if initialed by both buyer and seller. Note that four of them contain the line which causes them to be automatically considered approved unless the buyer notifies the seller of disapproval before a deadline. Always make such notification in writing.

(A) *Physical inspection* provides that the buyer may have the property inspected by professionals and may cancel the deal if the inspections reveal problems the buyer won't accept and the seller won't correct. It is considered approved unless the buyer disapproves.

(B) *Geological inspection* provides that the buyer may have a professional inspect the land. In California we tend to think of this as inspection for earthquake or earth movement (landslide or settling) risk, but geologic inspection is by no means limited to that, or to this part of the country. In many rural areas, for example, it is very important to know the quality and quantity of well water available, and whether the soil will properly support septic tanks. It is considered approved unless the buyer disapproves.

(C) *Condition of property* is a seller's guarantee that the property will be in the same shape on close of escrow that it was when the offer was accepted, that the roof doesn't leak, and that everything works.

(D) *Seller representation* is the seller's warranty that there are no violations of any local, state, or national government regulations filed against the property.

(E) *Pest control* covers termite and pest inspections and correction (clearance) of the defects. This is an important clause which should be added to any contract which does not include it.

(F) *Flood hazard area disclosure* requires that the buyer be told if the property is in an area with flood risk. I recommend that you buy no property in any kind of flood zone; the risks are high and the insurance often prohibitive.
(End of page 3, with initials; top of page 4 with address.)

(G) *Special Studies Zone disclosure* is a California clause, usually relating to areas with actual or potential earthquake or earth movement hazard. The buyer is notified and given a set number of days to investigate what it means under terms of the Special Studies Zone Act and all local building, zoning, and other codes. I advise careful studies of any property in such an area. Note that this is accepted unless the buyer disapproves.

(H) *Energy conservation retrofit.* Many California communities require energy conservation measures, which are enforced upon sale of a property. This clause provides that the work be done and who pays for it (the seller, of course, in any deal we write as a buyer).

(I) *Home protection plan.* In California, buyer and seller must be informed that such plans are available. I recommend that you ask the seller to provide and pay for one. If you are selling, ask the buyer to pay. The clause provides space for the details.

(J) *Condominium/P.U.D.* (P.U.D. means "Planned Unit Development.") Requires seller to provide buyer with all information and costs regarding such property, and gives buyer time to disapprove. It is approved if buyer does not disapprove.

(22) provides space for other terms and conditions—space for you to be creative.

(23) is a California clause resulting from new legislation on the "laws of agency" which went into effect on January 1, 1988. It is a result of legal questions which kept arising from real estate practice, namely, who does an "agent" represent? Traditionally the real estate agent has been the agent of the *seller*, even though you, as a buyer, might think of an agent as "your" agent. The agent got paid from money paid by the seller, and thus was a seller's agent. Unless you had specifically, for a fee, retained an agent to represent you, "your" agent legally represented the seller.

This created a legal condition called "dual agency" in which one agent represented both parties, which got even more legally complicated when a brokerage or an individual agent was both the listing and selling broker or agent. The new law does not outlaw dual agency, but requires brokers to decide whether they will be one or the other or both, and to inform buyers and sellers which they have chosen to represent. This clause provides the information. You should expect to see more states dealing with the matter of agency. Check to see what the present requirements in your state may be.

(24) says that all amendments and changes between buyer and seller must be in writing.

(25) States that this is an offer to purchase property and sets the time allowed to accept or reject the offer. It automatically withdraws the offer if no response is made within the time allowed.

Normally you make this period as short as possible. One day is reasonable unless you are dealing with an out-of-town seller and must allow time for paperwork to go back and forth. (With Federal Express you should be able to get papers out and back in two days, not more than three.) The reason for limiting time so severely is not to pressure the seller into acceptance, but to reduce the possibility that another offer will be made before yours is accepted. The seller can always ask for more time to consider, and normally you would grant the time, but most don't ask.

Below (25) is space for the real estate broker's signature (unless a broker was not involved) and the buyer's signature(s), with addresses and phone numbers for both. Note that the broker's space is set up to show the name of the broker or brokerage and then the name of the agent who wrote the offer. This is legally important because the agent you work with, unless the agent is also the broker, works as a *subagent* of the broker-of-record who owns or manages the real estate office.

Under "Acceptance" is a space to identify the seller's broker and commission agreement (if a broker is involved) and then space for the signature, phone number, and address of the seller(s) and the date they signed the agreement, followed by signature and date spaces for both

seller's and buyer's brokers. As above, there is space to
name both the broker and the agent.

Note that wherever signatures are required, *all* persons
involved must sign. The seller's signature(s) must include
everyone on the title, and the buyer's signature(s) must
include everyone involved in making the offer.

No Purchase Offer
Is Really Standard

Remember that laws differ from state to state, and your state may
require certain language in a contract, or certain language may not
be allowable. Seek competent legal advice before using this or any
contract in your state.

This rundown covers basic purchase offer documents. Any
actual offer will have additional pages or addendum sheets, according
to the needs of the deal. And, I'll repeat, be certain any form you
use conforms to the laws of your state.

If your offer becomes greatly fattened by additional forms, don't
worry. That's normal. By the time you close, the stack will be even
thicker. A title insurance report and policy and a pest control report
by themselves can make your stack of closing documents impressively thick. Some states will require or customarily use more
documents than others. If you feel overwhelmed the first time you
sit down to sign everything at closing, you're normal.

A friend, who is not an investor, tells this story of signing closing
documents for a home he bought: He and his wife signed in the title
company's conference room. The title officer explained what everything was, and then, as they began signing, was called out of the
room.

About the time they finished writing their names and were
flexing their fingers to relieve writer's cramp the title officer returned, saying brightly, "Hey, what did you think of that earthquake?" Said they, amazed, "What earthquake?" Five pointsomething on the Richter Scale, it had knocked things off desks

elsewhere in the office. My friends had been so absorbed in trying to understand all their paperwork that they hadn't even noticed it!

You get used to the documents fast. There's one basic rule, which I can't say often enough or emphasize too strongly: Anything you don't understand, ask the real estate agent, title officer, or attorney to explain. It is their job and responsibility to do so. That's important if all you're doing is buying one house to live in. It is even more important to know what you are signing, and what it means, when you are buying for investment purposes.

REAL ESTATE PURCHASE CONTRACT AND RECEIPT FOR DEPOSIT

THIS IS MORE THAN A RECEIPT FOR MONEY. IT IS INTENDED TO BE A LEGALLY BINDING CONTRACT. READ IT CAREFULLY.

CALIFORNIA ASSOCIATION OF REALTORS® (CAR) STANDARD FORM

_______________________________________ , California. _______________ , 19_______

Received from ____

herein called Buyer, the sum of ____ Dollars $_______________

evidenced by cash ☐, cashier's check ☐, or _________________ ☐, personal check ☐ payable to_______________

_______________________ , to be held uncashed until acceptance of this offer, as deposit on account of purchase price of

____ Dollars $_______________

for the purchase of property, situated in _________________ , County of_________________ , California,

described as follows: ____

1. Buyer will deposit in escrow with_________________ the balance of purchase price as follows:

____

____

____

____

Set forth above any terms and conditions of a factual nature applicable to this sale, such as financing, prior sale of other property, the matter of structural pest control inspection, repairs and personal property to be included in the sale.

2. Deposit will ☐ will not ☐ be increased by $_________________ to $_________________ within_________________ days of acceptance of this offer.

3. Buyer does ☐ does not ☐ intend to occupy subject property as his residence.

4. The following supplements are incorporated as part of this agreement:

                      Other

☐ Structural Pest Control Certification Agreement ☐ Occupancy Agreement ☐ _______________

☐ Special Studies Zone Disclosure ☐ VA Amendment ☐ _______________

☐ Flood Insurance Disclosure ☐ FHA Amendment ☐ _______________

5. Buyer and Seller shall deliver signed instructions to the escrow holder within _________________ days from Seller's acceptance which shall provide for closing within_________________ days from Seller's acceptance. Escrow fees to be paid as follows:

____

6. Buyer and Seller acknowledge receipt of a copy of this page, which constitutes Page 1 of_________ Pages.

Buyer _______________________________ Seller _______________________________

Buyer _______________________________ Seller _______________________________

A REAL ESTATE BROKER IS THE PERSON QUALIFIED TO ADVISE ON REAL ESTATE. IF YOU DESIRE LEGAL ADVICE CONSULT YOUR ATTORNEY.

OFFICE USE ONLY

Reviewed by Broker or Designee _______________

Date _______________

FORM D-11-1

SF-Sept-88

FOR ILLUSTRATION ONLY - Consult your attorney for legal advice ON CONTRACTS IN YOUR STATE

Reprinted with permission, California Association of Realtors®, Endorsment not implied

REAL ESTATE PURCHASE CONTRACT AND RECEIPT FOR DEPOSIT

The following terms and conditions are hereby incorporated in and made a part of Buyer's Offer

7.   Title is to be free of liens, encumbrances, easements, restrictions, rights and conditions of record or known to Seller, other than the following: (1) Current property taxes, (b) covenants, conditions, restrictions, and public utility easements of record, if any, provided the same do not adversely affect the continued use of the property for the purposes for which it is presently being used, unless reasonably disapproved by Buyer in writing within _________________ days of receipt of a current preliminary title report furnished at ______________ ____ expense. and (c) ____

Seller shall furnish Buyer at _______________________________ expense a standard California Land Title Association policy issued by _______________________________ Company, showing title vested in Buyer subject only to the above. If Seller is unwilling or unable to eliminate any title matter disapproved by Buyer as above, Seller may terminate this agreement. If Seller fails to deliver title as above, Buyer may terminate this agreement; in either case, the deposit shall be returned to Buyer.

8.   Property taxes, premiums on insurance acceptable to Buyer, rents, interest, and _________________________________ shall be pro-rated as of (a) the date of recordation of deed; or (b)____ . Any bond or assessment which is a lien shall be ___paid___ by _________________ . Transfer taxes, if any, shall be paid by __________________

                                           assumed

9.   Possession shall be delivered to Buyer (a) on close of escrow, or (b) not later than _________________________ days after close of escrow or (c) ____

10.   Unless otherwise designated in the escrow instructions of Buyer, title shall vest as follows: _____________________

(The manner of taking title may have significant legal and tax consequences. Therefore, give this matter serious consideration.)

11.   If Broker is a participant of a Board multiple listing service ("MLS"), the Broker is authorized to report the sale, its price, terms, and financing for the information, publication, dissemination, and use of the authorized Board members.

12.   If Buyer fails to complete said purchase as herein provided by reason of any default of Buyer, Seller shall be released from his obligation to sell the property to Buyer and may proceed against Buyer upon any claim or remedy which he may have in law or equity; provided, however, that by placing their initials here Buyer: (   ) Seller: (   ) agree that Seller shall retain the deposit as his liquidated damages. If the described property is a dwelling with no more than four units, one of which the Buyer intends to occupy as his residence, Seller shall retain as liquidated damages the deposit actually paid, or an amount therefrom, not more than 3% of the purchase price and promptly return any excess to Buyer.

13.   If the only controversy or claim between the parties arises out of or relates to the disposition of the Buyer's deposit, such controversy or claim shall at the election of the parties be decided by arbitration. Such arbitration shall be determined in accordance with the Rules of the American Arbitration Association, and judgment upon the award rendered by the Arbitrator(s) may be entered in any court having jurisdiction thereof. The provisions of Code of Civil Procedure Section 1283.05 shall be applicable to such arbitration.

14.   In any action or proceeding arising out of this agreement, the prevailing party shall be entitled to reasonable attorney's fees and costs.

15.   Time is of the essence. All modification or extensions shall be in writing signed by the parties.

16.   This constitutes an offer to purchase the described property. Unless acceptance is signed by Seller and the signed copy delivered to Buyer, in person or by mail to the address below, within_______________ days, this offer shall be deemed revoked and the deposit shall be returned. Buyer acknowledges receipt of a copy hereof.

Real Estate Broker _________________________________   Buyer _________________________________

By _________________________________   Buyer _________________________________

Address _________________________________   Address _________________________________

Telephone _________________________________   Telephone _________________________________

ACCEPTANCE

The undersigned Seller accepts and agrees to sell the property on the above terms and conditions. Seller has employed _______________ as Broker(s) and agrees to pay for services the sum of ____ Dollars ($_____________________), payable as follows: (a) On recordation of the deed or other evidence of title, or (b) if completion of sale is prevented by default of Seller, upon Seller's default or (c) if completion of sale is prevented by default of Buyer, only if and when Seller collects damages from Buyer, by suit or otherwise and then in an amount not less than one-half of the damages recovered, but not to exceed the above fee, after first deducting title and escrow expenses and the expenses of collection, if any. In any action between Broker and Seller arising out of this agreement, the prevailing party shall be entitled to reasonable attorney's fees and costs. The undersigned acknowledges receipt of a copy and authorizes Broker(s) to deliver a signed copy to Buyer.

Dated _________________ Telephone_________________   Seller _________________________________

Address _________________________________   Seller _________________________________

Broker(s) agree to the foregoing. Broker _________________________   Broker _________________________

Dated_________________ By _________________________   Dated_________________ By _________________________

FORM D-11-2

____ California, _______________________________ , 19____

Received from ____

herein called Buyer, the sum of ____ Dollars $ __________

evidenced by ☐ cash, ☐ cashier's check, ☐ personal check or ☐ ___________________ , payable to __________

_________________________________ , to be held uncashed until acceptance of this offer as deposit on account of purchase price of

____ Dollars $ __________

for the purchase of property, situated in _______________________________ , County of __________________ California,

described as follows: ____

1. FINANCING: The obtaining of Buyer's financing is a contingency of this agreement.

A. DEPOSIT upon acceptance, to be deposited into _________________________________ $ __________

B. INCREASED DEPOSIT within ______ days of Seller's acceptance to be deposited into _____________ $ __________

C. BALANCE OF DOWN PAYMENT to be deposited into _______________ on or before ____________ $ __________

D. Buyer to apply, qualify for and obtain a NEW FIRST LOAN in the amount of .... $ __________

payable monthly at approximately $_______________________ including interest at origination not to exceed

______ %, ☐ fixed rate, ☐ other ___________________________ all due______ years from date of

origination. Loan fee not to exceed ________________ Seller agrees to pay a maximum of _____________

FHA/VA discount points. Additional terms ____

E. Buyer ☐ to assume, ☐ to take title subject to an EXISTING FIRST LOAN with an approximate balance of ... $ __________

in favor of____ payable monthly at $__________ including interest

at______ % ☐ fixed rate, ☐ other ____

Fees not to exceed__________ . Disposition of impound account ___________________________

Additional Terms ____

F. Buyer to execute a NOTE SECURED BY a ☐ first, ☐ second, ☐ third DEED OF TRUST in the amount of $ __________

IN FAVOR OF SELLER payable monthly at $___________ ☐ or more, including interest at______ % all due

___________ years from date of origination, ☐ or upon sale or transfer of subject property. A late charge of

___________________ shall be due on any installment not paid within__________ days of the due date.

☐ Deed of Trust to contain a request for notice of default or sale for the benefit of Seller. Buyer ☐ will, ☐ will not

execute a request for notice of delinquency. Additional terms_______________________________________

G. Buyer☐ to assume, ☐ to take title subject to an EXISTING SECOND LOAN with an approximate balance of . $ __________

in favor of_____________________________________ payable monthly at $__________ including interest

at______ % ☐ fixed rate, ☐ other ___________________ . Buyer fees not to exceed _______________

Additional terms ____

H. Buyer to apply, qualify for and obtain a NEW SECOND LOAN in the amount of .... $ __________

payable monthly at approximately $___________________ including interest at origination not to exceed

______ % ☐ fixed rate, ☐ other____

__________ , all due________ years from date of origination, Buyer's loan fee not to exceed_____________ .

Additional Terms ____

I. In the event Buyer assumes or takes title subject to an existing loan, Seller shall provide Buyer with copies of

applicable notes and Deeds of Trust. A loan may contain a number of features which affect the loan, such as

interest rate changes, monthly payment changes, balloon payments, etc. Buyer shall be allowed________ calendar

days after receipt of such copies to notify Seller in writing of disapproval. FAILURE TO NOTIFY SELLER SHALL

CONCLUSIVELY BE CONSIDERED APPROVAL. Buyer's approval shall not be unreasonably withheld.

Difference in existing loan balances shall be adjusted in ☐ Cash, ☐ Other____________________________

J. Buyer agrees to act diligently and in good faith to obtain all applicable financing. ____________________

K. ADDITIONAL FINANCING TERMS: ____

L. TOTAL PURCHASE PRICE .... $ __________

2. OCCUPANCY: Buyer ☐ does, ☐ does not intend to occupy subject property as Buyer's primary residence.

3. SUPPLEMENTS: The ATTACHED supplements are incorporated herein:

☐ Interim Occupancy Agreement (CAR FORM IOA-11)　　☐ ____________________________

☐ Residential Lease Agreement after Sale (CAR FORM RLAS-11)　　☐ ____________________________

☐ VA and FHA Amendments (CAR FORM VA/FHA-11)　　☐ ____________________________

Buyer and Seller acknowledge receipt of copy of this page, which constitutes Page 1 of ________ Pages.

Buyer's Initials (__________) (__________)　　Seller's Initials (__________) (__________)

REAL ESTATE PURCHASE CONTRACT AND RECEIPT FOR DEPOSIT (DLF-14 PAGE 1 OF 4)

Subject Property Address ____

4. **ESCROW:** Buyer and Seller shall deliver signed instructions to _________________________________ the escrow holder, within _____________ calendar days from Seller's acceptance which shall provide for closing within _____________ calendar days from Seller's acceptance. Escrow fees to be paid as follows: ____

5. **TITLE:** Title is to be free of liens, encumbrances, easements, restrictions, rights and conditions of record or known to Seller, other than the following: (a) Current property taxes, (b) covenants, conditions, restrictions, and public utility easements of record, if any, provided the same do not adversely affect the continued use of the property for the purposes for which it is presently being used, unless reasonably disapproved by Buyer in writing within _________________________ calendar days of receipt of a current preliminary report furnished at _________________ expense, and (c) ____. Seller shall furnish Buyer at _________________________ expense a standard California Land Title Association policy issued by _________________________ Company, showing title vested in Buyer subject only to the above. If Seller is unwilling or unable to eliminate any title matter disapproved by Buyer as above, Buyer may terminate this agreement. If Seller fails to deliver title as above, Buyer may terminate this agreement; in either case, the deposit shall be returned to Buyer.

6. **PRORATIONS:** Property taxes, payments on bonds and assessments assumed by Buyer, interest, rents, association dues, premiums on insurance acceptable to Buyer, and _________________________ shall be paid current and prorated as of: ☐ the day of recordation of the deed; or ☐ _________________________ . Bonds or assessments now a lien shall be ☐ paid current by Seller, payments not yet due to be assumed by Buyer; or ☐ paid in full by Seller, including payments not yet due; or ☐ _________________________. County Transfer tax shall be paid by _________________________ . The _________________________ transfer tax or transfer fee shall be paid by _________________________ . **PROPERTY WILL BE REASSESSED UPON CHANGE OF OWNERSHIP. THIS WILL AFFECT THE TAXES TO BE PAID.** A Supplemental tax bill will be issued, which shall be paid as follows: (a) for periods after close of escrow, by Buyer (or by final acquiring party if part of an exchange), and (b) for periods prior to close of escrow, by Seller. TAX BILLS ISSUED AFTER CLOSE OF ESCROW SHALL BE HANDLED DIRECTLY BETWEEN BUYER AND SELLER.

7. **POSSESSION:** Possession and occupancy shall be delivered to Buyer, ☐ on close of escrow, or ☐ not later than _________ days after close of escrow, or ☐ ____

8. **VESTING:** Unless otherwise designated in the escrow instructions of Buyer, title shall vest as follows: _________________________

(The manner of taking title may have significant legal and tax consequences. Therefore, give this matter serious consideration.)

9. **MULTIPLE LISTING SERVICE:** If Broker is a Participant of a Board multiple listing service ("MLS"), the Broker is authorized to report the sale, its price, terms, and financing for the publication, dissemination, information, and use of the authorized Board members. MLS Participants and Subscribers.

10. **LIQUIDATED DAMAGES:** If Buyer fails to complete said purchase as herein provided by reason of any default of Buyer, Seller shall be released from obligation to sell the property to Buyer and may proceed against Buyer upon any claim or remedy which he/she may have in law or equity; provided, however, that by placing their initials here Buyer: (   ) Seller: (   ) agree that Seller shall retain the deposit as liquidated damages. If the described property is a dwelling with no more than four units, one of which the Buyer intends to occupy as his/her residence, Seller shall retain as liquidated damages the deposit actually paid, or an amount therefrom, not more than 3% of the purchase price and promptly return any excess to Buyer. Buyer and Seller agree to execute a similar liquidated damages provision, such as California Association of Realtors® Receipt for Increased Deposit (RID-11), for any increased deposits. (Funds deposited in trust accounts or in escrow are not released automatically in the event of a dispute. Release of funds requires written agreement of the parties or adjudication.)

11. **ARBITRATION:** If the only controversy or claim between the parties arises out of or relates to the disposition of the Buyer's deposit, such controversy or claim shall at the election of the parties be decided by arbitration. Such arbitration shall be determined in accordance with the Rules of the American Arbitration Association, and judgment upon the award rendered by the Arbitrator(s) may be entered in any court having jurisdiction thereof. The provisions of Code of Civil Procedure Section 1283.05 shall be applicable to such arbitration.

12. **ATTORNEY'S FEES:** In any action or proceeding arising out of this agreement, the prevailing party shall be entitled to reasonable attorney's fees and costs.

13. **KEYS:** Seller shall, when possession is available to Buyer, provide keys and/or means to operate all property locks, and alarms, if any.

14. **PERSONAL PROPERTY:** The following items of personal property, free of liens and without warranty of condition, are included: _________ ____

15. **FIXTURES:** All permanently installed fixtures and fittings that are attached to the property or for which special openings have been made are included in the purchase price, including electrical, light, plumbing and heating fixtures, built-in appliances, screens, awnings, shutters, all window coverings, attached floor coverings, T.V. antennas, air cooler or conditioner, garage door openers and controls, attached fireplace equipment, mailbox, trees and shrubs, and _________________________ except _________________

16. **SMOKE DETECTOR(S):** Approved smoke detector(s) shall be installed as required by law, at the expense of ☐ Buyer, ☐ Seller.

17. **TRANSFER DISCLOSURE:** Unless exempt, Transferor (Seller), shall comply with Civil Code Sections 1102 et seq., by providing transferee (Buyer) with a Real Estate Transfer Disclosure Statement: a) ☐ Buyer has received and read a Real Estate Transfer Disclosure Statement; or b) ☐ Seller shall provide Buyer with a Real Estate Transfer Disclosure Statement within _________________ calendar days of Seller's acceptance after which Buyer shall have three (3) days after delivery to Buyer, in person, or five (5) days after delivery by deposit in the mail, to terminate this agreement by delivery of a written notice of termination to Seller or Seller's Agent.

18. **TAX WITHHOLDING:** Under the Foreign Investment in Real Property Tax Act (FIRPTA), IRC 1445, *every* Buyer of U.S. real property *must*, unless an exemption applies, deduct and withhold from Seller's proceeds ten percent (10%) of the gross sales price. The primary exemptions are: No withholding is required if (a) Seller provides Buyer with an affidavit under penalty of perjury, that Seller is not a "foreign person," or (b) Seller provides Buyer with a "qualifying statement" issued by the Internal Revenue Service, or (c) if Buyer purchases real property for use as a residence and the purchase price is $300,000.00 or less and if Buyer or a member of Buyer's family has definite plans to reside at the property for at least 50% of the number of days it is in use during each of the first two twelve-months periods after transfer. Seller and Buyer agree to execute and deliver as directed, any instrument, affidavit and statement, or to perform any act reasonably necessary to carry out the provisions of FIRPTA and regulations promulgated thereunder.

19. **ENTIRE CONTRACT:** Time is of the essence. All prior agreements between the parties are incorporated in this agreement which constitutes the entire contract. Its terms are intended by the parties as a final expression of their agreement with respect to such terms as are included herein and may not be contradicted by evidence of any prior agreement or contemporaneous oral agreement. The parties further intend that this agreement constitutes the complete and exclusive statement of its terms and that no extrinsic evidence whatsoever may be introduced in any judicial or arbitration proceeding, if any, involving this agreement.

Buyer and Seller acknowledge receipt of copy of this page, which constitutes Page 2 of _________ Pages.

Buyer's Initials (_________) (_________)   Seller's Initials (_________) (_________)

<table>
<tr><td rowspan="3">BROKER'S COPY</td><td>──── OFFICE USE ONLY ────</td></tr>
<tr><td>Reviewed by Broker or Designee _________</td></tr>
<tr><td>Date _________</td></tr>
</table>

REAL ESTATE PURCHASE CONTRACT AND RECEIPT FOR DEPOSIT (DLF-14 PAGE 2 OF 4)

     DAVE DEL DOTTO

20. CAPTIONS: The captions in this agreement are for convenience of reference only and are not intended as part of this agreement.

21. ADDITIONAL TERMS AND CONDITIONS:
ONLY THE FOLLOWING PARAGRAPHS A THROUGH J *WHEN INITIALED BY BOTH BUYER AND SELLER* ARE INCORPORATED IN THIS AGREEMENT.

Buyer's Initials   Seller's Initials

______/______ ______/______ **A. PHYSICAL INSPECTION:** Within ________________ calendar days after Seller's acceptance Buyer shall have the right, at Buyer's expense, to select a licensed contractor(s) or other qualified professional(s), to inspect and investigate the subject property, including but not limited to structural, plumbing, heating, electrical, built-in appliances, roof, soils, foundation, mechanical systems, pool, pool heater, pool filter, air conditioner, if any, possible environmental hazards such as asbestos, formaldehyde, radon gas and other substances / products. Buyer shall keep the subject property free and clear of any liens, indemnify and hold Seller harmless from all liability, claims, demands, damages or costs, and repair all damages to the property arising from the inspections. All claimed defects concerning the condition of the property that adversely affect the continued use of the property for the purposes for which it is presently being used shall be in writing, supported by written reports, if any, and delivered to Seller within________ calendar days after Seller's acceptance. Buyer shall furnish Seller copies, at no cost, of all reports concerning the property obtained by Buyer. When such reports disclose conditions or information unsatisfactory to the Buyer, which the Seller is unwilling or unable to correct, Buyer may cancel this agreement. Seller shall make the premises available for all inspections. BUYER'S FAILURE TO NOTIFY SELLER SHALL CONCLUSIVELY BE CONSIDERED APPROVAL.

Buyer's Initials   Seller's Initials

______/______ ______/______ **B. GEOLOGICAL INSPECTION:** Within ________________ calendar days after Seller's acceptance, Buyer shall have the right at Buyer's expense, to select a qualified professional to make tests, surveys, or other studies of the subject property. Buyer shall keep the subject property free and clear of any liens, indemnify and hold Seller harmless from all liability, claims, demands, damages or costs, and repair all damages to the property arising from the tests, surveys, or studies. All claimed defects concerning the condition of the property that adversely affect the continued use of the property for the purposes for which it is presently being used shall be in writing, supported by written reports, if any, and delivered to Seller within ________________ calendar days after Seller's acceptance. Buyer shall furnish Seller copies, at no cost, of all reports concerning the property obtained by Buyer. When such reports disclose conditions or information unsatisfactory to the Buyer, which the Seller is unwilling or unable to correct, Buyer may cancel this agreement. Seller shall make the premises available for all inspections. BUYER'S FAILURE TO NOTIFY SELLER SHALL CONCLUSIVELY BE CONSIDERED APPROVAL.

Buyer's Initials   Seller's Initials

______/______ ______/______ **C. CONDITION OF PROPERTY:** Seller warrants, through the date possession is made available to Buyer: (1) property and improvements thereon, including landscaping, grounds and pool/spa, if any, shall be maintained in the same condition as upon the date of Seller's acceptance; (2) the roof is free of all known leaks and that water, sewer, plumbing, heating, air conditioning, if any, and electrical systems and all built-in appliances are operative, (3) ____

Buyer's Initials   Seller's Initials

______/______ ______/______ **D. SELLER REPRESENTATION:** Seller warrants that Seller has no knowledge of any notice of violations of City, County, State, Federal, Building, Zoning, Fire, Health Codes or ordinances, or other governmental regulation filed or issued against the property. This warranty shall be effective until the date of close of escrow.

Buyer's Initials   Seller's Initials

______/______ ______/______ **E. PEST CONTROL:** Within ____________ calendar days from the date of Seller's acceptance Seller shall furnish Buyer, at the expense of ☐ Buyer, ☐ Seller, a current written report of an inspection by ____ , a licensed Structural Pest Control Operator, of the main building and all structures on the property, except ____

If no infestation or infection by wood destroying pests or organisms is found, the report shall include a written "Certification" as provided in Business and Professions Code 8519(a) that on the date of inspection "no evidence of active infestation or infection was found."

All work recommended in said report to repair damage caused by infestation or infection by wood-destroying pests or organisms found, including leaking shower stalls and replacing of tiles removed for repairs, and all work to correct conditions that causes such infestation or infection shall be done at the expense of Seller.

Funds for work to be performed shall be held in escrow and disbursed upon receipt of written Certification as provided in Business and Professions Code 8519(b) that the property "is now free of evidence of active infestation or infection".

Buyer agrees that any work to correct conditions usually deemed likely to lead to infestation or infection by wood-destroying pests or organisms, but where no evidence of existing infestation or infection is found with respect to such conditions is NOT the responsibility of Seller, and that such work shall be done only if requested by Buyer and then at the expense of Buyer.

If inspection of inaccessible areas is recommended by the report, Buyer has the option of accepting and approving the report or requesting further inspection be made at the Buyer's expense. If further inspection is made and infestation, infection, or damage is found, repair of such damage and all work to correct conditions that caused such infestation or infection and the cost of entry and closing of the inaccessible areas shall be at the expense of Seller. If no infestation, infection, or damage is found, the cost of entry and closing of the inaccessible areas shall be at the expense of Buyer.

Other ____

Buyer's Initials   Seller's Initials

______/______ ______/______ **F. FLOOD HAZARD AREA DISCLOSURE:** Buyer is informed that subject property is situated in a "Special Flood Hazard Area" as set forth on a Federal Emergency Management Agency (FEMA) "Flood Insurance Rate Map (FIRM) or "Flood Hazard Boundary Map" (FHBM). The law provides that, as a condition of obtaining financing on most structures located in a "Special Flood Hazard Area," lenders require flood insurance where the property or its attachments are security for a loan.

The extent of coverage and the cost may vary. For further information consult the lender or insurance carrier. No representation or recommendation is made by the Seller and the Brokers in this transaction as to the legal effect or economic consequences of the National Flood Insurance Program and related legislation.

Buyer and Seller acknowledge receipt of copy of this page, which constitutes Page 3 of________ Pages.

Buyer's Initials (________) (________)   Seller's Initials (________) (________)

<table>
<tr><td>——— OFFICE USE ONLY ———
Reviewed by Broker or Designee ________
Date ________</td></tr>
</table>

BROKER'S COPY

EQUAL HOUSING OPPORTUNITY
SF-July-87

REAL ESTATE PURCHASE CONTRACT AND RECEIPT FOR DEPOSIT (DLF-14 PAGE 3 OF 4)

Subject Property Address ____

<u>Buyer's Initials</u>   <u>Seller's Initials</u>

____/____   ____/____   **G. SPECIAL STUDIES ZONE DISCLOSURE:** Buyer is informed that subject property is situated in a Special Studies Zone as designated under Sections 2621-2625, inclusive, of the California Public Resources Code; and, as such, the construction or development on this property of any structure for human occupancy may be subject to the findings of a geologic report prepared by a geologist registered in the State of California, unless such a report is waived by the City or County under the terms of that act.

Buyer is allowed _______ calendar days from the date of Seller's acceptance to make further inquiries at appropriate governmental agencies concerning the use of the subject property under the terms of the Special Studies Zone Act and local building, zoning, fire, health and safety codes. When such inquiries disclose conditions or information unsatisfactory to the Buyer, which the Seller is unwilling or unable to correct, Buyer may cancel this agreement. BUYER'S FAILURE TO NOTIFY SELLER SHALL CONCLUSIVELY BE CONSIDERED APPROVAL.

<u>Buyer's Initials</u>   <u>Seller's Initials</u>

____/____   ____/____   **H. ENERGY CONSERVATION RETROFIT:** If local ordinance requires that the property be brought in compliance with minimum energy Conservation Standards as a condition of sale or transfer, ☐ Buyer, ☐ Seller shall comply with and pay for these requirements. Where permitted by law, Seller may, if obligated hereunder, satisfy the obligation by authorizing escrow to credit Buyer with sufficient funds to cover the cost of such retrofit.

<u>Buyer's Initials</u>   <u>Seller's Initials</u>

____/____   ____/____   **I. HOME PROTECTION PLAN:** Buyer and Seller have been informed that Home Protection Plans are available. Such plans may provide additional protection and benefit to a Seller or Buyer. California Association of Realtors® and the Broker(s) in this transaction do not endorse or approve any particular company or program:

a) ☐ A Buyer's coverage Home Protection Plan to be issued by ____
   Company, at a cost not to exceed $ _______________________________ , to be paid by ☐ Seller, ☐ Buyer; or
b) ☐ Buyer and Seller elect not to purchase a Home Protection Plan.

<u>Buyer's Initials</u>   <u>Seller's Initials</u>

____/____   ____/____   **J. CONDOMINIUM/P.U.D.:** The subject of this transaction is a condominium/planned unit development (P.U.D.) designated as unit __________ and __________ parking space(s) and an undivided __________ interest in all community areas, and ________________________________ . The current monthly assessment charge by the homeowner's association or other governing body(s) is $ __________________ . As soon as practicable, Seller shall provide Buyer with copies of covenants, conditions and restrictions, articles of incorporation, by-laws, current rules and regulations, most current financial statements, and any other documents as required by law. Seller shall disclose in writing any known pending special assessment, claims, or litigation to Buyer. Buyer shall be allowed _______ calendar days from receipt to review these documents. If such documents disclose conditions or information unsatisfactory to Buyer, Buyer may cancel this agreement. BUYER'S FAILURE TO NOTIFY SELLER SHALL CONCLUSIVELY BE CONSIDERED APPROVAL.

22. **OTHER TERMS AND CONDITIONS:** ____

____

____

____

____

23. **AGENCY CONFIRMATION:** The following agency relationship(s) are hereby confirmed for this transaction:

LISTING AGENT: ____ is the agent of (check one):
   ☐ the Seller exclusively; or   ☐ both the Buyer and Seller

SELLING AGENT: ____ (if not the same as Listing Agent) is the agent of (check one):
   ☐ the Buyer exclusively; or   ☐ the Seller exclusively; or   ☐ both the Buyer and Seller.

24. **AMENDMENTS: This agreement may not be amended, modified, altered or changed in any respect whatsoever except by a further agreement in writing executed by Buyer and Seller.**

25. **OFFER:** This constitutes an offer to purchase the described property. Unless acceptance is signed by Seller and the signed copy delivered in person or by mail to Buyer, or to _______________________________ who is authorized to receive it, in person or by mail at the address below, within _______ calendar days of the date hereof, this offer shall be deemed revoked and the deposit shall be returned. Buyer has read and acknowledges receipt of a copy of this offer.

REAL ESTATE BROKER _______________________________   BUYER _______________________________________

By ____   BUYER _______________________________________

Address ____   Address ______________________________________

____   ____

Telephone ____   Telephone ____________________________________

ACCEPTANCE

The undersigned Seller accepts and agrees to sell the property on the above terms and conditions and agrees to the above confirmation of agency relationships. Seller agrees to pay to Broker(s) ____

____

compensation for services as follows: ____

Payable: (a) On recordation of the deed or other evidence of title, or (b) if completion of sale is prevented by default of Seller, upon Seller's default, or (c) if completion of sale is prevented by default of Buyer, only if and when Seller collects damages from Buyer, by suit or otherwise, and then in an amount not less than one-half of the damages recovered, but not to exceed the above fee, after first deducting title and escrow expenses and the expenses of collection, if any. Seller shall execute and deliver an escrow instruction irrevocably assigning the compensation for service in an amount equal to the compensation agreed to above. In any action or proceeding between Broker(s) and Seller arising out of this agreement, the prevailing party shall be entitled to reasonable attorneys fees and costs. The undersigned has read and acknowledges receipt of a copy of this agreement and authorizes Broker(s) to deliver a signed copy to Buyer.

Date ____________________ Telephone ____________________   SELLER _______________________________________

Address ____

____   SELLER _______________________________________

Real Estate Broker(s) agree to the foregoing.

Broker ____   By ____________________________________ Date ________________

Broker ____   By ____________________________________ Date ________________

Page 4 of __________ Pages.

BROKER'S COPY

OFFICE USE ONLY

Reviewed by Broker or Designee __________

Date __________

SF-July-87

REAL ESTATE PURCHASE CONTRACT AND RECEIPT FOR DEPOSIT (DLF-14 PAGE 4 OF 4)

CHAPTER 7

WHAT MAKES A PURCHASE "CREATIVE"?

L et me tell you a secret. You can make a very creative deal with a perfectly normal purchase offer.

What I want you to do is think of the deal itself and the purchase offer on which you write it up as two separate, distinct, and entirely different things.

"The deal" involves finding the property, figuring out how you will make money from it, learning the seller's needs, figuring out how to meet them and make money, and deciding how you will buy the property and what you will do with it.

The purchase offer is the means you use to present the results of your deal planning to the seller and *the tool you use to protect yourself against loss.*

Certain things you should always do are not part of "conventional" purchase offers. Most of these are not so much "creative" as just common sense. But, because others don't think to do them, they usually get labeled creative.

What Is Creativity?

Think of the meaning of "creative." It means doing things differently and with imagination. Almost anyone would agree that "creativity" and "imagination" are good things and we need more of them—but look around you.

How many people do you know who go to work and are happy because they just go in and do the same thing they did yesterday and don't have to think about it? Not many, right? But how many, even among those who complain how dull it is, would actually be *happy* if you bought the business that gives them that dull, boring job and changed everything to make it creative and exciting? Again, not many.

How many co-workers do you hear people say things about like, "Gee, ol' Snodgrass was brilliant when he started with the company, but now he's just putting in time waiting to retire"?

That's what happens when people, and their jobs, are not creative and stimulating. They fall into a comfortable rut and hate it, but get so used to that comfortable rut that they fight change. Unfortunately, creativity in living and working is not common, and we're all poorer for it—but it gives you and me an advantage.

Creative purchases are made by a small minority, usually educated investors (like you and me) and a few real estate agents who look at "The System" and say to themselves, "Hey, there's *got* to be a better way!"

And there is a better way.

Creative deals, and the contracts which put them in writing, are the result of an investor's understanding of the principles of leverage (using a little money to control a lot of money or a valuable property), of using other people's money to do it, and of knowing how to satisfy the seller's needs and motivations. Creative purchase offers put those ideas in writing and protect the buyer.

These are very simple ideas, but like any other simple ideas, there are some things you need to know to make them work. Some of these things are very important and should be used in every deal. Others might be used in some deals and not others. (Creativity also

---

means picking and choosing which techniques will make an individual deal work.)

SOME SIMPLE
CREATIVE TACTICS

Instead of using just your name as buyer, write: Joe Investor *and/or assigns or nominee*. **Always** write it that way.

Why? What it does is give you the right to sell all or part of your interest in the deal at any time before closing, or to add a partner. Adding those words will enable you to assign (sell) the contract to another person at any time before closing without getting all the documents signed all over again by the seller, and without paying additional closing costs.

If you find someone who wants the property, all you do is sign over the rights, for a few thousand dollars, and you've made money by doing no more than finding a property, making an offer, and signing some papers. Another investor, or a buyer whose offer came in after yours, might still want the house and be willing to pay you that few thousand to purchase your rights to it.

Sure, maybe you'd make more if you kept it and sold it yourself, but if you can make a few thousand just by making an offer and signing a paper, think how many dollars per hour you've made for your time! At most, you'd have spent some money on inspections, which you could include in the price. You can go spend your time on another money-making property. Now, is that easy money or what?

You might want to add a partner for several reasons. Most obvious, you might see a deal you couldn't quite work yourself, but you don't have a partner lined up. The "and/or assigns or nominee" clause will let you make an offer and tie up the property long enough to find a partner. It can even be a useful tool in finding partners—you may look better to a prospective partner if you come to him or her saying, "I have a great deal pending on—" instead of, "Why don't you put up your money and financial statement and I'll go looking for property?"

Cashless Deposits

Suppose you made half a dozen offers expecting to get one or two accepted, and put up a $2,000 cash deposit on each one. You don't need a calculator to know you'd have a lot of money tied up. But you have to put cash down for the deposit, right?

No, you don't have to.

You can make a deposit using a *promissory note*. This is simply a *promise to pay* the required amount. It won't always work (some sellers won't accept it) and in some states you may be required to put up a certain amount of actual cash. Check with an attorney in your area to learn what is required and acceptable.

Your real estate agent may never have heard of this idea, or may be uncomfortable with it, but don't let that worry you. If it conforms to the laws of your state and the seller accepts, then you're all right.

Use a promissory note form accepted in your area. You can get forms from your title company or a stationery or office supply store. On the next page is an example of a promissory note. As with any legal document, check with an attorney before using this exact wording to be certain it conforms with the laws of your state.

PROMISSORY NOTE

$_____________________________   ____________19____

____after
date and for value received, I, ___________________________prom-
ise to pay to____or
order at_____ (address)___________________________________
the sum ____________________Dollars with interest only from
(date)_____________to (date)__________________at the rate of___
percent, per annum, payable____________________ and the principal due and payable as of____________________19____

Should interest not be so paid, it shall thereafter bear like interest
as the principal, but such unpaid interest so compounded shall not
exceed an amount equal to simple interest on the unpaid principal
at the maximum rate permitted by law. Should default be made in
an installment of interest when due, the whole sum of interest and
principal shall become immediately due and payable at the option
of the holder of this note. Should suit be commenced or an attorney
employed to enforce the payment of this note, I agree to pay such
additional sums as the court may adjudge reasonable as attorney's
fees in said suit. Principal and interest payable in lawful money of
the United States.

Borrower ___________________________________

Borrower ___________________________________

Lender___________________________________

Lender___________________________________

WATCH THOSE TERMS AND CONDITIONS

In the general terms and conditions section (number [1] on the two-page purchase offer form), we list almost all the things that make our offer "creative." The key creative elements are financial—how we'll pay for everything. If you're a licensed real estate agent, you must disclose the fact (by California law) in this section, usually at the bottom, after all other terms. Even if this is not required in your state, it's still a good idea to include it. We also list everything else that must happen for the deal to work.

In the longer form, many of these terms and conditions are written out, so we only need to fill in blanks or initial them if they are to become part of the offer. This makes writing out the financial details easier. The exact wording of some of the "condition" clauses makes it harder for us to use them as I recommend, but the "other terms" line lets us add the language we need. I'll tell you how to do it.

In this chapter, I'm talking about creative terms as if you were using the short form, which, as I've said, is probably similar to most non-California forms.

Why are these terms important?

Our deal is "conditional" upon all of these things being acceptable to the seller, and, most important, to us as the buyer. If anything doesn't happen as we state it, we have the option of *getting out of the deal.*

The ability to get out is our safety net, our protection against getting into a deal and discovering that it isn't what we thought it was. I always write a number of escape clauses into my contracts. Some of them are quite routine and appear in most deals. The difference in those, for me and for you, is that we include these clauses knowingly, and intend to use them if there is any reason to get out of the deal.

I call these "Houdini clauses," after Harry Houdini, the famed magician and escape artist who performed so many "impossible" escapes and unexplained feats of "magic" that to this day people are trying to contact his ghost because he said he'd come back if he could. (They haven't succeeded, so I guess that proves there's at least one thing you can't escape.)

How Houdini Clauses Work

An ordinary deal might routinely have a clause reading: "Conditional upon buyer's acceptance of pest control report." Most people assume that means if the report is clear or the seller corrects the deficiencies, the deal goes.

No!

The clause says nothing of the kind. It says *conditional upon buyer's acceptance of* the report. It doesn't say a thing about what the report must contain!

One of my favorite stories, which I'll tell again because it makes the point so well, is about the time I made a deal and found myself stuck with some liens the seller had not disclosed to me. Now, I could have sued him, but a court action costs time and money, so I'd rather not get involved in that. The only conditional item left in the deal was the pest control report, which came back perfect—not a single termite or any other pest in sight.

I disapproved the report. The seller didn't believe it, but there was nothing he could do. Now I'd never do that to anyone who'd dealt honestly with me, of course, but it shows the principle of how the Houdini clause works, even under the most severe and unusual conditions.

The key words in any Houdini clause are "conditional upon buyer's approval of—." If for any reason your spouse or partner are not on the contract as "buyers," you can also make it conditional upon their approval.

You'll notice in the long California form that the clauses for inspections, pest control work, and so on, are written on the assumption that seller will make corrections and that if seller does, buyer will accept. This is normally adequate for our needs, but is not as absolute as "conditional upon buyer's approval of—." So, in the "additional terms" section, write: "Sale is conditional upon buyer's approval and acceptance of—" (pest control report, physical inspection, and whatever else you have made a condition.)

If a seller or agent questions the condition, saying that it is already covered, point out that it would be possible for an inspection to uncover a problem which would make you not want the house, even if it were repaired, and the clauses as written don't quite cover that.

Routinely, any sale should be subject to buyer's approval of all inspections. You, or any other buyer, want to be certain the property is as it appears and is represented to be. You should list, separately, each inspection to be made. If you want an inspection not listed on the long form, be sure to write it in. You should put "subject to buyer's approval of" in front of each one, rather than using a general clause. *All* inspection clauses can serve the purpose of a Houdini clause.

I suggest also using a clause saying, "conditional upon buyer's approval of a final walk-through inspection not more than x days before closing." Make it within a day or two of close, unless this would cause problems for the seller and you're reasonably sure the deal will be free of problems. Normally, the seller will have moved out by then, so you can see what the house looks like empty. In the case of a vacant house, you might even want to make the inspection the morning of closing, to be sure there's been no vandalism.

SPELL OUT FINANCING

Every deal is (or should be) conditional upon the buyer obtaining financing as specified. For that reason, be sure to spell out in the offer not just the amount of the cash down payment to the seller, if any, the terms of existing financing to be taken over or assumed by the buyer, and/or any new financing which must be obtained by the buyer, but also the interest rates and monthly payments of each loan.

If there is seller financing involved, be extra sure all terms are spelled out clearly so the seller knows exactly what you ask. That can save lots of misunderstanding later. (If the seller seems even a little uncertain about your terms, take whatever time is needed to be explain.) If you work a deal which gives cash back to the seller, the details are written out here. Again, be sure the seller understands what you're doing.

MORE VALUABLE
CLAUSES

Some other clauses we might want to include are:

A HOME
WARRANTY CLAUSE

Ask the seller to obtain and pay for a home warranty policy covering electrical, plumbing, and mechanical devices in the home, including all appliances and pools or spas. Always ask for this, and always specify that the seller pays the premium.

Many sellers will not want the extra expense (usually a few hundred dollars). If so, you have a negotiating point. If you can see that everything is in good condition, you can be generous and give up on this point to get something more important. If you have any doubt, or if there is a pool or spa, then hold firm on the warranty clause, or as a last resort, get something else in negotiations and pay the premium yourself.

This is less important if you plan to sell at once, but vital if you plan to hold the property as a rental, lease-option or equity-share deal. The cost of replacing a stove or refrigerator will usually pay for the premium. Pools can develop very expensive problems. Spas are usually less troublesome, but if they need repair it can be expensive.

Include Personal Property

List all personal property to be included in the sale. The basic principle is, if it's there, ask for it. You can always generously concede the point (to help get something else), and you may be surprised and find the seller quite willing to part with valuable items in order to sell the house.

Some contract forms will have a separate clause for personal property. Otherwise, we include them as part of the "general terms and conditions." In either case, this is important and deserves more discussion.

The simplified definition is that "real property" is land and buildings, and "personal property" is everything else.

There are some fine points and hair-splitting in the application of the definition. The most important is that personal property "attached" to real property becomes real property. For example, the kitchen range is personal property, but if the cooktop and oven are built in, they become real property. If you have an old family heirloom lamp hanging in the living room, the fact that it's attached to the ceiling might be considered to make it real property. (Take it down before you sell to be sure it stays with you.)

When we make an offer on real estate, it is assumed we are offering to buy the real property. Any personal property to be included must be specifically listed.

Part of our creative purchase strategy is that we ask the seller to include many personal items not normally included in the sale of a house, for instance: "Sale to include range, refrigerator, dishwasher, microwave, freezer, washer, dryer, large-screen TV, stereo, all furniture including antiques, oriental rugs in living room, dining room, and bedroom, power tools, and the Porsche 911 Turbo in the garage."

You may laugh and say this is ridiculous, but that's (partly) the idea.

First, you may get some of what you ask. (Appliances are frequently included in a sale. Note that we listed them; just writing "all appliances" could lead to an argument if you bought the house and the microwave and portable dishwasher were gone when you took possession.) You never know what a seller really values. Antique buffs will never part with their stuff, but if it all came from relatives and the sellers have considered it not "antiques" but as a house furnished in "early in-law style," they may be delighted to have you take it off their hands. It comes down that basic principle: if you don't ask, you won't get. When you do ask, you may be surprised by what you get.

Now what would you do if you got the microwave, washer, dryer, stereo, and bandsaw?

You might use the appliances to increase the value and salability of the house. You could turn them into cash by selling them through classified ads or a garage sale. That might make you a few hundred to a few thousand dollars—or more, if you got the Porsche! Or, you might add them to your own possessions. You might never go out and spend your money for a stereo system if you have one already, but if you got one "free" to put in the family room or give to your kids, would you turn it down?

Repairs and Buyer's Approval

If any work is to be done on the house before closing, the deal is conditional upon the work being done and your approval of it. This is most important—any work the seller does, you won't have to pay for. Even in a property you buy as a fixer- upper, ask for some or all of the work to be done. Again, this is a negotiable point. If you don't ask for it, you can be sure you'll never get it.

Contingent on Sale of Property

If you need to sell another property to make the deal, include a contingency clause that buyer must sell his or her home (or other property) before closing, and use the proceeds to buy.

You can use this to shorten the time between investments. If you have an accepted offer on a property you're selling, you can offer at once on another property, with the sale contingent on the first deal closing.

When you are selling property, you'll find buyers who want this clause. Take a good, hard look at the probability that they will sell, and whether they are expecting a realistic price. If you accept that contingency as a seller, keep the property on the market looking for a "back-up offer"- -an offer from someone else who will buy if the first deal falls through.

Another trick to use if your buyer wants that clause is to see whether you can make an advantageous deal for the house they are trying to sell. If it is a property you want, you have a perfect example of a motivated seller—they want your house and can't do the deal until they sell theirs. If they are being realistic, you could have two deals in one.

If there is not enough space to write all you need, you use an addendum (usually there will be a standard addendum form for this purpose) to continue your lists of terms and conditions.

You can, quite literally, write anything you want (as long as it's legal) in this section. That's what it's there for, and that's where we have our chance to be creative. Whatever the circumstances of the deal, you can write them here.

You can make the deal "subject to buyer's approval of" just about everything you write in the terms and conditions of a contract. Be sure, as a safety measure, that you have at least one good Houdini clause in every contract.

SUBORDINATION

The *subordination clause* is a clause which states that a loan is in a subordinate (lower, or junior) position. A second loan is subordinate to a first loan, a third is subordinate to a second, and so on.

Now, you might think that this is automatic and you don't have to worry about it. Mostly, that's right. But—there are times when it is very important, or when you can use it to help make money. There could be an entire book written about the finer points of using subordination clauses, but I won't take that much time (or make you read that much).

The subordination clause simply states that you may obtain any new financing you wish at any time in the future, and the seller agrees to subordinate his note to your new loan(s).

Whenever we have a seller take back a note and deed of trust or mortgage, a subordination clause in the note allows us to take out loans and record them in positions superior to the seller's note (a new first and second, with the seller's note a third, for example) and have the seller's note remain in the same subordinate position. This is important, because you can get better interest rates on a first than on a second, and some banks either won't make third loans, or will charge an arm and a leg in interest.

A seller or seller's agent may want to strike out the subordination clause. This is understandable, because it is possible to misuse such a clause. You and I know we would never do so, but the buyer doesn't know us that well. Don't give up a deal if you can't get a subordination clause (unless the deal won't work any other way), but try, and keep trying. You'll get your share accepted.

When you're the seller, accept a subordination clause from the buyer only when it's necessary to make the deal work and you have confidence in the buyer. (If you put yourself in the seller's shoes and think what it would take to convince *you* that you could trust a buyer, you'll go a long way to understanding how to convince a seller to trust you.)

If interest rates are high, you can say that you may wish to refinance when rates are lower. If they are low, point out that you are in the investment business, which is why you can offer to buy his home, and to make your business work efficiently, you need to keep your financial options open and your loan rates as low as possible. If you change the loans ahead of his, he is not losing anything, since all the terms of his loan remain unchanged. If you are using the new first to obtain the cash the seller needs, you have a very good argument that the seller should accept the idea. He or she is benefitting, not just you.

SUBSTITUTION OF COLLATERAL

A *substitution of collateral* clause can be useful in times of high interest or in difficult markets. You can expect a harder time selling the idea in low interest or "hot" markets.

In this clause, the seller agrees to substitution of collateral (for his seller-carried loan) on a property of equal or greater equity. That means you transfer his loan to another piece of property (collateral) as the thing of value which supports the loan. Instead of having a note against his former house, he has a note against another of your properties, one of equal or greater value.

Suppose you have a five-year $20,000 seller-carried second on a house. You also own, free and clear, a piece of raw land appraised at $25,000, which you picked up at a tax sale. The land will be worth considerably more in five years, as business and housing develop toward it, so you want to hold the lot for its future appreciation. But right now that lot isn't doing you any good—it just sits there while you pay taxes and cut weeds. If you transfer the seller's loan to different collateral, your lot, you can then borrow additional money on his house, giving you cash for further investment.

In this example, the seller benefits too—his second or third becomes a first, which puts him in a better position. That's an explanation you can use to convince those who doubt.

PREPAYMENT PENALTIES

A *no-prepayment-penalty* clause should be contained in **all** your offers if the seller is taking back a loan. You *must* also be certain that any bank loan contains the clause. Most do, but don't take a chance. Always ask when taking out the loan.

A prepayment penalty is a charge made for paying off the loan early. Since you do not plan to hold your property for the life of the loan, you certainly don't want to get hit with an extra fee when you sell.

The clause simply states that you, as buyer, may pay off the loan at any time without paying a prepayment penalty.

Never accept any loan without a no-prepayment-penalty clause.

In these last two chapters you've learned how to write a contract, how to protect and advance your interests by the way you write it, and how to make creative use of various clauses.

You'll find some of these ideas work in your area and your market, and some won't, and some work better in high or low interest markets. All of them will work under the right conditions. Use them, and find out what works for you.

CHAPTER 8

CREATING A "NOTHING DOWN" DEAL

I n Chapter 2 I talked about ways to buy with no or little money down. In this chapter, I'll give a couple of examples of how some of those methods might work. Let me emphasize that there are many ways to structure a deal; these examples, and those in the section of example purchase offers, are only a few of the possibilities, with notes on ways around some problems you may or may not encounter.

You'll find that the pure "nothing down" deal works better (or more often) in times of high interest or in a very slow market. Under those circumstances, more people are more highly motivated, and lenders, who need to make loans to make money, are often more willing to cooperate.

WHEN INTEREST IS HIGH

For our first example, let's assume we've returned to the bad old days of 18 percent interest.

We find a $100,000 house (appraised value) with an assumable FHA loan of $60,000 at 10.5 percent interest. The seller, knowing that asking prices are negotiable, started out asking $110,000, dropped it to $105,000, and, because he was a motivated seller, accepted our offer of $100,000.

That negotiation pattern is not unusual. Sellers typically feel their houses are worth more than the market will pay, no matter whether the market is good or bad. Real estate agents fight a constant battle to convince their clients that reality is real. In this case, in a slow, high-interest market, the price we have offered is very generous. More likely, we'd end with a deal at $95,000 in this market, but in a hot market the same property might easily bring $105,000, or even the original asking price.

Now, how do we structure this deal to work with nothing down?

First, of course, we assume the $60,000 FHA loan. Then, most lenders will loan up to 80 percent of the purchase price, so we obtain an assumable adjustable second mortgage for $20,000. And finally, we ask the seller to carry the remaining 20 percent ($20,000).

Now, second loans usually carry a higher interest rate than firsts, so if first loan interest is 18 percent, we'll pay more for the second—but we're only paying the high interest on $20,000!

We ask the seller for good terms. We want his $20,000 at 12 percent for five years, interest-only payments, with a balloon for the principle due at the end and an option to renew the loan. This lowers our total (combined) interest rate to below what we could get on the current market, and the interest-only third lowers our total monthly payments, helping our cash flow. We expect to sell the property before the five-year balloon payment comes due. The seller gets monthly income from the interest on his $20,000.

Variations would be to have the interest come due with the

principle in five years (you make *no* interest payments during the life of the loan), to have interest payable quarterly or annually, or to pay both principle and interest, if the deal will support that expense.

We might have trouble with some lenders, who would not want to give us the second if we were putting no cash down. Then we just look for a lender who's willing.

Another possibility in this deal would be to have the seller take a second note for the entire balance! The problem with this is that most sellers want some cash out of the deal, at least enough to pay the costs of sale. You'll find some sellers willing to sell without getting any immediate cash, though, so try it.

A LOW-INTEREST DEAL

What if interest is low?

Take the same deal with interest at 10 percent. We'd have to assume the selling price was higher, say $105,000. (It might be more.) Most sellers would be less motivated to accept a second or third loan, so we'd have to look longer and harder to find someone who was open to the idea, but we'd find sellers who like the idea of income.

We have several options. One is to simply pay a small amount down (5 percent) and get a new assumable adjustable loan. If we want a no-down deal, we find a seller willing to carry the balance on an assumable second, and assume the old loan. Or, we have the seller obtain an assumable second, or we obtain the second.

Because interest is lower and the market better, property is appreciating in value more rapidly. This gives us more flexibility in what we offer the seller as a second loan. We can offer higher interest than the seller could get at a bank, or we can offer payments of principle and interest more easily. Rapid appreciation means we can resell at a larger profit sooner.

What about a slow market in times of low interest? This is what my student in Texas, who I mentioned earlier, is facing. He is able to simply assume VA loans from people leaving the area. Those sellers have paid little down, and made monthly payments about the same as or perhaps lower than rent. They are ahead to walk away from the houses and have someone else assume the loan. He gets the houses for the assumption fee. He can lease option for a positive cash flow and wait for values to rise.

In his case, there is no structuring to be done. He just assumes the loan and takes possession.

Now suppose you assumed a loan at 12 1/2 percent, but current rates were 10 percent. Is that foolish? Who would you find to assume such a loan from *you*? You'd find the person who couldn't make a down payment, but could afford the monthly payments. You'd point out to that buyer that he or she could refinance at a lower rate after taking possession of the house. (Some of these buyers would have to wait until they could qualify for the refinance.)

You'll note that a key in all these deals, as I've mentioned before, is that as much as possible, you deal in assumable loans, because assumable loans make it easier for more buyers to buy the house from you.

USING CONVENTIONAL FINANCING

Can you make a nothing-down deal with conventional financing? In most cases, probably not. As I said in Chapter 2, banks are not happy when you borrow the down payment, and no conventional lender will finance more than 95 percent of the appraised value.

But there is a way around this. You can "recycle" your down payment, if you make careful deals. Go ahead and make your cash down payment, and then, after the sale is closed, refinance or take a second loan to cover the amount of the down.

This technique requires that you buy a property with enough equity to support the new first or second loan, and that you be certain of your ability to get the loan. It's a useful method if you have a limited amount of actual cash to use in your investment program and don't want it tied up in one property. You are "recycling" one down payment from one property to the next.

You can use a variation of this idea in seller financing of the full remaining balance when you assume loans. It requires that you earn the seller's trust because you cannot (and should not) write it into the deal as a binding condition. Tell the seller, "Give me a second loan for the balance, with a subordination clause, and after I have title to the house I will refinance or get a second for X dollars, from which I will pay off X dollars of your loan."

You can't make this agreement binding, because you have not yet gotten the loan, and no lender is likely to give you one in advance. What you can do, in writing the seller's note, is include a "memorandum of understanding" in which you state that it is your intention to get the new loan and pay off part of the seller's loan as agreed.

If you are using any new financing, you'll find lenders object to even this much written promise. As an alternative, you could use a memorandum of understanding stating that you are selling another property and promise to pay the seller X dollars of his loan, conditional upon sale of that property and closing of the deal. Banks will usually accept this because it involves money from a transaction independent of the one they are lending on. As you can see, once you have several properties in your portfolio, you can use one of them to help make a deal on another.

CHAPTER 9

THE PROCESS
OF A SALE

N o two states have exactly the same laws governing the way real estate is sold, nor will the expenses be the same. The actual cost of each expense will not be the same from deal to deal, even in the same state, so it's impossible to tell you that if you buy or sell a $100,000 property, your costs will be so many dollars. The expenses of a sale, in addition to varying from deal to deal, will vary according to who pays what, or in what percentage.

California is an "escrow" state, in which the paperwork of a deal is handled by the title company (also called the "escrow office.") In non-escrow states, the deal may be treated as a legal action, with the paperwork handled by attorneys; and the county recorder's office or other government office may have the job of making sure everything happens correctly and in accordance with law. My discussion here is based on California practice.

At the end of this chapter is a sample of estimated closing costs, comparing FHA/VA and conventional financing. This is an *example* only.

You will have to find out what the process is in your state and locality. Real estate agents will know—that's their job—or you can call your county courthouse and ask.

The purchase offer is the primary instruction document. You remember that the purchase offer sets a time by which buyer and seller must deliver signed escrow instructions to a designated title company.

Escrow instructions tell the title company all the details of the deal: who has agreed to what, all financial arrangements, including the lender(s) used, how much money has been deposited in what form and whether the deposit will be increased, all the conditions, such as inspections, which must be met, and the times allowed for everything, including closing.

THE TITLE COMPANY'S ROLE

The title company's main reason for being in business is, as the name suggests, to ensure that buyers get a clear and legal title to property they buy. The purchase offer provides that the title company will furnish a "preliminary title report" and issue a policy of title insurance.

The cost of title insurance is based on the purchase price of the property, because if the title turns out to be other than reported, the title company must pay the buyer (and the lenders) the purchase price. You can understand why banks won't lend without title insurance!

The matter of making a title search and assuring that the buyer purchases a clear title is handled differently in different states, and sometimes even varies in different counties within the same state. To find out how it is done in your area, call your county courthouse and ask. You'll be referred to the correct department (usually the county recorder's office) and they will explain how it is done and what is important to the process.

"Tracking" Progress

In a deal handled by a real estate agent, the agents of both parties are responsible not only for delivering the signed instructions to the title company, but also for "tracking" the progress of the deal—making certain all inspections are done within the time specified, that the financing is arranged, etc.

If you are dealing directly with an owner, you and the seller are responsible for delivering the documents and meeting the deadlines, whether you are dealing with an escrow office or a different system for tracking and enforcing the process of a sale.

Failure to meet a deadline specified either in the purchase offer or in additional instructions is reason to call off the deal. In cases where both parties want the deal to go through, a missed deadline is usually forgiven and extended. For an investor, failure of the other party to meet a deadline can provide a "free" Houdini clause if there is reason to get out of the deal.

Fees and Expenses

You'll find, on any closing statement, a list of expenses (or credits) assigned to buyer and seller. These will include the title insurance cost, fees, prorations, commission, costs of insurance, and so on, shown on the purchase offer, and some fees, usually small, that are not, such as a charge for drawing up the closing documents, notary fee, appraiser's fee, tax service fee, and whatever else may be required by law or local practice.

Any expenses which are being paid out of escrow, or from the purchase price of the house, will be listed. These may include pest control work, inspections, repairs, or anything else you have specified in the deal.

There will be a balance sheet on which all the money involved in the sale is accounted for—where it came from and to whom it was disbursed.

The escrow (or closing) papers will include everything of record that has taken place from the acceptance of the offer to the closing—loan documents, title insurance, pest control inspection and clearance, and so on.

Because things are different in every state, I'll repeat that you should take the time to find out how it works, and what the average expenses you should expect to pay may be. If you live in California or a similar state, where the paperwork is done by a title company, just call a title company and say you are planning to buy property and would like to know how a sale is handled and what expenses you should expect. If they are too busy to talk to you, call another one—you'll find someone who wants your business. If you live in a non-escrow state and don't have a handy title company, find out who is responsible for sale paperwork, and find someone who's willing to talk.

Don't fail to do this. Remember what I said when talking about the purchase offer: There are many fees which can be paid by either party. Each of those fees is money which you or the seller must pay in order to buy or sell a home. As an investor, you want to pay as few of them as possible. More important, you want to know approximately what your costs will be each time you buy a piece of property.

In most deals, you'll expect to make enough money that a few dollars in sale expenses, plus or minus, will make little difference. But, if the deal is close to the "works/doesn't work" point, then those dollars can mean a lot. And, over the course of a number a deals, saving even as little as a hundred dollars on each deal will add up.

Most important, once you *know* what the local practice and normal expenses are, you'll have the security and peace of mind that comes with understanding that part of a deal, and be able to keep the creative part of your mind worry-free to deal with other, more major, parts of your deals.

ESTIMATED CLOSING COSTS*

EXAMPLE ONLY: 95% LOAN, $85,000

	FHA/VA	CONV.
Appraisal fee	100.00	150.00
Credit report	40.00	40.00
Loan origination (points)	850.00	1700.00
1/2 escrow fee	210.00	210.00
Title Insurance	100.00	100.00
Recording fee	8.00	8.00
Tax and insurance impounds (6 mo.)	525.00	525.00
Prepaid interest (30 days)	850.00	850.00
Funding fee (.5%)	424.00	-0-
Document prep fee	-0-	125.00
Tax service	-0-	35.00
Demand fee	-0-	25.00
1 year prepaid H.0. or fire insurance	200.00	200.00
Private Mortgage Insurance (PMI) 1st year premium	-0-	850.00
	$3,308.00	$4,818.00

* These estimates are shown and intended as *general guidelines* only, and are not *absolutely accurate*. In any given deal, there may be additional fees or charges, in amounts varying according to individual lender policies, insurance rates, state laws, local government fees, and accepted practices in various areas or for other causes.

PART II

FINDING SELLERS

Chapter 10

FSBOs and Real Estate Agents

The two basic sources of property are real estate agents and private owners. You could add foreclosures, tax sales, and government agencies, of course, but except for tax sales and IRS auctions, most property available through government agencies and foreclosure is first available through the private owner and later through a real estate brokerage.

How to Make a Fortune in Foreclosures and *The Land of Opportunity: How to Buy and Use Tax Sale Land* are part of the Cash Flow package.

Working With FSBOs

There are advantages in dealing with a private owner, or FSBO (For Sale by Owner), which come from the reason a FSBO is a FSBO in the first place.

The FSBO wants to save money.

So do you.

A private owner selling his or her house without an agent expects to save the agent's commission. The commission is not a minor expense. It is not set by law, and can run as high as 8 percent of the purchase price. That's $8,000 on a $100,000 home. Six percent is the most common figure, or $6,000 on the same home.

To the seller, who usually pays the commission, a $100,000 home becomes a $94,000 or even $92,000 home, if the sale is made through a real estate brokerage, before other expenses of sale are added on. An average homeowner, not wise in the ways of selling property, could see a home appreciate 10 percent in a year, and lose it all, or even more, in expenses of sale. Isn't that a powerful motivation to sell it himself?

Why use an agent at all when it costs that much?

Because selling a home, for a person untrained in real estate, is difficult, time-consuming, and a nervous, mysterious process. A FSBO does not have an agent's access to the Multiple Listing Service, nor expertise in preparing a home for sale, nor, usually, expertise in salesmanship or negotiation. Most owners do not know what is important in a real estate deal, nor how to convince a buyer to love *this* home and not some other.

Real estate agents know this. So, if you are a FSBO, one result of putting a "For Sale by Owner" sign on your front lawn or an ad in the paper is that every real estate brokerage in town will tell its new agents to call you. It's standard training for new agents to call every FSBO they can find in the hope of talking them into listing with the brokerage. Even some experienced agents have found the FSBO contact route works for them, so they keep right on calling.

Now, if a poor FSBO has suffered through a dozen or two calls from beginning real estate agents, all saying, "List with me and I'll *try* to sell your house," and you call and say, "I'd like to *buy* your house," does that give you an advantage? Does that make you look like the cavalry arriving in the nick of time? Sure does. And that's your first advantage: you have a seller who is motivated to save money, who is having a hard time selling his home, and all his calls have been from agents.

Your second advantage is that, if the seller has priced the home realistically, you have more room to bargain. If the seller balks at giving up part of the commission he or she would pay a real estate agent, point out that in normal real estate practice, the broker for the buyer and the broker for the seller split the commission. Since in effect the seller and you, as buyer, are replacing the brokers in this deal, it is only fair to split whatever the normal commission in your area happens to be.

Your third advantage is that when you present your deal to the seller, there is no old-fashioned agent at his or her shoulder looking at the way you've written your terms and saying, "But you can't do *that!*" Since you're presenting your offer directly, you are the one explaining what you want the seller to do, and why. Your offer is not being presented by an agent who may not understand or believe in what you're doing.

You can see that dealing with FSBOs offers significant advantages.

But just the fact that a property is offered by a FSBO is not enough to make it a good deal. FSBOs are like any other sellers—they may have unrealistic expectations of the value of their property, they may be unwilling to bargain, they may be unwilling to accept creative terms, or any terms that will make the deal work for you.

Any seller, of whatever kind, *must* be both motivated and realistic if we are to make deals that work for us and make money.

In the next chapter, I'll talk about motivations, how to recognize them, and how to use them.

How do you find FSBOs?

The easiest, obvious way is to see a sign or ad that says, "For Sale by Owner." Many FSBOs do that, and you may find plenty of deals just from those "marked" sources.

One of my Florida students finds properties by simply getting in her new car—which she bought with her real estate income—and driving up and down streets looking for property. That's a good way, but can be time-consuming. (She has the time.) If you work a full-time job, try setting aside a certain number of hours on the weekend to just drive and look in areas where you'd like to buy.

Wherever you drive, for whatever reason, keep a notepad and pen in the car. When you see a property that looks interesting, stop long enough to write down the address, phone number, and, if it happens to be offered by a Realtor instead of the owner, the name and phone number of the brokerage and agent.

If you have time to knock on the door of a FSBO, do so. If not, call.

If your driving is usually so rushed that you can't even take time to stop and write down a phone number, try buying a small cassette recorder, or, even better, a microcassette recorder, so you can pick it up, push "record," and say, "FSBO in the 2100 block of Elm Street," or whatever other information you have time to notice and talk into the recorder.

The reason a microcassette recorder may be preferable to a standard cassette recorder is that they are very small. You can carry one around in your purse, or shirt or jacket pocket, and hardly know it's there. If you're really high-tech, you could use a phone in your car and the answering machine at home to make your notes! (The recorder is cheaper.)

What about FSBOs who don't label themselves?

Usually, a lawn sign will say "By Owner," but some don't. If a brokerage is not listed on the sign, assume it's a FSBO.

In the classified ads of your paper, many will say "By Owner," but a surprising number will not. Now you get to play detective. You know that any ads with a brokerage name are not FSBOs, so you look at all the ads that don't say one or the other.

Some of those ads will be from agents. Why would an individual agent place an ad, at his or her own expense, when the brokerage is already advertising? The answer is the same reason a brokerage places ads, which is also the reason the FSBO has not been getting much response from his ad: A brokerage does not advertise to sell the home in the ad, it places a bunch of ads in the paper *to make the phone ring!*

Reality in the real estate sales world is that property rarely sells directly from an ad, or even from an open house. Instead, the ad or open house brings potential buyers into contact with the brokerage and agent, whose job is to turn those people into committed clients who will work exclusively with the agent and brokerage. This is something you must always be aware of when trying to sell the property you buy, and which you should always (carefully and diplomatically) point out to a FSBO who is reluctant to consider your deal.

An agent trying to increase his or her personal business will spend the money for ads to accomplish the same thing. The agent wants to be called personally, so that when the phone rings, it's for him.

Usually, when an unlabeled ad has one phone number, it will be a genuine FSBO. Not always, however; some agents will give just a home number to avoid other agents "stealing" their customers. In some brokerages, agents respect and help each other, but at others it is pure tooth and claw, with everyone out for themselves. If the ad has two numbers, especially if one number is followed by "ask for Dave," there's an even or better chance that it's an agent. It may also, of course, be a FSBO's work number.

I suggest calling the single-number ads first, and then calling, in the evening, the numbers without the "ask for Dave" line. If it is a FSBO, he may be grateful you didn't call him at work. If it's an agent, make sure you get the agent who placed the ad (or his or her spouse or answering machine) instead of someone else in the brokerage. Why? You can use contact with bright, ambitious agents, and those who do their own advertising are more likely to be that kind.

There is one more way to screen ads before calling: by carefully reading the way they are written. Agents and brokerages write ads for a living. They know what will catch a buyer's eye and make that person pick up the phone. The FSBO doesn't. A smart FSBO will read brokerage ads carefully to get the style right, but even those will tend to be simpler, more direct, less embellished, and with less use of "sell phrases" like "must see," "won't last long," "super kitchen,"

"great yard," and so on. The FSBO's ad may just say something like:
"3br 2ba ranch. 000-0000." Call the simplest ads first.

CHOOSING THE
RIGHT REALTOR

Now, what about real estate agents?

Why use an agent at all, when there are FSBOs and foreclosures out there? Well, you may find all the property you can handle from those sources. Or, depending on your area, or your local market, or your preferred way of working, you may find it easier to work through agents. If you're trying to begin an investment career while working a demanding job, and perhaps your spouse has an equally demanding job, and you've got children, you may find an agent saves you time and hassle.

I've been a little hard on agents so far, and rightly so, because they often think only about doing deals the same old way. They can actually get in the way of creative deals, or fail to present your offer with the kind of conviction needed to convince the seller to sell.

In 1982, almost all agents were like that; but today there's a whole new crop of agents, and some smart survivors of the old era, who have seen people like you and me go out and make creative deals and make money at it, and have said to themselves, "Hey, there *is* a better way!"

Such agents will not only listen to you and present your deals positively and sincerely, they may welcome you with open arms because they understand what you're doing and know that you're money in their bank if they can make you their client. And, they make you their client by doing the job for you, the way you want it done, with bright-eyed and bushy-tailed enthusiasm.

Finding such a gem of an agent may take time, but it can be done. You may have to try several agents before you find the one who is just right for you.

Understand the Agent's Viewpoint

You'll be helped in your search, and any time you deal with an agent, if you understand how reality looks to an agent. Real estate is a commission sales business. In some offices, the agent pays a fee for the privilege of having a desk and phone, in addition to fees for membership in the local Board of Realtors (which gives him or her access to the Multiple Listing Service) and the costs of obtaining and maintaining a real estate license.

How much does an agent earn from commissions? Let's assume we bought a $100,000 house, sold at 6 percent commission. Our agent's broker and the seller's broker split the $6,000—$3,000 to each. Our agent's broker then splits that commission with the agent.

Commission splits vary widely. A new agent might get a 50 percent split or less; or the split schedule might say that each year, the split is 50 percent for the first $15,000 of commissions, 55 percent to $25,000, and so on until the top split is reached, whatever it may be. An agent who sold well in the past year might start the new one at a higher split.

So, our agent may only get $1,500—a quarter of $6,000. If our agent sold one $100,000 house a month for a year, that would be an income of only $18,000—gross. All expenses—office, fees, car, clothing, insurance, phone, etc., come off the top of that amount.

An agent's basic reality is that it is necessary to sell a couple of houses a month to make a reasonable income—more, in areas where the average home price is under $100,000. This is not easy—there are a lot of good agents who don't sell one house a month, and the tougher the market, the harder it is for agents to survive.

So, if your investments provide an agent with a steady, dependable stream of commissions, that agent is going to be very grateful—or should be—and will do anything you want. He or she will keep an eye open for the kind of properties you seek, and generally give you priority service when you need it.

For a new agent, reality is even tougher. A few people go into the business with natural sales talent and a wealth of contacts in the community, and make $70,000 the first year. There are not many like that. Most have to learn how to sell while they learn about real estate, and have to work to build up a base of contacts which provide referrals for future business.

Some brokers provide excellent training programs; others figure the good agents will swim and the rest will sink, and the brokers have to go through a bunch of sales duds in order to find one who can make them some money. That's a little like teaching people to swim by tossing them off the Golden Gate Bridge and saying, "See you at the marina."

What this means to you, when you walk into a real estate office for the first time, is that you should think of yourself a little like the proverbial Christian walking into a den of lions—all those smiling faces in real estate agent suits are very, very hungry for your business. You can use this to your advantage. You have what they want—the ability to buy a property and make them a commission.

IMPRESS THE AGENT

You may encounter an obstacle when you first walk into a real estate office. Many offices assign their agents to "floor duty." This means that you talk to (and become the client of) the agent whose turn it was to sit at the front desk and wait for the phone to ring or the door to open. It could be any agent, from the best in the office to a beginner sitting there for the first time.

In some offices, a walk-in customer is fair game for whoever sees him first, which may at least get you a fairly aggressive agent, but may also indicate a brokerage in which agents don't respect and help each other. I'll talk about picking an agent in a moment.

Let me take a little time now to talk about *you* when you walk into the lion's den. If you are to be taken seriously as an investor, you have to convince an agent that you know what you're doing. Any agent who has been around even six months or a year has seen plenty of people come in and talk about "investment property" without the slightest idea what it means, and often without the slightest means to do anything about it.

I used to suggest that the best approach was to quietly blow the agent's mind. The technique was to put on your very best suit, buying or renting a new one if need be, rent a Mercedes or Cadillac, spend the money for an elegant leather briefcase, and walk in like you were Donald Trump looking for another office tower. The idea was to look through the MLS book, pick out ten or so properties that fit your requirements, and write up nothing-down deals on all of them, hand them to the agent, and ask to be called after they'd all been presented.

In the 18 percent interest era, this worked—you could be almost certain that of ten offers you'd get one or two accepted. It still can be done, but is a little more difficult in times of low interest. You could probably do it in slow markets like Houston.

The thing that is important in this scenario, which *always* applies, is that your appearance is vital.

When I made my first deal, I didn't stop at the real estate office on the way home from a day of sweating over drywall, park my muddy truck in front of the office, and walk in wearing a t-shirt and faded jeans, covered with drywall dust.

I went home, showered, had supper, put on my best suit and tie, got out my briefcase, and drove to the office in a nice car. I walked in with my best smile and acted as if I owned the place. And I might as well have owned it, because I was walking in with something they wanted—the ability to buy property and earn them a commission— and *I looked as though I could!*

When I told agents what I wanted, I was believable in their judgment. When they believe in you, they'll do what you want.

That's why I say, if you don't have a good suit, buy one. If you can't afford it, rent one. If you don't have a nice car, rent a Mercedes, or find a friend who'll loan you a shiny new car that looks prosperous. Spend the money for a professional-looking briefcase.

You are a real estate investor, so *look like one*.

And the interesting thing is, if *you* know you look like a successful investor, you'll begin to feel like one, too!

Look at the agents. If they're smart, they'll be well-dressed. They know they have to impress clients with their competence. They'll drive the nicest car they can afford. And yes, the top agents will be driving Mercedes, BMWs, and Cadillacs.

The agents are playing a power game called "look how successful I look," so you should play the game right back at them. If they figure out that you're playing the game, too, and the good ones will, they'll respect you for understanding the rules.

So let's review a moment: What does that real estate agent need? Right, you got it—sales and commissions! What happens for him when he makes a deal work for us? Right—sales and commissions. And what happens for us when he makes our deals work? Profits!

CHOOSING AN AGENT

So, you've walked into the lion's den, and they're all smiling and hungry. How do you find the agent who can make it happen? How can you tell?

If you know another investor or a friend who can make a recommendation ("Oh, Mary Jo is just the greatest!"), that makes life easy. You try Mary Jo and see if she works as well for you as for your friend. She may not. Part of what makes your "perfect" agent is a personality match. If she doesn't work out for you, try someone else.

I'm going to assume you have no recommendations and are starting cold.

Any agent will be a combination of talents and personality traits, some good, some bad, and the way the combination works for you is what matters. So, I'll talk about some of the things I've found important, some positive, some negative. Don't forget that agents are people just like you and me, and they're all different. Just because an agent has or lacks some quality does not mean that agent can't do a super job for you. Look for a combination of traits that accentuates positive thinking and goals, enthusiasm, and willingness to try new things.

First, where should you start looking? There are pages and pages of real estate broker listings in most phone books. The best place to start, unless your knowledge of agents and brokerages in your city tells you otherwise, is with the largest and best-known broker in town.

My reasoning is that more often than not, such a brokerage will have more listings than any other, and more agents to choose from than any other. Its agents will range from very experienced to totally green. It will probably have a training program for new agents, and a large number of agents who are in the first few years of their careers. From this talent pool the odds are better of finding the agent who will help you than if you go into a small neighborhood broker-age which consists of one broker and half a dozen agents.

Having a large number of its own listings can make a difference. In any brokerage, agents tend to be more familiar with in-house listings than with those of other brokerages— that is, they'll have better up-front knowledge of which of those listings is a seller who will listen to your deal.

But which agent? Well, you could try asking for the agent who owns, manages, or personally buys and sells the most property. That may just be someone who believes in the product he or she is selling, but more likely it will be someone who understands investment and investment methods. If that person hasn't heard of your methods, the chances are good he or she will be happy to learn. (Of course, that agent may be so busy he or she doesn't want to work with you, and there will always be old traditional agents who buy property the old way, and will tell you it can't be done any other.)

An absolutely green agent can be a good prospect, if that person is smart, eager, and willing to learn. That gives you a chance to train your own agent, but it may mean you lose a few deals while the agent develops negotiating skills and familiarity with real estate.

In most cases, I suspect, your best bet will turn out to be an agent with a few years' experience and a good but not spectacular track record who has invested in at least one property. Why not an agent with a spectacular track record? Easy—that kind of agent is too busy to give us the attention we need, and, more important, that agent *doesn't need us!*

An agent with a few years' experience and average success has been around long enough to know that real estate sales is not all peaches and cream and easy profit, but not long enough to burn out and settle into a rut of mediocrity. In short, this is a hungry agent— and we want a hungry, eager agent with a flexible mind.

INGREDIENTS OF THE SUCCESSFUL AGENT

Now let's talk about ingredients which could go into making the agent you want. Consider this discussion as being like a list of things you *might* use to make sauce for your pasta. You can make sauce from a *lot* of things, in an incredible number of combinations. Ever notice that *nobody* makes a sauce like your mom makes, even if Mom has a couple dozen different recipes, some going back seven generations to the Old Country? Right, and agents are just as unique. These are the "ingredients" for the "sauce" (agent) you use on your "pasta" (deals) to make each deal leave the right kind of good taste in everyone's mouth.

Okay, (now that we've all dashed off to the kitchen to whip up our favorite sauce and indulged ourselves) here's what to look for.

1. You want someone with enthusiasm and energy who backs it up by getting things done. That *can* be a person who is very quiet, low-key, and methodical, but usually those are harder to spot on a first meeting. The odds favor someone visibly bursting with energy.

2. You want a hungry, ambitious agent who is just as anxious as you to make *lots* of money—ideally, one who has a real, pressing need to make more than he or she has been earning, or who has a burning desire to live a financially better life. Exceptions to this ingredient occur, but they're **very rare.**

3. The agent should be willing to listen to you, respect what you say, learn from your knowledge, and be willing to try whatever you write up. An agent who won't listen is useless.

4. The agent should be someone who has made enough deals to know his or her way around the world of real estate, and be knowledgeable in the ways and needs of buyers, sellers, and lenders.

   This may seem the opposite of Number 3, but it isn't. Part of what you pay an agent for (via commissions) is this kind of knowledge. Such an agent can advise you on the effect of state and local laws and zoning regulations on deals you propose, and if he or she thinks you have a deal that won't fly, he or she should be able to suggest a way to make it work, or give you real reasons why you should dump this one and try another. This agent will also know his or her way around lenders and government loan programs.

   A knowledgeable agent got that way by being willing to listen and learn. Such an agent will listen to what you say, try your deals, and learn from you while teaching you how to do your kind of deals better.

5. The agent should be a good negotiator. That's another thing you

pay the agent to do, if you don't have natural deal-making talent, or lack the time to develop it. This is the skill a new, green agent will most likely lack. A good agent with some experience will know a variety of negotiating methods, and have developed the sensitivity and judgment to know when to use each. (This is a skill you'll develop if you work with FSBOs.)

6. The agent should be willing to ask for the moon with green cheese on the side—this goes with Number 5. If an agent (or you) is confident in his or her negotiating ability, then asking for the antiques and the Porsche in the garage is easy, and seen as one more good negotiating tool.

7. Your agent *must* have a positive attitude—this is one trait you can't do without. You already know that if *you* don't have a positive attitude, you'll never get what you want. The same is true for your agent. An agent with a positive attitude will get what you ask.

   Positive agents will talk about how they are going to make your deal work. If they start talking about things that might not work, they do so in a *positive* manner. Their attitude is analytical, a discussion of *why* things may or may not work, how they expect a particular seller to react, how to make the deal more attractive to the seller's *agent*, because the agent's recommendation can sway a seller in either direction, and what alternate techniques might be used instead of what you propose.

   They will present your deal with their best efforts even if they don't think it will work. (In California, agents are required by law to present *all* offers, but the law doesn't require them to recommend their acceptance or even to work hard for the buyer.)

TRAITS TO WATCH OUT FOR

It would be easy to say, don't touch any agent with negative attitudes. But these traits, like all others, may be a little present or a lot present in a person, and may be counterbalanced by other, positive traits. And, sometimes, prudent caution can look like some of these negatives. Generally, if any of these seem strong or dominant in an agent, you can do better.

These are some negative traits to look out for, and avoid:

1. If the agent "knows it all" and makes sure you understand that he or she does, you've encountered the opposite of "knowledge-able." This agent may actually know a great deal, but is so convinced of the greatness and completeness of his or her knowledge that any idea he's never heard of before can't possibly work.

2. If the agent doesn't listen to you, that's a sure sign of the "knows it all," or, worse, the "doesn't really care." This agent will sit there while you explain what you want to do and say you can't, and then write up a perfectly standard offer. And, chances are, he or she will present even that offer with all the enthusiasm of a dead mouse.

3. If the agent won't listen to any but conventional financing methods, he or she is probably still living in the 1970s. There are less of these around now than there were in 1982. Those that aren't around probably wonder why real estate became such a bad place to make a living—they're out of the business because they stopped making deals and never figured out why.

4. The doughnut-hole inspector. You've probably met people who, if you offer them a doughnut, will complain at length about the size and shape of the hole before even taking a bite to see whether the doughnut is tasty—and by then it could be the best doughnut ever made and they'd never know. This is the agent with a negative attitude for everything, whose sole mission in life seems to be to point out everything that could possibly go wrong. They are not usually very successful in real estate.

5. Some people are unwilling to take a risk. They are afraid of being turned down. Such agents (and people in general who are not agents) consider a refused offer to be a personal affront, or a personal failure, or both. They are not very secure. Such agents try to present only offers they are *absolutely certain* will be accepted. They get very resentful when anything is turned down and may blame you, not themselves or the seller. They don't understand that a turned-down deal is not failure or rejection, just a deal that was tried and didn't work. They

certainly can't see that they might have turned it around with a more positive attitude.

These people are often doughnut-hole inspectors.

6. An agent unwilling to ask for what you want is an agent we *must* stay away from, since a key part of our strategy is to ask for the moon. This is often a shy person, who really has no business in real estate, but may be the kind of agent who has been moderately successful by developing a narrow range of personal methods that work and is afraid to try anything else. He or she is probably also afraid of being refused.

7. A part-time or semi-retired agent may be someone who is an absolute gem, but the odds are against it. A semi- retired agent, by definition, is almost always old, and may cling to old ideas about the way things should be done and what will work. Being a successful, go-getting, part-time agent is possible, but difficult. Real estate sales is a profession that demands an agent's full attention and time.

    The worst bet among agents is someone who's trying to start a real estate career part-time. That person is trying to learn a career and establish a client base on perhaps twenty hours a week when other beginning agents may be putting in sixty to eighty hours a week.

    There are exceptions, of course. Some people are "naturals," and can do eighty hours' work in twenty, even starting out. And, more and more, age does not always mean "old fashioned." A skilled older agent who doesn't need full- time income may be looking for a challenge and be delighted to find a client who wants to do it differently. Such an agent can be a real find, as can a really good, experienced agent who for some reason can't devote full time to the job.

In general, the agents to stay away from will be those who tell you it won't work, are convinced no seller will accept your offer, and try to tell you that you can't do things that investors all over the country do every day. They may say things like, "Well, I'll present this offer, but there's *no way* they'll accept!"

And *you* have no need to accept their services as agents!

CHAPTER 11

SELLER'S MOTIVATIONS: HOW TO RECOGNIZE THEM

"**M**otivated seller" merely means that someone has a pressing need to sell a property. That person is willing to listen to creative offers and willing to bargain on price or other terms in order to sell.

An "unmotivated seller" may seriously and sincerely want to sell, but can afford to wait for the right offer to come along. He or she can be picky and patient, and has no need to bargain or listen to creative terms.

And, of course, there are always sellers in a third category: those who really don't want to sell because of emotional attachment to the property, because of wanting an unrealistically high price, or, among those in financial difficulty, those unable to sell for a realistic price because the house is over-encumbered.

How can you tell the difference?

The key lies in the *reason for selling*. Additional keys are circumstances which make it necessary to sell *now*, and the minimum amount of money the seller *must* have to make the deal. I'm talking about the first two categories here; the third kind are usually pretty obvious.

REASONS FOR SELLING

Let's looks at some different sellers and their motivations.

Perhaps someone merely wishes to buy a better house. That isn't a great motivation—that person can afford to wait for the right price. But, if that person has *already bought* a better house and is making payments on *two* houses, *then* we may find motivation. What we need to find out is what the person must have, minimum, from the old house. Then perhaps we can work out a deal which will give the seller what he needs and let us make a profit. It depends, as always, on the numbers.

A couple may be ready to retire and wish to sell the big old family home and move to smaller condo, apartment, or perhaps a cottage in the hills. Again, the motivation—from our viewpoint—is not strong. They can afford to wait for their price, unless they've already bought their new home.

Someone who has been transferred to a new job has stronger motivation—his family can't follow him until the house is sold, or, if he goes ahead and buys in the new city, he's *got* to sell the old place.

There can be some interesting variations here. If the person is transferred from an expensive location (say San Francisco) to an area of much lower property value (say, Dayton, Ohio) that person can afford to take a low price or creative terms in order to sell. Someone transferred from Dayton to San Francisco (after recovering from sticker shock at SF prices) will hold out for full price, and need it. But if houses aren't moving in Dayton, and his home (and family) sit there for six months, the motivation to accept a lower offer will increase.

Many major corporations have a relocation program for employees they transfer. The company will buy the house for an agreed price (usually a bit low) if it does not sell by a certain date. Some companies are generous, and others not so generous, in the price they'll offer. You may find nice deals by offering a transferee a thousand or two over the company price.

After a company has bought a home, it wants to get rid of it fast. A corporate relocation property that hasn't sold in a few months can sometimes be bought at a good price. (These are called "relo's," which is both a generic industry term and the name of one of the national relocation services, "ReLo.")

You'll notice that I began with low motivation and have moved to higher motivation.

STRONGLY MOTIVATED SELLERS

What about someone who is facing foreclosure or about to lose the home for nonpayment of back taxes? Is that person motivated? You'd better believe they are.

Foreclosures happen for many reasons. Whether loss of job, medical expense, or simply poor financial planning, they all come down to a person who must sell the house or lose it, and if the person is foreclosed against, that puts a black mark on the person's credit record.

You can make your best deals with people who face foreclosure but have not yet been foreclosed upon. These people are in a position where they will not only lose everything if they don't sell, but also have their credit record messed up.

You'll find two kinds of foreclosure victims: those who have equity in the house and those who don't.

If the seller has equity, he wants to save some of it. He may be able to get a bank loan on the equity to tide him over until he's back on his feet, or the bank may not be willing to loan to him because he has no income. If you can offer a deal which gives him *some* of his equity, there's a good chance he'll take the deal rather than be foreclosed. Even if he's managed to get an equity loan, he may still be willing to accept a creative deal, or almost any reasonable deal, to get out of the payments the house represents.

If the seller does not have equity in the house, then there is no use talking, unless you think there is a possibility the lender may discount the original loan. This can happen if the lender would prefer to accept a known loss rather than risk a larger loss by taking back the house and having the expense of fixing it up and selling it.

You may not think of banks or the FHA or VA as motivated sellers, but they are. They are not in the business of *selling* real estate, they are in the business of *loaning money* on real estate. But, as I've discussed before, the fact that they loan money means that a certain number of loans will turn bad, and they'll have to foreclose, and so you find banks with REOs and FHA and VA foreclosures.

Lenders that have foreclosed are usually interested in getting rid of the property even if it means a loss. They'll try to get fair market value, of course, but they'll listen when you offer. If they've had the property on their books for a while, they'll listen harder. If the property is not in the best shape, they'll be even more willing to accept a below-market offer.

SELLERS TO PURSUE

Let's review motivation for a moment.

The sellers you want to deal with are those who have a strong, pressing reason to sell.

The strongest reasons and greatest pressures are financial.

A motivated seller *must* sell, because he or she needs the money. "Needing the money" can be a matter of avoiding foreclosure, or be the only way to pay off major debts—very strong motivation—or needing the money to buy another home or pay for a new home already purchased—strong motivation, but not as strong as a "must have money" motivation.

Financial motivations usually also come with a time pressure motivation. The seller *must have* money by a certain date, or *must have* money to relieve financial pressure, such as payments on the old house and the new one at the same time, and the sooner the better.

All other reasons to sell, no matter how real and sincere, put less pressure on the seller, and are less motivating.

You will make more deals, and better ones, in less time, if you concentrate your efforts on strongly motivated sellers.

CHAPTER 12

HOW MEETING YOUR SELLER'S NEEDS CAN HELP YOU MEET YOUR NEEDS

I've talked a lot about motivation. Another term is "need." A seller's needs are the source of his or her motivation.

You're motivated by a need to make money. You've chosen to meet your need by buying property. You are, therefore, motivated to find and buy property, but not just any old property. You're looking for property which will make money. That's obvious, isn't it? We've been talking about that since page one.

I've restated your need *because* it is obvious. It's easy to see and understand our own needs and motivations. If we stop and think of our needs, and then try to stand in the seller's shoes, it is easier to see things from the seller's point of view. To deal effectively, bargaining for the right price and convincing sellers to accept our creative terms, we must know and understand the needs behind a seller's motivation and understand what needs are most important.

UNDERSTAND THE SELLER'S NEEDS

Earlier, I talked about sellers facing foreclosure. Motivated? You can't get much more motivated than that. But the *need* behind the motivation can take many forms.

I'm going to assume that the needs are something we can meet. He or she may not even be facing foreclosure, but just the financial pressure of several months without work, followed by reduced income which cannot maintain the house payments, much less pay off debt from the out-of-work period. Sale of the home is the only way out. Obviously, if a seller has over-encumbered the property we can't meet his needs no matter how much we'd like to help him out.

Let's suppose Mr. Seller lost his job. He was out of work for three months and, as is often the case today, he found work, but it pays less than the old job. His home and his spending patterns and debt structure were based on the assumption that he'd always have the higher-paying job, plus raises.

Why is this "often the case today"? I chose this example because it is. Three main economic trends are producing this type of seller.

ECONOMIC TRENDS PRODUCING MOTIVATED SELLERS

One trend is the tendency of major corporations to engage in "cost cutting" or "reduction of overhead." What this often means is that people who thought they had secure, well-paying white-collar jobs suddenly find themselves out of work, sometimes with only an afternoon's notice to clean out their desks.

Unless they are still upwardly mobile in their careers, and still actively looking for the next better job, these people usually aren't prepared for a job search. When they look for work in their field, they discover that their company's competitors have also been

reducing overhead, meaning no openings; or that openings in that
skill are being filled with people willing to work for a lower salary.
They may need more than the three months in the example to find
a new job; and when they do find one, it may not be in their specialty,
or it may be in a different city.

If these displaced workers survive by starting their own business, they can count on it taking some time to match their former
income. They may even need to sell their home to raise capital for
the business or to keep the business operating.

A second trend, related to the first, affects blue-collar workers.
It's called "lay-offs," which may in fact be permanent, or "plant
closings," which almost always are. These occur when a company
has more plant capacity than orders and decides not to keep a plant
open, or a job filled, while waiting for orders to improve. The effect
is the same, except that the blue-collar worker may have had more
warning, and that a laid-off worker may decide to sit and wait to be
called back to work rather than start looking for a new job. Unfortunately, this choice may mean that the person is much deeper in the
hole when he finally realizes that he's got to do something about it.

The third trend, which overlaps the first two, is the shift from a
manufacturing-based economy to a service-oriented economy. If
you read employment statistics, you find that for quite some years
the largest increases in new jobs have been in the service sector. And
guess what? Service jobs always have and still do average lower pay
than manufacturing jobs.

Yes, I know you may not believe this when you get a bill for your
plumber's services. There have always been good-paying service
jobs, but the average is lower. The plumber's assistant may not make
much more than the kid at McDonald's, and the plumber himself
was once a plumber's assistant, and has to pay the overhead for his
shop, his truck, workman's compensation for the assistant, and so
on.

More important to us, a staff plumber who worked for a closed
plant has to either go to work for another plumber or start his own
business. He probably won't make his former wage, especially if he
worked in a union-contract plant, for some time.

What all this means is none of us can count on putting in thirty
loyal years at one job and getting a gold watch. All the people I've
described above should have done exactly what you are doing
now—learn to make money without relying on an employer.

They're not, so you will find them selling homes they thought they'd have for the rest of their lives. And wherever you are, there will always be some, if not many, families facing the problem.

HOW YOU CAN HELP
THE MOTIVATED SELLER

Back to Mr. Seller. He is someone we can help, because he was out of work only a short time and had equity in his home. He has a job, but he's wiped out his savings and the new job won't support his house payments. His numbers might look like this:

$100,000 house.
 $25,000 equity, most of it from appreciation in value.
He needs:
 $2,000 to pay off credit card debt incurred while out of work.
 $2,000 in costs of sale. (He's a FSBO, and we're going to ask him to pay most of the costs.)
    A down payment on a less expensive home. He can qualify for payments on a $60,000 house, if he has ten percent down, so he needs another $6,000.
Total cash needed, after payoff of loan: $10,000.

That means he'll need $85,000 total.

If we get a 95 percent loan, we could give him *more* than he needs. He might like that—it would give him money in the bank against any future job loss or financial problem. He could also buy $10,000 more house to replace the one he's selling. This is the standard, old-fashioned way of buying a house and meeting a seller's needs.

But what if we offer to put 5 percent down ($5,000) and get a loan for $80,000, with the seller carrying the $15,000 balance? The seller is trying to live on less income than before, and having a hard time of it. Carrying $15,000 at 10 percent interest, with interest-only payments, would give him an extra $125 a month. At 12 percent interest, it would produce $150 a month.

That might mean the difference between the seller and his family "just getting by" and living comfortably. And, he'd have the balance coming whenever the balloon payment is due, or whenever you sell the house. The trick here is that you offer higher interest than he could get from a bank if he put that much money in CDs, but less than you're paying for your commercial loan, so you both win. Be sure you write the loan so you can renew after five years, in case you have reason to hold the property.

What if the seller doesn't want an interest-only loan? You can offer to make payments at a thirty-year loan rate for the duration of the loan, still with a balloon payment due in five years, renewable. Your payment would then be only $131.84 a month, at 10 percent, a small increase from interest-only.

If the seller wanted the whole loan paid off in five years, with amortized payments, it wouldn't work—you'd be paying $318.73 a month, and you'd do better with the regular loan. The purpose of this kind of seller-carry financing is to give the seller an income while giving you lower monthly payments. Each of you has a need to improve your cash flow, and this kind of financing meets both your needs.

Suppose this seller didn't have income to qualify to buy a new home, or not enough to buy a home he'd want?

Then your seller-carried loan might look even better. The seller's real need, after paying off the existing debts, is more income. That's exactly what your deal offers. You write the deal to provide enough cash from the sale to cover the seller's debts, and perhaps a small amount of cash so the seller can have the comfort of money in the bank and use the rest to provide income. Without changing the above deal in any way except to change the seller's need for a down payment to a need for a bank account, we can give the seller the same income plus $6,000 in the bank. Anyone who has been in financial difficulty or has had to take a lower-paying job should appreciate the offer.

WHEN THE SELLER
HAS LESS EQUITY

I can hear you asking, "Okay, but what happens when the seller doesn't have so much equity in his house?" Well, as I said earlier, the seller has to have enough equity to make the house saleable. The more equity, the easier it is for us to help him. If the house has been over-encumbered, we can't help. But we can help sellers who bought their homes wisely and have paid a few years on the mortgage.

Let's suppose our seller bought the home for $92,500 at 10 percent two years ago, paying 5 percent down. We'll assume appreciation has been slow, less than 5 percent per year, and the house is now worth $100,000. His down payment was $4,625, leaving a balance of $87,875 financed. After two years, he'd still owe 98.8 percent of the original balance, or $86,820.50. His equity would be $13,179.50. We could still buy the house, but we couldn't help the seller as much. He has enough equity to pay his debts and cover costs of sale, and we have a little room to bargain on price.

We can't meet as much of his need as before, but we can still meet the important needs—the ones which motivate the sale. We can't meet our needs for low-cost financing. If the deal depends on shaving our costs to get a positive cash flow, we may not be able to buy the property. If our cash flow works, we meet the seller's needs and have a deal.

You can meet your needs and a seller's needs in a wide variety of deals, with widely differing circumstances, needs, and amounts of equity. The key is *always* to know what you can afford to spend to control title to the house, and *always* to find out what the seller needs, so you can offer a creative way to meet those needs and benefit yourself.

LET YOUR TELEPHONE DO THE DRIVING: HOW TO BUY PROPERTY YOU'VE NEVER SEEN

S o far, I've talked about the motivations of sellers and the importance of meeting their needs. Now it's time to turn our attention to *finding those sellers*.

In this chapter I'll talk about negotiating with FSBOs by telephone. In Chapter 10 I talked about FSBOs and how to determine which ones to call first. Now, you'd like to know, *what do I say when I call them?* (Telephone negotiating and information-gathering techniques work just as well when you deal face to face, as you would when talking to an agent or with an owner who is selling through an agent.)

The reason for telephone negotiating is to save time. You could knock on the door of every house you saw with a "For Sale by Owner" sign in the yard, and you could call every ad in the paper and make an appointment to go see the house and talk to the owner.

Do you get a feeling that all that talking and looking would take a tremendous amount of time?

You should—it would. You'd never cover all the possibilities, and you might well miss the best deals simply for lack of time to look for them.

The real purpose of telephone negotiation is not negotiation at all, but a process known in the sales industries as *qualifying*. In sales, it means finding out how much the person can afford, or whether the person can afford what he says he wants to buy—that is, is the potential customer realistic?

When you call FSBOs you are "qualifying" them in a similar but somewhat different sense. You want to find out the important information about the house and seller: the motivation, details about the house, the existing financing, and whether the owner is willing to listen to a creative offer.

The last item is not something you will ask directly, but will learn from asking other questions. You'll find that many FSBOs are not sophisticated and will listen to creative offers. They haven't been listening to real estate agents telling them that the only way to deal is the way things have always been done—which too often is negative advice; telling the seller all the things that "can't be done."

Agents should be protective of their clients, which is what they get paid for, but often they are over-protective and avoid selling by any method other than the way property has been sold for the last forty years. That attitude is changing, as I discussed in Chapter 10, and I expect it to continue to change.

INTERVIEWING THE SELLER

You want to learn the same things a salesperson would: Is this seller realistic? Will he or she listen to your proposal?

And, you want to know as much about the property as you can learn on the phone, and all the details of existing financing.

You might think, "It's easier talking to someone face to face. I'll make my first contacts that way, until I learn what I have to do."

No, don't do it.

Why?

Because you can expect to talk to a number of sellers before all the questions you need to ask are second nature.

If you do your first interviews over the phone, however, you can have all your notes in front of you, reminding you what to say and what you want to learn. You can even have your questions written out so you can read a question and be sure you ask it just the way you want to. You don't have to think about what you're going to ask; you need only think about the seller's responses.

What you will be doing is very similar to what many beginning real estate agents are trained to do—except that your success rate will be far higher!

In real estate sales, it is called "farming," or "cold calling." The agent is told to take a section of the city, get the names and phone numbers of everyone who lives there, and sit down and call them all, asking, "Are you interested in selling your home, or do you know anyone who is thinking of selling their home?" I don't have to tell you that they get rejected a lot! Even people who love to talk on the phone can get to hate the idea of making that kind of call!

What you'll be doing is that agent's dream—you're calling only people that you *know* have what you want, who will be happy to get your call! You're calling to pick which, of the many possible sellers, are the ones you want to work with—not only are you calling people who want you to call, they have to sell *you* on the idea that they can offer you more house on better terms than the last or next person you call!

I'd suggest that you use one technique used by those poor agents. They are often told to commit themselves to making a certain number of cold calls each day. You should do the same. Suppose you want to use your weekend to view property. During the week, you can call all the FSBOs and possible FSBOs in the classified ads.

In any moderately large city, there will be a lot of them, so select them according to the probability that they'll be what you want, using the methods I discussed earlier. Make copies of the qualification sheet, clip and paste the ads on each one, and you'll have a stack of prospective sellers.

Each night, call some of them. Commit yourself to calling a certain number. If you feel a little nervous or unsure of yourself, that's normal and will pass as you make more calls. The first night, talk to at least five FSBOs. If you feel like talking to more, great! Go do it. But at least talk to five.

Once you've done it a few times, you'll feel comfortable and you'll know about how long you're going to take on an average call. Then you can either decide that each night you'll call a larger number—ten would be good—or set aside a period of time—say, 7:30 to 9:00 PM—during which you will call as many as you can. Make your calls Monday through Thursday, and on Friday look over your sheets and decide who you want to call back to set up a weekend viewing appointment.

You can also make calls one night and set up appointments to view the next, if that works for you. There are many possible ways to arrange your time. The important thing is to commit the time and commit yourself to doing it.

Usually, a phone call is all you need to determine whether it is worth your time to check out the house and make an offer.

PREPARATION PAYS OFF

Now, you know what? Lots of people are afraid to pick up the telephone and call a total stranger, even to offer such good news as, "I'd like to buy your house." If you're not one of them, consider yourself lucky—but don't go pick up the phone quite yet. Whether it is hard or easy for you to pick up the phone and make that first call, you should be prepared to ask all the right questions and get all the right answers, the first time. And if making that first call is hard for you, being prepared will make it much easier.

As I said above, it's a good idea to write down what you're going to say to the person, especially if you're someone who hates to make phone calls. Think what you want to say and how you'll say it, and practice a few times, even if you love talking on the phone. That way you'll sound confident, assured, friendly, and professional when you make your call. It's all right to read your questions, but you don't want to *sound* as though you're reading from a script.

A little practice will do it. You also want to sound humble, not overbearing, and show a deep concern for helping the people get where they want to go. The sellers should feel as if they're talking to good old Uncle Harry, not a heartless investor.

The tool you use to do all this is a *qualifying sheet*. An example of a complete qualifying sheet follows this discussion. The sheet presented here includes some blanks for things you will determine later, rather than in conversation with the seller. They are included so that you can keep most of your information about the house and seller on one form, making it easier to use.

You can use the same sheet and method when talking to sellers face to face. The sheet enables you to both collect the information you need and remember to ask all the needed questions.

USING THE
QUALIFYING SHEET

Paste the ad at the top of the sheet. Take whatever information is in the ad and write it in the appropriate spaces, so you won't have to ask for information the seller has already given. Write the date on which you made the call. There is space to make notes if you get no answer, an answering machine, or someone who cannot talk about the sale (a child, friend, roomer, etc.), and space to log follow-up calls.

If you reached someone other than the owner, there is a space to say who it was. That way, when you call back, you can say, "I talked to your daughter, Mary..." instead of something more negative like, "I called last night but you weren't home..."

If you got no answer the first time, don't mention it. If you left a message on the answering machine, say that you did. If their answering machine "I'm not here now" message was pleasant or creative, tell them how nice it was. Everyone thinks most answering machine messages are awful (most really aren't; people think so because they're mad they didn't get the person they called), so if you can honestly compliment them on the message, you've made them feel good about you right away.

Okay, the seller answered.

You give your name and say you saw their ad. Now, what's the first question you ask?

The seller's name, of course! ("Hello, my name is Dave Del Dotto, and I saw your ad in the *Chronicle*. What's your name?")

People instinctively feel that using their name is a sign that you care. Use their name whenever it is natural in the conversation. (Not in every sentence! That would sound phony and forced.) For some of us, using a stranger's name is hard to learn. If you have trouble, or it seems awkward, just do it. After you've made enough phone calls or talked to enough agents and sellers, it will become natural. Use the name often enough that the person knows you know it, and care enough to use it. After all, we all like to be recognized as individuals and called by our names.

Next, ask the address and, if needed, directions for getting there.

Before you make your first call, get street maps of the entire area in which you may be buying, and study them so you at least know the names of the main streets. This is especially important if you are investing in an area you've just moved to or are not familiar with. In that case, take the time to study the maps, drive through all the neighborhoods, and find people who've lived in the area long enough to tell you what the neighborhoods are like, before you begin making calls.

Next, you say something like: "Your ad sounded like a house I might be interested in. Can you tell me more about it?" You may elaborate, using information in the ad: "You say it has three bed-rooms, two baths, a family room, and a large yard. How big are the rooms? Is the yard landscaped?" or whatever seems reasonable to ask. This gives the seller a chance to tell you what a wonderful home it is.

You'll find that almost every seller loves his home and will fondly go into great detail, giving you all kinds of information. If you encounter someone who gives you only the barest bones, you can ask more questions. Remember that those who live in a home see all the good things, while we have to look at its investment value. *Don't* let a seller sell you on how wonderful it is! You can determine that when and if you decide it is worth inspecting and you see the reality behind the seller's pride.

On the qualifying sheet I've put blanks for the standard features you will or may find in most homes, followed by three blank lines for other information. You may want to add extra lines here, or you can keep a notebook or steno pad next to the qualifying sheet, on which you can write any information which does not fit in the space provided. When you ask the seller to "tell me about your house," you may get a lot of information that doesn't fit the neat categories of a form, and much of it may be useful, so be prepared to write it down on a separate sheet.

When the seller seems to have told us all about the house, we have the opportunity to say, "That sounds like a lovely house. Why are you selling?" The response will tell us the seller's motivation. Listen carefully. You may find some sellers who don't want you to know that they are facing financial difficulty, and will give some excuse—but when they give you an excuse you can usually hear it in a hesitation in their voice.

You'll notice that we have not said a thing about price yet, although price is the most important single piece of information. We're interested in numbers, the financial reality, not the neat kitchen and cute green shutters, right?

Right, but what we've done so far is make the seller feel happy by letting him talk about his house to an interested listener, *and* we've found out enough about the house to begin to give us an idea what it should be worth. We've got a lot of information which suggests how easy it will be for us to rent, lease, or sell the property after we buy it.

This is a time to ask about things the seller may not think to tell you, like the size of the home in square feet, and the lot size, if the seller knows (they should, but may not). With the square footage, you can calculate the price per square foot that is being asked. If you find out what an average lot in that neighborhood sells for and the cost per square foot for construction in your area, you can add them up and see how the seller's asking price compares with the cost of new construction. This is a quick way to determine value and will work in most tract home areas of most cities. There will always be cases where the value is not in the cost to replace, but in the rarity of the type of construction or uniqueness of setting.

You want to know about schools, shopping, and transportation, because all three can add or subtract value. Some features may be important in one city but not in another. For example, here in

Modesto, where summer temperatures usually are in or near the 90s, central air conditioning and swimming pools are much more important (and common) than they would be in Duluth, Minnesota.

GET THE NUMBERS LAST— AND GET THEM ALL

Once you've learned everything else the seller has to tell you about the property, it's time to ask about price. (If the price was in the ad, we have a good idea of whether it is realistic.) So, we ask the price, and ask about existing financing.

When we learn the existing financing on the house we can figure the maximum second loan we could get, whether the first is assumable, and determine whether the seller will carry a second or third. Banks will usually lend up to 80 percent of appraised value on a second loan.

We will not usually wish to ask the seller whether he or she will carry a second or third at this time. The spaces are for our use later, in working out the kind of offer we might want to make on this property. (If the seller brings up owner financing, then go ahead and talk about it.) The first spaces are for existing financing and whether or not it is assumable. You want the remaining balance, the interest rate, and the monthly payments. If existing financing is not assumable, the remaining balance is all that is important. It will have to be paid off when the house is sold, from the purchase price.

"Least amount down" and "cash needed by seller" sound like they might be the same thing (and could be), but usually are not. The amount down is how much cash *you* need to come up with to make the deal work. That will usually depend on the kind of financing that exists on the house or can be worked out.

The cash needed by seller means the money the seller needs to pay sales costs plus the cash he or she needs to get after all loans and fees have been paid. This amount is one of the needs you should determine while talking about the reasons for selling, because the need for a certain amount of cash is a powerful motivating factor in the sale of a home.

Seller's Knowledge Can Work For Us

Why would we want to note how knowledgeable the owner appears? First, a very knowledgeable owner might be another investor like ourselves, who would not be likely to offer us a good deal. He or she will be motivated to make money, not sell as quickly as possible on creative terms. We cannot expect to make money on a property on which someone else has already made the profit. We might, however, find a person who could be a partner, should we encounter such a seller. Second, our approach and attitude toward a seller who clearly knows nothing of real estate is different from the way we can deal with a seller with average knowledge.

If the seller knows nothing, we have an obligation to explain not only what we are doing but also how real estate dealing works. We have the opportunity to "train" our seller to appreciate our deal, and at the same time do the seller the favor of giving him or her greater knowledge about making the biggest investment most people make in their lives.

A seller with "average" knowledge may be the most difficult to work with. That's usually a person who may have bought and sold several homes due to job change, transfers, or income growth. Such a person may feel he or she "knows it all," or may "know" enough to be afraid of any deal that's proposed.

On the other hand, such a person may appreciate how much he or she *does not* know, and be very willing to listen to you and grateful for your information. You won't have to talk with many sellers before you develop a sense of which one falls in which category. And, when you have talked with a number of sellers of all motivations and levels of knowledge, you'll find you have a personal style for dealing with each kind of seller.

You make notes on what kind of a seller you think the person is so when you call back or make an offer you can remind yourself how to ask questions and how much explanation you should be prepared to make. If you've called ten FSBOs a night for a week and decided to follow up on six of them on the weekend, you'll have to depend on your notes to remember what you talked about, because you won't remember unless you have a very rare memory.

Estimate the Property's Potential

Finally, the sheet contains space to analyze the property. You'll do this after the phone call, perhaps in pencil, so that you can make changes after you actually see the property. Will it produce a profit? How? How soon? How much? And, if it will, what terms will you offer the seller?

Of course, what you are doing is *estimating* the financial performance of the property. No one can *guarantee* the real estate market, though it is a lot more dependable than the stock market and most other forms of investment. By making this estimate, you can be more certain that your investments will pay off. What you will find, if you do a week of calls and make that many estimates, is that certain properties will stand out as more likely to make more money sooner. Those are the ones you go after first. By making your offers on the highest-probability properties you minimize the time you spend and maximize your potential profit.

The rest of the last page of the qualifying sheet is space for comments, because no form can cover all the possible notes you might want to make about a property, either while talking to the seller or afterward. If you need more space, use another sheet.

If you have called ten sellers a night Monday through Thursday, you've got a lot of forms to keep track of. You could put each in its own file folder, but at this stage it is simpler to buy a three-hole punch and a three-ring binder. Put the forms in the binder, then go through them on Friday and pull out the ones you decide to work with.

Seller Qualifying Sheet

Phone number___________

Date Called___________2nd call_________3rd call______

Response: OK____ Not home____ Answering Machine_______

Person other than seller____who_________________________________

Call back at_______________________________

Address____

Directions (if needed)_______________________________________

____

____

Details about house:

Bedrooms_______________ Baths______________________________

Living room (size)____________ Family room (size)_______________

Dining room_________________ Garage_________Other__________

____

Yard______________________ Basement_________Attic____________

Pool________________ Spa___________

Schools: Elementary__________________

Jr. High_______________________________

High School___________________________

Shopping____

Transportation_______________ Freeway access__________________

Square feet_________________ Lot size______________________

Type of construction______________Style_____________________

Number of floors____________ Finished attic?____Basement?______

Other information and features:______________________________

____

____

____

Reasons for selling____

____

____

Motivating needs____

____

____

____

Price______________
Loans:
    1st: ____________________________ %______
    2nd: ____________________________ %______
    3rd: ____________________________ %______
Payments:
    1st: ____________________________
    2nd: ____________________________
    3rd: ____________________________
Equity____________________________________Assumable?
1st______2nd______3rd________________________________
Least Amount Down ________________________________
Cash needed by seller ________________________________
Maximum possible 2nd loan ____________________________
Seller carried? ________________________________
Terms: Interest rate________ Years______Mo. payment__________
3rd loan______________Seller carried?__________________
Terms: Interest rate________ Years______Mo. payment__________
Other financial information____________________________

____

Net to Seller______________ Cash to buyer?______________
Owner knowledge? much________average__________little______
Market value if sold now______________________________
Market value if rehabilitated____________________________
Current rate of probable appreciation__________________
Appreciated value in one year__________ Two years__________
Probable rental income________________________________
Cash flow: Positive______________ Negative______________
Lease option?____
Equity share?____
Terms to be offered seller:____________________________

____

Comments____

____

Now you understand how to talk to a seller on the phone and
find out almost as much about the house and his or her motivations
as you could learn had you knocked on the door, been given a grand
tour, and sat in the living room for an hour or more.

BUYING WITHOUT
VISITING THE PROPERTY

In the title of this chapter I promised to tell you how to buy a house
you'd never seen. Now, I don't recommend that you actually do
that, because you don't have to. (There might be an occasional
exception, but not many.) But my point is that you *could*. What you
have done with your telephone qualifying is learned a lot about the
seller and the property, saved yourself lots of time, and "visited" far
more property than you could have by driving around seeing every
one.

If you were to buy this way, you would tell the seller that you are
interested in the property, but that you need a little time to work out
the terms of your offer, and will call him back. Then you'd call and
say, "Your price seems fair," (if it is) or, "I can offer you $100,000,
which seems fair to me, given the price of similar homes in your
neighborhood, and my terms are—" And then you'd explain the
terms.

In actual practice, that part of a deal is best done face to face.
However, some investors do work this way. One of my students told
me he was so frightened of dealing with people, he made all his
offers over the phone or by mail. Of course, every purchase offer
contained a "subject to inspection" clause. When someone accepted
his terms and sent back a signed purchase offer, he would then visit
the property for the first time and look it over. That's where he made
his final decision on whether or not to complete the deal.

By using this qualifying sheet and these methods of telephone
qualification and negotiation, and getting in the habit of calling all
the FSBOs in the paper, you can easily buy property with little or no
money out of your pocket. If you buy just one a month, or twelve

houses a year, you'll be sipping cocktails on the beach in Hawaii or the Bahamas before you know it!

PART III

WHEN YOU ARE THE SELLER

CHAPTER 14

HOLD IT OR SELL IT?

You're about to buy your first property. You've found a good deal and are ready to make your offer.

Your first question, before you begin to write up the offer, should be, "How can I best make money on this property?" And, as I've discussed in previous chapters, there are basically two ways—you can sell it right away if you can see that it will make a profit, or you can hold it, waiting for its value to rise.

I prefer to think of the third way, buying property which will produce an income ("income property") as a tool for controlling an investment, not a means to produce wealth. If you buy property to produce large amounts of rental income, you're talking about buying and holding a lot of property, or a multi-unit building.

For most of you I expect that will come later, after you've made deals on single family homes, duplexes, or perhaps up to four-unit apartment buildings. Some of my students have made deals on million-dollar apartment complexes early in their investment careers, and perhaps you will, too, but I expect that most of you will make a number of one-to four-unit residential deals first.

Usually, however, the greatest profit in real estate comes from the increase in value of the property itself. Income, even when a building has an excellent cash flow and is profitable, is a secondary source of wealth. That million-dollar apartment building may produce a nice positive cash flow, but if property is appreciating at 10 percent per year, it will be worth 1.1 million in a year, 1.21 million in two years, and so on. Whatever it cost you to control title to that building will have earned you $100,000 the first year and another $110,000 the second.

Let's look at the factors that make us decide to either sell or hold a property.

Knowing When to Sell

This is, partly, a review of things I've said before, but I want to put them all in one place, where you can refer back to them, and I want to talk a little more about knowing when to sell. You might even say there are only two important things to learn in real estate: knowing what to buy, and knowing when to sell it. That oversimplifies things, of course—if it were that obvious I wouldn't need to write this book. I've talked mostly about buying and knowing how and what to buy.

Let's take our standard $100,000 house.

If we bought it for that price, and the price was fair market value on the day we closed, then we could not resell it at a profit any time very soon. We'd have to hold it until its value appreciated.

If its fair market value was $110,000, then—it would seem—we should be able to make $10,000, less our expenses of sale, by selling at once. But we should ask ourselves: If the seller we bought it from couldn't get $110,000, can we expect to? Chances are we can't, and each month it remains unsold, we're paying interest on the loans.

Okay, now do you see why I place so much importance on lease options and equity-sharing deals? Such deals, if done properly, give us a positive cash flow—it isn't costing us anything to control the title to the house—*and* give us a buyer for a guaranteed profitable price, without having to put the house on the market and make payments while it sits empty. If the person does not complete the deal, then we have an appreciated house that didn't cost us anything, so we can sell if the market looks good, or do another lease option or equity share if it does not.

The same reasons apply to my insistence that you write *and/or assigns or nominee* after your name on the offer. That gives you the opportunity to make money instantly without needing to spend monthly payments while the home is on the market.

Now suppose the fair market value is $100,000, but the home was an FHA foreclosure, the former owner left it in a mess, and we buy it for $70,000. If we can do most of the work ourselves, we might bring it back to being worth fair market value for $10,000 in materials, our own time, and labor costs for those things we couldn't do ourselves. Then we'd have a choice: we could sell it now and take our profit, or we could decide to hold it and let the value rise still further.

LET THE MARKET
GUIDE YOU

We would look at our local market, find out what the rate of appreciation was now and what it seemed likely to be over the next year or two. Then we'd estimate what our cash flow would earn us, and decide whether we would benefit more by taking our money out and reinvesting it, or whether this investment will pay off better if allowed to stand.

What I'm saying is that some properties *must* be held if they are to produce a profit, and others give you a choice. You almost never find a situation where selling is the *only* choice. In times of high interest rates or a slow market, you are more likely to have to hold a property. You may be able to buy below market more easily, but selling at market will be more difficult. That's when you're glad to be able to lease option or equity share.

In times of moderate interest or an average market, things are usually more balanced. You can find properties which give you either choice.

In times of low interest, or in a hot market, you may find it harder (but not impossible) to buy below market, but you may have appreciation of as much as 20 percent per year (usually not quite that high!), so you can hold for a year or two and make money. Sometimes in this kind of market you can't buy low enough for a positive cash flow from rent, so once more lease options and equity sharing come to your rescue. If you can buy below market—like that foreclosure which had been trashed by its former owner—you can be assured of getting market value or better, and selling quickly, when you have the property put in shape.

Make your sell-or-hold decisions based on the price you paid and the current value of your property, the state of your local market and interest rates, your cash flow, and your best estimate of the way each property will produce the most money.

CHAPTER 15

PREPARING A PROPERTY FOR SALE

I f there is one single thing which will most often allow you to buy property below market, it is the failure of sellers to properly prepare their homes for sale.

I'm thinking mostly of private owners in saying that, but it applies to many foreclosures as well—the bank or agency which has taken over the property may not spend the money needed to prepare the home to show to its best advantage.

When you sell, you don't want to fall into the trap of believing that appearances don't matter. Think of it this way:

If you're about to sell your dingy old car, does it make sense to drive down to the dealer, park it next to shiny new cars or used cars which have been cleaned up and waxed until they glow in the dark, and ask how much it's worth as a trade-in? Can you expect to get a top-dollar trade-in if your car's interior is filthy and strewn with kids toys and old McDonalds' bags, and the outside is dull and dirty and

---

hasn't been waxed in years? If you were trying to sell it yourself, would you leave it in that shape and expect a good price? Or even a sale?

No way!

And, if you were *buying* a used car, you'd certainly go right past anything in that condition, looking for the one that was clean and well cared for. Right?

I used the car example because we've all bought more cars than homes, and because in a car it is so obvious. (Even so, if you remember the last time you went looking at used cars which were for sale by their owners, I'll bet you found more than one that had not been cleaned up and made to look its best.)

Now you'd think than anyone selling anything as important as a home would *just know* that it will sell faster, for more money, if it's in perfect shape and spotlessly clean. But, who knows why, you'll find many, many owners who apparently figure that the new owner will want to fix it up their way anyhow, so why should they waste their time and effort? And so you walk into perfectly good homes that haven't seen a paintbrush in ten years, weren't cleaned since last month, have dirty dishes in the sink and kids toys scattered from one end to the other. The sellers expect the average buyer to see past all this filth and junk and know what the home will look like when it is clean and painted, with new carpet and all the buyer's furniture moved in.

Profit From
Seller's Mistakes

Well, buyers are far too often faced with trying to imagine what houses might look like cleaned up, and they don't do too well at it. Result? The home that is clean and bright and fixed up—the equivalent of the used car which has been waxed until it glows in the dark—will sell faster and for more money.

As I discussed in the last chapter, we want to sell for a higher price, and we want to sell as quickly as possible. And, as I've mentioned repeatedly, we want to buy below market so that we can make a reasonable profit.

Now, you and I, when we are buyers, need to train our eyes to look at homes in the mess described above, and see a sound house that can be fixed up with a little paint and carpet or whatever, and *which can be bought below market because the owner has left it in below-market condition!*

We will, almost certainly, need to do some work on almost every home we buy. Exceptions would be those rare "perfect" homes, and those which we are able to sell using the "and/or assigns or nominee" technique, or which we are able to lease option or equity share before closing.

We can divide "preparing a property for sale" into two general categories. It can mean taking care of minor things and cleaning everything up—making it sparkle—or it can mean more extensive work—the kind of house often called a "fixer-upper," the house that has deteriorated or has been trashed, but which can be restored economically. If repairs plus purchase price cost more than fair market value, it isn't a good buy and may be beyond economical repair.

Think of a car you can sell if you just clean it up and give it a real good wax job, or a car you can't sell without doing all that plus a new set of tires, brakes, a valve job, and a new muffler.

I'll talk first about the basic rules and tricks of making a house look attractive to every buyer who walks in the door. Then I'll talk about fixer-uppers.

MAKING IT SPARKLE

Drive down any street in any town. Drive slowly, and look carefully at each house on the block. Even in areas that convey an impression of neatness and perfection, as if you are looking at a picture-postcard city, you'll see, if you look, some peeling paint, drooping gutters, untrimmed hedges, and so on—lots of little things that all of us

---

decide not to get around to fixing *this* weekend.

If you visit friends' houses, even if they've cleaned and picked up the house because company was coming, look around and you'll see cracks in the plaster, scuff-marks on the door frames, rooms that should have a fresh coat of paint, and all the other things that result from the normal wear and tear of actually living in a house.

It does not take long for any house, even one lived in by the home-owning equivalent of the "little old lady who only drove her car to church on Sunday," to accumulate its share of these "battle scars." If a home is occupied, tastefully furnished, and kept spotless, such problems will be less evident. If the home is empty, every scuff will jump out at a prospective buyer, to be added up as one more thing the buyer will have to paint or fix before moving in.

The two most obvious areas to freshen up are paint and carpets. You may not have to do much to either, or may need to do a lot. Sometimes paint can be washed and carpet cleaned. (If carpet needs more than a good vacuuming, call a professional carpet cleaning service.) The more you have to do, the closer a house comes to being considered a fixer- upper.

Painting is something you can do yourself. Even if you've never held a paintbrush or roller in your hand, even if you think you have ten thumbs, painting is easy. You can learn, and it is worth taking the time to learn.

With a few gallons of paint and a couple of weeks of evenings, you can paint the entire inside of an average house. (A big house or one with lots of windows or trim may take longer; and if you're painting for the first time, you won't be as fast as if you'd done ten houses already.) Again, you may not need to do it all; sometimes just little good clean-up will do the job.

USE THE RIGHT
TOOLS FOR THE JOB

Paint is cheap, especially if you watch the sales, and there are almost always paint sales. Just be sure you buy a good brand of paint. Believe it or not, the better brands do go on more easily and cover better than the discount brands. The time and hassle you save is well worth the few dollars extra you pay. You need only a few tools, and they are cheap, too.

You'll need drop cloths. You can buy heavy professional ones, if you expect to be fixing up a lot of houses, or plastic throw-away cloths. Avoid the cheapest plastic cloths, which tear easily and are so light it is hard to get them to stay where you put them.

You'll need a pan and roller for painting walls and ceilings. If you are using more than one color, you'll want a pan and roller for each color—saves a lot of clean-up time, and they're cheap.

For windows and trim, you'll need paintbrushes. You can buy cheap brushes or expensive ones (even expensive brushes are cheap, compared to what you're gaining) and here I'd recommend that you avoid the cheap stuff. A good brush can make work much easier and faster, and avoid lots of frustration. Ask the person at the paint store about the best brushes and the best way to care for them. If the salesperson doesn't know, shop somewhere else. Your paint store should be a source of expertise any time you have a question about the best way to solve a painting problem.

For window trim you'll want a small brush, with an angled cut on the bristles. A larger angle-cut brush, perhaps 2" wide, will do nicely for edging. For door frames and such, you'll want a wider brush. If you have large flat surfaces, painted kitchen cabinets, for example, you'll need a still wider brush. You can make some brushes do double duty. The edging brush could also do door frames and kitchen cabinets, but it would take longer to get the job done.

Exterior painting is a different process. You still have trim, which you paint the same way you paint inside trim. A masonry exterior doesn't need paint, nor does aluminum siding and some kinds of shingles. You may be able to spray paint a frame exterior. An equipment rental store can provide the equipment and instructions on how to use it. If you do it by brush, you'll want a wide brush, but no wider than the siding boards. Rollers will work on some frame siding, and on stucco. You should be even more careful in your preparations, because exterior paint is subject to wider extremes of heat and cold, and will crack or peel more easily.

Try to find out what kind of paint was used (oil-based or latex-based) and use the same kind. Latex does not always stick properly over oil, and vice-versa. If you use both kinds of paint, use a separate set of brushes for each. That will save lots of clean-up time and eliminate risk of contamination.

Always scrub the surfaces before painting. A layer of dirt or grease will prevent paint from sticking.

Carpeting is not something you should do yourself, unless you happen to be a professional carpet layer, but can be a major value-adding selling point. You don't have to buy expensive carpet; just buy carpet that looks good. We're after appearance, right?

Many large cities have discount warehouses where you can buy carpet seconds and discontinued patterns at bargain prices. Also, carpet mills sometimes have factory outlets where you can get really good buys. Most of these are located in the southern states, so if you live near one, you could find nice-looking carpets at deep reductions.

If you plan to lease option or equity share, you might want to pay a little more attention to buying carpet which lasts and cleans well, so you don't have to replace it again if your tenant walks out on the lease or equity share agreement.

DON'T GO OVER
THE RAINBOW

Now, what kind of appearance do we want?

We'll follow the lessons learned by generations of real estate agents, corporate relocation services, and banks that fix up their REOs. It's very simple. Paint the ceilings white and the walls off-white. The carpeting should be light colored, usually "earth tones," with little or no pattern.

Does that sound bland and neutral? Experience has shown that no matter what people *like* and would choose for themselves, almost no one *objects* to light colors. Perhaps more important, light colors make a house look cleaner, bigger, and brighter, and therefore more attractive. This is especially important if you are selling a vacant house.

There's a story I've heard in so many versions that I'm sure it's true and happened more than once. An agent returns to his broker with the good news that he got the listing. The bad news is that it has *horrible* orange shag carpet. The good news is that the carpet is worn out, and the owner has agreed to replace it.

In a few days the agent gets a call that the new carpet has been

installed, and would he like to see how nice it makes the house look?
Of course he would, so he goes to the house and gets the bad news—
it has been recarpeted in brand new livid orange shag! Now, you
may like orange shag, and in some rooms for some people it is the
perfect choice. But a lot, if not most, people won't like it. That's why
you use white or off-white paint and earth tone carpets and, if
needed, drapes.

If the house has hardwood floors, you have a choice of carpeting
them if they're in bad condition, refinishing them if they need it, or
simply going over them with a cleaner and fresh wax. The cleaner
is important. Most houses that have been lived in will have a number
of layers of wax on top of any hardwood floor, and after a time the
wax build-up will get thick and dull. A cleaner will remove the old
wax and make your coat of wax look better.

You can refinish floors yourself. Equipment rental stores have
the sanders and will tell you how to use them. If you can find a friend
or someone who has done it before to help you the first time, that's
a good idea. Use a good-quality urethane varnish.

That takes care of the most obvious items of appearance. If you
did them all, you're nearer to a fixer-upper than a "make it sparkle"
job, but usually you won't need to do them all. You may not have
spent more than a thousand dollars and your time. If you didn't
recarpet, you may only have spent a few hundred dollars and your
time.

LITTLE THINGS
COUNT FOR A LOT

Now think of the things that annoy you in a house—the light switch
that doesn't work, the toilet that drips, the cupboard door that sticks,
and so on. Most of these are things you can fix yourself, and the
repairs are usually cheap and quick. Of course, if you need major
plumbing or electrical repair, you're better off to hire a professional
unless you happen to have those skills. (Some of my students have
taken the time to learn plumbing and electrical work so they can do
it all themselves.)

Okay, you've never done any of that stuff?

Chances are you know some of it—basic home repair is something we all should know, and most of us have fixed one thing or another, once or twice. I'd suggest you go to your local library and look up books on home repair. Check out those that look most like they explain it so you understand what they're saying. When you decide which one you like, check your bookstore to see whether they have that book, or a current version of it, so you have a book you can always refer to when you have to do something you've never done before. (Libraries keep books that are quite old, which may not make any difference at all in a home repair book, but an old book will probably be out of print.)

You'll find that a small amount of knowledge and a few tools will take care of minor problems, both around your own house and in those you buy for investment.

I'd suggest you start out with a hammer, several sizes of screwdrivers, both regular and phillips head, a pair of regular pliers, and a pair of needle-nose pliers. You might add a set of hex wrenches (also call hex key wrenches) because you'll sometimes find bathroom fixtures or other things using set screws which require them. If you get into plumbing you'll want a pipe wrench (monkey wrench). That's basic, and will do a lot of jobs. You can add tools as you find a need for them.

CREATE A GOOD FIRST IMPRESSION

Mowing the grass, landscaping, and gardening are easy to do, and important. A potential buyer driving up to a scruffy lawn and scraggly shrubbery will enter the house with the beginnings of a negative impression, rather than the beginnings of a positive impression. Everyone likes to come home at night to a home that looks nice. If you're trying to sell one that doesn't, the buyer is going to look at it, wonder whether he or she wants to come home to *that*, and wonder how much work it will be to make it something they are proud of.

THE FIXER-UPPER PROPERTY

Everything I've said about making it sparkle applies to the fixer-upper. The difference is that there is more of it to do. A home in good condition will need *some* of what I listed; a fixer-upper probably needs it all, and may need some major repairs as well—a new bathroom, a new roof, new wiring. Anything that can wear out on a house may be worn out or trashed in a fixer-upper. You may need to carpet the whole house, not just a hall or living room.

One thing you should *not* do, whether the house is a fixer-upper or not, is feel you must do everything you would do if you were going to live there.

What you are trying to do is make the house liveable and saleable with the least amount of time and expense. So, the things which create a good appearance are the most important: the paint, the carpets, the landscaping, the attention to little details like whether the bathroom towel bars match and are all firmly attached, and no faucets drip.

If you get into fixer-upper properties, you have two choices: You can learn to do all or most of the repair yourself, or you can search out professionals who do the job the way you want for a reasonable price.

One of my students took the first route, and made it a family affair with in-laws from both sides of the family pitching in to fix up the house fast. Her husband found friends who taught him how to put on a roof, replace plumbing, and do electrical work. They have little need to hire outside help now.

IF YOU CAN'T "DO IT YOURSELF"

Another student, who worked in the building trades until a disabling accident, turned to investing as a source of income and called on people he'd worked with to do his work, knowing that it would be done well and for a fair price.

Obviously, you will make more money if you can do the work yourself, but that won't work for everyone.

If, for example, you are a professional couple with demanding jobs, it may be all you can do to find the properties and make offers. For you, fixer-uppers may not be the ideal properties. But suppose you find one? Buy it, and look for professionals to do the work. If you don't have the contacts of my student who worked in the building trade himself, you can still use his method.

Suppose you have an electrician look at the house first. Say to him, "I'm going to need plumbing, painting, and a new roof, too. Who would you use? Can you recommend three people in each trade?" He'll recommend his friends, of course, which is why you ask for three—you'll probably get someone besides his best buddy.

Then you get estimates from those people and try to judge which you'd rather work with, and see how they work out. If they deliver quality work, on time and within budget, you know you have someone to call the next time you have a fixer-upper. If they don't work out, you try someone else next time. When you've done several like that, you'll have a "staff" of people you can rely on, and you'll know what it will cost to have them do a job, so you can look at a fixer-upper and decide whether it will make money for you.

I'd suggest that you should not start with a fixer-upper that's been really trashed. Look for something in between—it needs more work than an average lived-in home, but it's not a disaster. The reason is that a really trashed house, while it offers the opportunity to make a lot of money, can conceal a need for major repairs and major expense. That could wipe out your gains. If your first properties need some work, but not a huge amount, you have the chance to learn what each kind of repair costs in your area, what you can do yourself and what you cannot, and to develop your ability to judge the extent and costs of needed repairs.

When you sell, the way to get the best price is to make the property look its best. This is usually simple, you can do it yourself, and it won't cost much.

The fixer-upper property offers an opportunity to buy well below market and, if selected and repaired carefully, to sell at market for a good profit. The more you can do yourself, the more you will make.

If you use professionals, shop for the best work at the lowest price.

CHAPTER 16

ADVERTISING AND NEGOTIATIONS

W hen your property is prepared for sale, the final steps are to advertise it and negotiate with a buyer. Now *you* are in the position of the seller we talked about in earlier chapters. You do not want to be in a position where your motivation is that you *must* sell. Your motivation is to sell for top dollar.

If you have worked out a lease-option or equity-sharing agreement, you don't have to worry about advertising and you've already done your negotiating.

If you sell through a real estate brokerage, you can let them worry about the costs of advertising and the process of seeking out buyers. If not, you become a FSBO yourself. You face all the selling problems of a FSBO, except that you know much more about the process of selling real estate. You should have an easier time selling the property, because you know what you're doing.

There is an in-between alternative in some cities. These are offices which, for a flat fee, will help a FSBO sell a property. They provide advice, counseling, signs, advertising, and other services, may or may not put the property into the MLS service (they may charge extra for that), answer questions, and have an office for potential buyers to phone or walk into.

From reading this book, you know about the selling process. What such a service might do for you, on your first sale or two, is provide you with knowledge of your state and local real estate laws and practices, for less that you'd pay if you got the information by working with a full-service real estate broker. I'd suggest that if such an office is in your area, you investigate them when you are *buying* and find out how knowledgeable they are, and how hard they work to sell *you* on the properties of the sellers they represent. That will tell you the kind of job they'll do for you when you sell—and that applies to full-service brokers, as well.

ADVERTISING

Before writing your first ad, take a good, close look at the ads run by real estate brokers. How are they written? What do they say? What features do they stress? What language do they use?

Then think how you would respond if you were a buyer reading those ads. Which would you be more likely to call?

3br 2ba N. Modesto
$100,000. 000-0000

Or:

SPOTLESS 3BR 2BA RANCH! Great N. Modesto
schools. Spacious kitchen & family room, lg
mstr br suite, lg yard with almonds, nu carpet
$100,000. 000-0000 121 Elm St. Open Sun. 12-6

The second one will get your eye, right? Right. But many a FSBO will check out the cost of running a classified ad and run the first version because it's cheaper. What the thrifty FSBO fails to realize is that if no one reads the ad—if it does not make your phone ring—the cheap ad is much *more* expensive, because the money was spent and didn't do any good.

Your ad will do no good if no one sees it or, if they see it, if no one responds to it. You'll also find that various abbreviations are common, and just which ones are used will vary from one city to another. When you study the ads, notice which are used, and use them. You'll write a more professional-looking ad, and using abbreviations will make it cost less.

In the "good" ad, I included information on an open house. When you do that, give the address. Open house shoppers won't go to the trouble of calling to find out where the open house is.

But, if you are not advertising an open house, *do not* include the address! Why? Another lesson learned from real estate agents. They don't (or shouldn't) give addresses over the phone or in anything but open house ads, because most house shoppers use that information to drive by and decide they *don't want to look at that house!* They use it to *eliminate* property from consideration rather than to actually *find* a house! (Another reason to make certain the front of the house is spotlessly painted, the lawn is mowed, and the shrubbery and garden trimmed and weeded.)

So, when you get a call, *always* ask the caller to make an appointment to come see the house before you give the address.

When you advertise for lease-option or equity-sharing buyers, don't advertise in the "Homes for Sale" section, unless you run two ads. The place you are most likely to find those tenant-buyers is in the "Homes for Rent" section, so run the ad there. You could try running the ad both places and see what response you get. You might find renters looking wishfully in "Homes for Sale" who would respond. Or, you could run a regular "For Sale" ad in addition to the lease-option or equity-share ad, with an added line, "will consider lease option." That would reach both kinds of potential buyers.

NEGOTIATIONS

If you have a real estate agent come to talk to you about listing a property, the agent will probably tell you something like, "Your house should sell for about $100,000, and you should list it for $107,500." Depending on the current market, the condition of the property, and the price it should sell for, the agent will tell you to ask between 5 percent and 10 percent more than the property should bring. That's your "negotiating room."

It is traditional in real estate that whatever price is asked, the buyer will offer less. Then the seller usually counter-offers somewhere between the asked and offered prices, and eventually the offer is negotiated to acceptance or is rejected.

When you are buying, your object is to obtain the lowest price, and the best terms. When selling, your object is to sell for the highest price, and the most favorable terms. This is not a contradiction; this is the way you make money.

I've told you to seek motivated sellers. Another way of putting it is that you seek sellers who are negotiating from a position of weakness—they *must* sell, and the property may not be in perfect condition.

When *you* sell, you negotiate from a position of strength: Your property is in good to perfect condition, and you should never put yourself in a position where you *must* sell. You can always rent, lease option, or equity share if you can't get the price you need.

When you're buying, you ask the seller to pay all the expenses that can be paid by either party or split between the parties. If the seller doesn't want to do that, you ask for more favorable terms on price or other things.

When you're selling, you ask the buyer to pay all those expenses or give you a better price. By doing this, whether buying or selling, you can make the "hidden" profits that result from not having to pay expenses that you might "normally" pay.

Let's take a look at one possible negotiation. I won't call it "typical," because each purchase and sale is different from any other, and the minute you start thinking "typical," or "standard," or "routine," you're on the road away from creative deals.

We'll take the $100,000 house which the agent advised us to list for $107,500. We're going to sell it ourselves, so we can expect that any buyer is going to want a piece of the commission we're saving—which is fair enough, but we don't want to give it up if we don't have to, do we?

We look at the market. What are similar homes (our competition) listed for, and what have they sold for? This is one reason for asking an agent to evaluate the home. A good agent will bring a list of "comparables," similar homes now on the market and those recently sold. Some agents will let you keep the information to study at leisure; others will tell you that all MLS information is confidential (it is supposed to be) and they can show it to you but not leave it with you. If the latter, take all the time you need to study it, and make notes, before handing it back.

The question we ask ourselves is whether we will get offers if our asking price is a little higher. If the market is hot and interest rates are low, there's a good chance we will. In that case, we can raise the price, perhaps to $109,900, and see whether we get action. If we don't, we can always lower it. If the market is slow, we'll get more action by pricing low—$105,000, $102,500, perhaps even at $100,000!

When we set the price low, we make it a point to tell all interested buyers that we are asking "less than market," and expect to be fairly firm on the price. If we ask $100,000, we are very firm, but look for a way to offer something attractive in the way of terms. Normally, if you have to list at market value, the market is slow enough and tough enough that you may be better off with a lease option or equity share.

So, for this house, we listed at $107,500, as the agent suggested. After a few weeks, we get an offer of $92,500.

Well, that's ridiculous, isn't it?

Not from the buyer's point of view. He wants to see how you'll respond; he does not seriously think you'll sell at that price, unless he's living in fantasyland. He'd be delighted if you did, of course. He's also asked us to pay for all the inspections and repairs, pay transfer taxes and other expenses of sale. (Sound familiar? If the buyer is an investor like you, you haven't got a deal—you don't want to sell for a price that would let him make money at your expense.)

You could simply reject the offer, and that might be the end of that. But as long as there is an offer on the table and an interested buyer, it pays to counter-offer. Since he was way low, we'll counter high: $105,000, and he pays the expenses. If he's really a low-ball buyer, a wishful buyer, or an investor, he'll probably drop out now.

This buyer doesn't, so we begin to get a sense that he really wants the house. He offers $97,000 and offers to split a few of the expenses.

Okay, that's getting closer. We can try $102,500, and he pays the expenses. Now we're close, a little over $5,000 apart on price and probably a thousand or so in expenses.

If he comes back at $100,000 and a reasonable split on expenses, it's usually time for us to smile, take the money, and run to our next deal. If he comes back at $98,500 and doesn't budge on the expenses, we have a sense that we may be close to what this buyer will offer. We look at what we have in the house and what we need to get out of it, and how much it is costing us to keep it on the market each month, and decide whether the offer will work. Chances are, we counter at $100,000 with a split on expenses. And, chances are, we'll get an acceptance.

This is very simplified, of course. In an actual deal, you'd be looking at all the other terms and conditions of the offer, too. I didn't put them in, because they can vary so much from one deal to the next. You know from my discussion of terms and conditions, from your viewpoint when you are the buyer, how you should evaluate them when you are selling.

I've also not included the things in a deal which will give you clues to how far the buyer will go, because that will be unique to each deal. If you're selling and showing the house yourself, you have a chance to watch each potential buyer react to the house when it is shown to them. This can give you a sense of how much they like the house, who likes it most, and whether the husband or wife will really make the decision.

When you know they really like the house, you can hold out for more money. If they are so careless as to let financial information slip, you might know in advance that the most they could offer (and get bank approval) would be $97,000. All these bits of information are useful, so keep your eyes and ears open when you show a person your house.

The bad thing about using an agent is that you pay a commission. If, however, you simply don't have the time to market the home properly yourself (say you're that busy professional couple I talked about) then an agent is the only way to go. It means your property must gain more value before you sell it, because you have to pay the commission from the sales price. And, it means that you should pay extra close attention to finding the right agent, one who will work hard for you and negotiate for your point of view when it comes time to make counter-offers and counter-counters and so on.

Look at it this way:

In the example above, if the agent was right and the house sold for $100,000, you'd pay the agent 6 to 8 percent commission. That means your actual net would be $92,000 to $94,000. If you were selling it yourself, you could look at your "real estate agent profit point" as being one of those figures, or whatever the commission in your area happens to be.

That would mean that the buyer's original offer of $92,500 would be better than an 8 percent commission sale, if the expenses were split, and almost as good as a 6 percent commission sale. If you negotiate to a sale at $100,000, you've saved the entire cost of the commission. If you took the $97,000 offer with a split on costs, you'd be sharing a 6 percent commission with the buyer—a good point to make if you're trying to close a deal.

There is one more thing to be said for selling through an agent. Although you pay a commission, you'll usually find that you sell for a higher price, sooner. The higher sale price will make the net expense of commission less.

If, in our example, we sold the property ourselves for $97,000 but the agent sold it for $100,000, the net cost of the commission would be $3,000—3 percent, not 6 percent. That is, by selling ourselves, we net $97,000; by selling through an agent who gets $100,000 for the house and takes a 6 percent commission, we net $94,000. Due to the higher sales price, we actually only net $3,000 less than we would have without the agent—well worth the price of letting someone else handle showing the property, negotiations, and tracking all the paperwork through escrow.

If the agent sold it in a month or two less than it would take us to make a sale, and the house was vacant, creating no cash flow to make the loan payments, the payments we didn't have to make would reduce the effective commission cost still further. It might only cost us $1,000 or $2,000 to sell through an agent, and it might be worth that much to us to be able to spend the time it takes to sell a property in the search for the next one we want to buy.

I'm not suggesting that any of these possibilities is *exactly* what you need, but rather that you should look at your needs and the selling methods available and choose what will work best for you. If you're not sure, try selling one property yourself and let an agent sell another one. You may want to sell several properties, alternating the methods, until you're sure you know which works best for you.

I mentioned the cost of keeping a vacant house on the market. Your monthly payments are mostly interest, of course, and you don't get that back when you sell. You recover your tax savings, which are less than they used to be, under the 1986 Tax Reform Act, but the rest of the interest is out-of-pocket expense.

If you have rented a property, the cash flow from the rental will keep making those payments, if the renter holds over until the sale. The same is true if a lease-option or equity-sharing tenant is unable to meet the contractual terms, but wishes to remain in the house until it is sold.

EVALUATING
YOUR OFFERS

When the house is vacant—the tenant has moved out, or you bought a house, fixed it up, and put it on the market—you have the monthly expense of payments to consider when evaluating an offer. If you are selling in a hot market, this is not likely to be a major problem. But what if the market is slow, you've been paying for the house for three or four months while fixing it up and trying to market it, and an offer comes in that will make money, but is less than you expected and want to get for your efforts?

Suppose we bought the house in our example for $80,000 as a trashed VA foreclosure, spent $8,000 and six weeks putting it in saleable shape, and it has been on the market for three months at an after-tax net cost per month of $700? We've got $91,050 invested so far, and someone comes along with an offer of $93,000 net to us? You negotiate, but that's as far as the potential buyer will go.

Should you take it?

Again, I can't give you a firm yes or no answer, because too many other factors may affect your judgment. Under most circumstances, I'd say hold on to it; you have a $100,000 property and can do better. I might decide that now is the time to try for a lease option or equity share. Or, if that offer was the only interest expressed in the property the whole time you had it on the market, I might suggest that you're better to take what you can get and go on to the next investment. You're making almost $2,000. If you held it and got no more offers for several months, you would spend that much in payments.

With each property, and each offer, evaluate all the circumstances of the deal, and make your decision. Remember that each deal is different. Be as creative when you sell as you were when you bought.

CHAPTER 17

PUTTING YOUR PROFITS TO WORK:

HOW TO KEEP WHAT'S YOURS

O kay, you've completed your first deal—you bought a property, chose a way to make money on it, and sold it at a profit. Let's say you netted $10,000. (It might be more or less, depending on housing values in your part of the country and what kind of a deal you made.)

You breathe a sigh of relief—you did it! And it worked! And now you have ten grand to pay off a few bills, buy a new car, and—hey, wait a minute!

You did this as an *investment*, didn't you? You were planning on *building* wealth, weren't you?

Do you think you'll build wealth if you spend your profit as fast as you make it?

You said, "No," right? If you did, you got it. But there's a catch (isn't there always?), and the catch is taxes.

If you spend ten cents of your ten grand, you have to pay taxes on the whole thing. At current rates, that will usually mean 28 percent, for some of you 33 percent, and for probably very, very few of you, 15 percent. You'd have to be making *very* little from other sources to make ten grand on a property and stay out of the 28 percent bracket. At 28 percent, Uncle Sam gets $2,800 of your ten grand, leaving you an after-tax net of $7,200. (This assumes *all* of the $10,000 was taxed at 28 percent; the figure would be less if only part of the profit was in the 28 percent bracket.)

PUT OFF
PAYING TAXES

Now, I don't object to paying taxes—they're our share of the cost of running the country. You and I might be upset at some of the things our tax money goes for, or feel it could be better managed and all that, but we do have to pay for government services, and we should be glad to—we'd be awfully unhappy if some of the things we take for granted suddenly weren't there any more.

And you can count on it, sooner or later Uncle Sam will get his— *but*, you don't have to give it to him *now*.

Yes, I know some of you will need that profit right now for everyday expenses. If baby needs shoes, then you'd sure better buy shoes for baby.

But if you can buy baby's shoes from your other income, just as you would have if you hadn't made ten grand on a property, your investment career will move faster. At the beginning, when you've made one deal, or several, try to put all your money right back into investment. After you've built your wealth, *then* is the time to decide that you're ready to enjoy the fruits of your work, and use some of your profits to live the way you always wanted to, and have fun.

But for now, try looking at that $2,800 you'd pay in taxes as "free" money for your next investment.

How do you do it?

Well, you may think, that's easy; as long as you buy another property of equal or greater value within two years, you're covered.

Wrong!

That's the rule for your personal residence.

We're talking about investment property, which goes under different rules. The basic belief of tax law is that if you are engaged in business to make a profit, the profits ought to be taxed. Investments in property are considered a business. Under the old tax law, your profits were considered "capital gains" and taxed at the favorable capital gains rate. Under the new law, your profits are regular income and taxed at regular, higher, rates.

Your solution is a device called the *tax-deferred exchange*, also called a "like-kind exchange," and sometimes called a 1031 exchange, after the Federal Tax Code section which covers it. It is a technique which has been available to investors, and was used frequently in California before the new tax code wiped out some of the old tax advantages of real estate. Now it is being used more widely across the country, because it's one of the best deals left in the tax code, and looks even better because of the higher tax rates. An attempt to eliminate the idea was beaten down in Congress late in 1987.

You might think, from the "like-kind" terminology, that if you sold a three-bedroom, two-bath house, you could only exchange for another three-bedroom, two-bath house. Not so—the definition is very, very broad. You can exchange just about any kind of real property, as long as it is of "equal or greater value" than the property you sold.

Our key advantage, beyond saving taxes, is the improvement in our leverage. Look at it this way: Say you bought a $100,000 house and sold it at a $10,000 profit. Let's also suppose you bought the house with 5 percent down, which, of course, you got back when you sold. Now, instead of having $5,000 to invest, you have $15,000—the original $5,000 plus your $10,000 profit. You can buy a more expensive property.

Suppose you bought a $300,000 house, or a income property of the same value. Housing in the same area appreciates at about the same rate whether you paid $100,000 or $300,000 for it. (Sure, there will be variations from one neighborhood to another, and perhaps between single family residential and income property, but usually not wide variations.) So, in the same time that a $100,000 property will appreciate enough to make you $10,000, a $300,000 property will make you $30,000. And, it doesn't take much imagination to see that if you invest your $30,000 in a more expensive property, you'll make even more when you sell that one.

Do you remember what I said earlier about real estate profits not being based on the value of the property, but on how much money it costs to control the title from purchase to sale? See how it works to build wealth? Suddenly, you sell a property and the profits are wealth you once thought you could only dream of.

Well, you dreamed, and you did it, and your dreams came true. Now, if you want to give Uncle Sam his share and enjoy some of your gains, you'll still have plenty of cash left to make your next deal. Or, you might want to make several deals, so you could take your profits on one property and re-invest the profits from others through exchanges.

So, how does it work?

USING EXCHANGES FOR PROFIT

It isn't as simple as selling your personal residence and buying another within two years. When you do an exchange, *always* consult an attorney who is expert in the field. You not only want to be sure your deal conforms to all the requirements of the law, you want to be certain there have been no changes since the last time you did an exchange—or since anything you read about it (including this book) was written.

The first requirement (and limitation) is that property to be exchanged must be "held for productive use in trade or business or for investment."

That means just about any property which is not your principal residence or a vacation home. A vacation home may qualify if you rent it out most of the year and show it as investment property on your tax return. (Be sure you get accurate advice on what you must do to make a vacation home qualify as an investment. The IRS can get awfully upset and want a lot of your money if they decide you've done it wrong.)

There are two kinds of exchanges: simultaneous and delayed.

A *simultaneous exchange* means that you close the deal on both the property you are selling and the property you are buying at the same time. You give your buyer the keys, and the seller of your new property hands you his or her keys. This sounds simple, but in practice is hard to arrange and less common than the delayed exchange.

A *delayed exchange*, in addition to being more common, is also legally more complicated, so I'll repeat my advice to be certain you work with an attorney who knows the field.

The delay allowed is not unlimited. After you sell your property (close and turn over the keys to the new owner) you have 45 days to identify your new property and 180 days to complete the exchange transaction. This is, really, plenty of time—about 6 weeks and almost half a year. If we are working hard to build our wealth, we want to put our money back to work faster than that.

My recommendation is that you begin looking for potential exchange properties the day you put your property on the market, or even before, if you know that you will be putting your property on the market soon, or by a known date. (One mark of a good investor is the habit of thinking ahead.) That way, if you find something ideal, you can tie it up with an offer conditional upon sale of your property and conditional upon meeting all the conditions needed for a 1031 exchange.

You improve the possibility that you may be able to arrange a simultaneous exchange. You could even write in a condition that would pay the seller more if a simultaneous exchange takes place, because, usually, you'll save on fees if you can arrange a simultaneous exchange; another case of arranging to meet your needs by meeting the needs of a seller.

The biggest complication of a delayed exchange is that it involves the use of an intermediary. The IRS, apparently, wants to be very sure you don't have the use (profit, which would be taxable) of your money during the time between the first close and the final close.

What happens is that you deed the property you are selling to a neutral third party, who sells it for cash to the buyer you have selected and accepted in advance. The intermediary holds your money until it is needed for the purchase (closing), and then hands it over to complete your deal.

You can see that when you place your money in the hands of a third party, you want to be very certain that the person is someone you trust, *and who is bonded to assure that your money is safe.* Be sure that anyone who holds your money is bonded, or is covered by a bank letter of credit or a surety agreement which guarantees that you will get your money if the intermediary fails in performance of his or her duties, absconds to a tax haven in the Caribbean, or dies, any of which could leave you without your money, and with an unbelievable tax mess.

In California, you can talk to a commercial broker, tax lawyer, accountant, escrow company, or someone who specializes in facilitating exchanges. In other parts of the country, look for a commercial real estate broker or a tax or real estate lawyer knowledgeable in the exchange laws and practices of your state. The National Association of Realtors awards the designation of Certified Commercial Investment Member (CCIM) to qualified members.

You will, of course, pay a fee for the services (and bonding) of a person to perform this function, and there are other fees and expenses associated with an exchange transaction, including normal real estate sale costs—but you will save far more in taxes.

This is something you should investigate as soon as you buy your first property. If you need to take time finding the right person, or time to understand federal and state law, and what you can or cannot do, then you shouldn't wait until the last minute to begin.

OTHER TAX SAVINGS

Are there other ways to save taxes? Of course.

It is *possible* to use the "principal residence" rule for your first deal, or maybe several. You should do so carefully, because the IRS will get very unhappy if they think you're abusing the rule.

The technique is one I would suggest to those who enter investment very cautiously. My idea of the best, safest cautious way is to tell someone who is hesitant, hey, go buy a house for yourself, but buy it like it was an investment. Make sure it meets all the requirements for a profitable property. Go ahead, move in, fix it up, maybe live in it a while, and then put it on the market.

When you get an offer, give them a counter-offer making sale
contingent on your finding another home, with closing on your new
home to take place on the date of closing for the sale of your home.
You'd also need to ask for a couple of days occupancy after closing,
to give you time to move out and clean the house for its new owners.
A buyer shouldn't object to that.

I'd expect that if you did a house every couple of years, you could
do it that way without challenge—but if you do, check with your
accountant, or, better, a tax lawyer.

If you were buying and moving every four to six months, I think
the IRS would be justifiably upset, and would run you through an
audit wringer.

I don't, in any case, suggest this method as an ongoing investment strategy, simply because working with one house and turning
it over every couple of years isn't going to make the money you
dream about. It's a beginning tactic for someone who is hesitant
about taking the full investment plunge right off. Once you've done
it and know you can do it, you should have no trouble buying and
selling property as investments.

KEEP YOUR MONEY
EARNING MONEY

What if you really do need cash from that first ten grand, or however
much you make on your first deal?

Let me make a few general suggestions. Use them if they seem
to fit your situation.

First, try making yourself a promise that a certain dollar amount
or percentage of anything you sell (after taxes) will go back into real
estate.

If, as in our example, you began with $5,000, don't let *anything* eat
into that basic capital. Then, of the $7,200 you have left after taxes,
add $5,000, or $2,000, or even $1,000 to your original investment
capital. Even if you can only manage $500, make sure that *something*
is added from every deal. The more the better, of course. Then you

can make an offer on a more expensive property and, because it is worth more, its appreciation will mean more dollars in profit for you. Keep building up your investment nest egg.

If you don't shelter your income by an exchange, then perhaps you want to divide your investment capitol and offer on *two* properties. That would provide you with the option, when you sell, of taking your profit and paying your taxes on one, and doing an exchange on the other. Once again, you see how techniques can be combined and how you can find creative answers to investment profit problems.

A FINAL SUGGESTION

And finally, I have a suggestion for anyone who has read this far and is thinking, well, that's all very fine, but I could never do it. Well, first, don't say that. Of course you can.

But I know—because I've talked to many people and listened to many problems—and because my Customer Service department talks to people every day who just can't believe they can do it, or who are not willing to take the time and put forth the energy to do it—that some of you *will* get this far and quit.

And I don't want you to do that.

You've read the guarantee which comes with the Cash Flow package (at least I hope you've read it), and you've seen that it is a *conditional* guarantee, which requires that you try my methods and do the things required to make investment work.

But some of you, in spite of all of that, will take this book and this package and stick it on the back shelf of your least-opened closet and give up.

And I don't want *you* to be one of those people.

I want you to have the joy of success and know the pleasure of having enough money for the things you always wanted.

So I have one last, money-making suggestion for those who still, for whatever reason, don't want to do what I've taught.

You can make money in real estate without even being (quite) an investor. You see people doing it all around you, and you don't think they are investors, and chances are they don't either, but they are.

Every time you buy a house for your family, and every time you sell it, you're being an investor.

That's right.

And, if you are a good investor (not everyone is) when you sell the house you discover that it is worth a lot more than you paid for it. You've been saving on taxes as long as you paid interest on your mortgage, but I'll bet neither you nor your accountant ever tried to separate out how much you saved on taxes by owning your home.

So—even if you don't begin an investing career, *read* this book, and the others in the package. What they will do for you is make you a smarter investor every time you invest in your own home.

Now, I really want you to make money. But let me accept that maybe all you'll ever buy is your own home. You can tell how hard it is for me to accept that, so I've got one more idea to help you make money even if you never think of yourself as an investor.

I'll have to admit it isn't my idea. I heard about it from a friend, who told me (with delight) the story of a friend of his who bought houses to live in, with, apparently, no more attention to investment potential than any average home buyer—*but*, when she moved, *she didn't sell her homes!* She always managed, no matter how hard it was, to come up with a down payment on a new home, and then rented out the old one.

Now she has a small but nice portfolio of real estate; the first home she bought is free and clear; and she's got an easy quarter-million in equity sitting there appreciating each year, not to mention a nice positive cash flow. After years of "not being an investor," she's thinking of selling one or two and using the proceeds to buy more expensive income property—which will make her wealth appreciate at an even faster rate.

And how does she plan to do it? Well, she took a college evening course in foreclosures and decided she probably didn't want to go that route, but has been very carefully and thoroughly learning all about tax-free exchanges, while going out and looking at the kind of properties she could buy if she sold.

Now, how about that? Isn't that about as safe and cautious as you can get? And look what happened.

Even if the idea of investing in real estate terrifies you, now that you've read the book and know what's involved (it shouldn't, but I know some of you will find it terrifying), *this* is something *anyone* can do.

So why don't you?

Conclusion

Part IV of this book is examples of contracts for some kinds of deals you might use. The contracts deserve your careful study.

In the Introduction and the first three parts, I've told you how to purchase property creatively and sell it at a profit. I've even, in the last chapter, told you how to invest without being an investor. There's more valuable information in the cassettes which accompany this book, and in the other books which make up the Cash Flow package.

I've tried to make this book as authoritative and accurate as I can, but, as I've said often, real estate law differs from state to state, and sometime from county to county, or city to city. It also changes, especially in regard to tax and banking laws. It's your responsibility to know and understand your local laws and practices, just as only you can understand your local market, and to keep current on tax and financial laws and practices.

And, you have one most important responsibility, one thing I can't put in the pages of this or any other book or do for you:

You must take the information in this and my other books and go out and find the properties and make the deals.

You, and only you, can make the commitment to yourself that you will go out and *do it!*

And that's the most important thing. It is your life and your dream, and it won't happen unless *you* do it.

Go for your dreams of financial independence, and may you make them all come true.

PART IV

EXAMPLES OF PURCHASE OFFERS

Introduction to The Examples

I f you're looking at the offers first:

You have, I hope, read the rest of the book before looking at these examples. It's not that it's no fair peeking, but that you need the things you've learned from the rest of the book to make the best use of these offers. If you haven't read the book, they may seem like Greek to you. If you want to look at the offers first and then read the book, fine—but if you don't understand them, don't be discouraged. They'll talk about things you've never heard of, and you bought this course to learn just those things. You *need* the rest of the book to know what the offers mean, and how to use them creatively. So, look at them now if you wish, but then read the book.

Okay, now you've read the book—

The first edition of CREATIVE FINANCING was called 101
PURCHASE OFFERS SELLERS CAN'T RESIST, because it had 101
purchase offers in this section. This edition is called HOW TO
WRITE 1,001 PURCHASE OFFERS SELLERS CAN'T RESIST, and
the difference in the titles is important. 101 was my first attempt at
sharing my ideas with other people who wanted to invest and make
money, just like I had. I felt, then, that my readers needed contracts
they could follow as exactly as the laws of their states allowed.

Boy, was I surprised!

What I learned (along with a lot more, in the last six years) was
that my students didn't use the exact offers I had in the book, but
used the *ideas* contained in the offers!

Let me say that again, in big letters:

My Students Used The Ideas in My PurchaseOffers!

I want you to read these offers for the ideas in them, and then use
those ideas to write the most creative offers you can think of, making
each offer you write fit your needs, the needs of the individual deal
you're making, the needs of the seller, and the needs of the real estate
market wherever you are and whatever the interest rates and
economic conditions may be.

Remember when I talked about making "combination of ingredients deals?" You'll find many of the offers are exactly that. Most
of these offers combine more than one idea, and the combinations
suggest others. If you've studied this book and studied these offers,
you'll find not 101 offers, nor 1,001, but limitless, infinite possibilities. You have only to let your imagination run free to find that there
is a way to do almost any deal.

All the offers come with a standard disclaimer, which states:
"For illustration only—consult your attorney for legal advice on
contracts in your state." The disclaimer is important, too, because,
as I've said repeatedly in this book, state laws differ, and it is part of
your job to know the laws of your state and make your deals in ways
which conform to them—and which make the fullest and best use of
everything you are legally allowed to do.

For this edition, I went through the original set of purchase offers
and found many that were no longer useful, or which relied on loan
programs no longer available, or otherwise were not appropriate. I
wrote a number of new, updated offers, and edited many of the
remaining offers to reflect 1988 market reality. However, I feel that
it is quite possible that we will return to the days of high interest

during which I wrote 101 PURCHASE OFFERS, so for a number of offers I left the old high interest rates alone. I wanted you to see how it can be done under such conditions, should you need to. I suspect many of us will have an easier time looking at a deal which worked when interest was 16 percent or worse, and then being able to see how it can work with 10 1/2 percent interest, than the reverse.

You'll also notice that in most cases I haven't filled out the entire offer form, but have shown only the parts of the offer that are different and important to that particular creative deal. This is not intended to suggest that you should write only what is shown. You studied purchase offer forms, and what you should put in them, in Chapters 6, 7, and 8. You might want to review those chapters before studying the offers in this section. Be sure, when you write your offers, that you cover every important item, and be sure you include enough Houdini clauses!

Don't feel you should read the offers straight through, as you would read a novel or any of the other chapters of this book. Take them a few at a time, and give yourself time to stop and think about them, and allow the ideas they give you time to grow. Take time to think about each one.

Your ideal goal is to train yourself to think about deals and possibilities and all the elements of an irresistible offer, so that when the time comes to write your first one, you don't have to get out the book and worry about whether you've thought of everything.

In reality, you'll probably write a number of offers before you think of all the possibilities right off the top of your head each time, so don't worry if you feel the need to get out the book when you write your offers. Just remember that your goal is to be able to think in terms of the possibilities, all the time.

Study these offers, study your local market, and go for your dreams!

LIST OF CONTRACTS

(1) 80% Fixed Rate Conventional with 20% down

(2) 80% Variable Rate GPM Loan with 20% Down

(3) FHA - 203-B Loan - Minimum Down

(4) FHA - 245 Plan I - Low Down

(5) FHA - 245 Plan II

(6) FHA - 245 Plan III

(7) FHA - 245 B

(8) VA Graduated Plan I

(9) VA Graduated Plan II

(10) FHA - VA

(11) VA Loan - No Down

(12) Cal-Vet Loan - Low Down

(13) No Interest Loan - 30% Cash Down

(14) 75% Fixed Rate - 15% 2nd - 10% down

(15) Owner Finance - 20% down

(16) Wrap-Around - All Inclusive Deed of Trust

(17) Contract of Sale

(18) Bond Money Loan -First time buyer - 12% loan

(19) Conventional Loan - Second

(20) 80% Conventional - No payment second

(21) 50% Conventional - interest only 2nd

(22) 60% FHA loan - less than interest 2nd

(23) 60% conventional - Graduated 2nd

(24) 60% Variable loan - unsecured note

(25a and 25b) 2- Escrow Contracts

(26) I.R.A. Account Contract

(27) Credit Card Down

(28) Diamond Down

(29) Jewelry as Down

(30) Bonds for Down

(31) Stocks as Down

(32) R.E. Commission as Down

(33) Note from Another Property Owner

(34) Corporate Guarantee

(35) 75% FNMA Refi - 25% 2nd with annual payments

(36) 80% FNMA Resale Loan - Created note as down

(37) 95% FNMA Resale loan - at appraisal value

(38) 70% FHA Investor Loan - Interest only 2nd

(39) Land-Trust Purchases

(40) Wrap-Around 2nd - Seller 3rd

(41) Take Over 1st - Seller creates 2nd and sells in escrow -
carries 3rd

(42) Seller gets 1st for 50% - seller caries 50% 2nd

(43) Buyer obtains 1st for 60% - seller caries 40% 2nd - annual
payments

(44) Seller creates 1st for 60% - Buyer gets 20% 2nd - Seller carries
20% 3rd

(45) Sell the Option while in Escrow

(46) Contingent on Dividing into Multi-Units

(47) Contingent on Approval for Shared Use

(48) Contingent on Seller Assisted Subdividing

(49) Offer to Trustee in Bankruptcy

(50) I.R.S. Seized Property Bid

(51) Probate Sale

(52) 30% Refi - House for down - no payment second

(53) 50% Refi - prepay 1st - 50% 2nd

(54) Buyer obtains New Farmer's Home 1st for 40% - 60% 2nd - pocket crop

(55) Assume 1st - new 2nd - 3rd with principal balloons

(56) Refi 1st 50% - wrap-around annual payment

(57) Lease - Option on Foreclosure

(58) Farmer's Home - Low income loan

(59) Land Bank 70% First - 30% Second

(60) New Income Property Exchange - 60% Refinance

(61) Land Bank 40% Refinance - Annual Payments - Split Second and Third

(62) Land Bank 30% Created First - 40% Second - Wrap-Around

(63) Take Over First - Take Over Second - Lender Advances Payments - $2,000 Down Prepaid Payments

(64) Take Over First - New Second from Another Second Lender - Discount on Price

(65) Take Over First - New Second by Existing Lender at Less Interest - No Points

(66) Foreclosure - Create New 50 Percent First at a Discount over Former Loan - New 50 Percent Second - Prepay First in Price

(67) Foreclosure - Create New First at lower rate- New Second with Construction Draws

(68) Take Over First - New Second - Larger than Previous Second - Construction Loan to Finish

(69) Take Over First - Renegotiate First to Waive Interest - Second Lender Waives Second Interest

(70) Lease Option from Lender - Rehabilitate at Set Price

(71) Equity Share with Lender

(72) Buyer Takes Over Existing First - Seller Obtains New Second -
Buyer Makes Payments on First - Seller Makes Payments on
Second (50/50 Ownership) - Duplex - Live Together

(73) Buyer Assumes Existing First - Seller Lives Free

(74) Seller Refinances Existing First - Seller Keeps 50% Ownership
in Lieu of Note

(75) Partnership Makes Down Payment - Occupant Owns 50% with
no Down

(76) Co-Mortgage Helps get New First for 25% Ownership

(77) Private Lender Loans on Second for Lower Interest and 20%
Ownership

(78) Trust Funds Provide Low Interest Loan and 20% down Payment for 33% Ownership

(79) Six Month Lease-Option

(80) One-Year Lease-Option - No Credit Back

(81) Two-Year Lease Option - $200 Credit Back

(82) One-Year Lease-Option - Buydown

(83) Two-Year Lease-Option - Equity Share

(84) Seller held to Guaranties

(85) Realtor held to Guaranties

(86) Buy - Lease Back

CONVENTIONAL CONTRACTS

(1) 80% Fixed Rate with 20% Down

(2) 80% Variable Rate GPM Loan with 20% Down

(3) FHA - 203-B Loan - Minimum Down

(4) FHA - 245 Plan I - Low Down

(5) FHA - 245 Plan II

(6) FHA - 245 Plan III

(7) FHA - 245 B

(8) VA Graduated Plan I

(9) VA Graduated Plan II

(10) FHA - VA

(11) VA Loan - No Down

(12) Cal-Vet Loan - Low Down

(13) No Interest Loan - 30% Cash Down

(14) 75% Fixed Rate - 15% 2nd - 10% down

(15) Owner Finance - 20% down

(16) Wrap-Around - All Inclusive Deed of Trust

(17) Contract of Sale

(18) Bond Money Loan -First time buyer - 12% loan

REAL ESTATE PURCHASE CONTRACT AND RECEIPT FOR DEPOSIT
THIS IS MORE THAN A RECEIPT FOR MONEY. IT IS INTENDED TO BE A LEGALLY BINDING CONTRACT. READ IT CAREFULLY.
CALIFORNIA ASSOCIATION OF REALTORS® (CAR) STANDARD FORM

_______________________________, California. _______________, 19______

Received from _______________________________
herein called Buyer, the sum of ________ -Five Hundred- ________ Dollars $ **$500.00**
evidenced by cash ☐, cashier's check ☐, or _______________ ☒, personal check ☐ payable to_______________
_______________, to be held uncashed until acceptance of this offer, as deposit on account of purchase price of
-Eighty Thousand- _______________ Dollars $ **80,000.00**
for the purchase of property, situated in _______________, County of _______________, California,
described as follows: ________ **158 Cherry Lane**

1. Buyer will deposit in escrow with _______________ the balance of purchase price as follows:

A. Buyer to put $16,000 cash as down payment including above deposit.

B. Subject to buyer qualifying and obtaining an 80% conventional
loan for $64,000 from American National Bank. Interest rate
not to exceed current rate of 10.5% or selling price to be
renegotiated. Loan will be for 30 years at a fixed interest
rate with monthly payments of approximately $585.43 per month.

C. Seller to pay $1,200 for buyer's loan fees.

D. Sale to include washer, dryer, and all existing drapes.

E. Seller to provide a clear pest report at no cost to buyer.

Set forth above any terms and conditions of a factual nature applicable to this sale, such as financing, prior sale of other property, the matter of structural pest control inspection, repairs and personal property to be included in the sale.

2. Deposit will ☐ will not ☒ be increased by $ ______ - - - ______ to $ ______ - - - ______ within ______ - - - ______ days of acceptance of this offer.

3. Buyer does ☐ does not ☐ intend to occupy subject property as his residence.

4. The following supplements are incorporated as part of this agreement:

Other
☐ Structural Pest Control Certification Agreement ☐ Occupancy Agreement ☐ _______________
☐ Special Studies Zone Disclosure ☐ VA Amendment ☐ _______________
☐ Flood Insurance Disclosure ☐ FHA Amendment ☐ _______________

5. Buyer and Seller shall deliver signed instructions to the escrow holder within ______ days from Seller's acceptance which shall provide for closing within______ days from Seller's acceptance. Escrow fees to be paid as follows:

6. Buyer and Seller acknowledge receipt of a copy of this page, which constitutes Page 1 of______ Pages.

Buyer_______________________ Seller _______________________

Buyer_______________________ Seller _______________________

A REAL ESTATE BROKER IS THE PERSON QUALIFIED TO ADVISE ON REAL ESTATE. IF YOU DESIRE LEGAL ADVICE CONSULT YOUR ATTORNEY.

FOR ILLUSTRATION ONLY - Consult your attorney for legal advice ON CONTRACTS IN YOUR STATE
Reprinted with permission, California Association of Realtors®, Endorsment not implied

(2) 80% Variable Rate GPM Loan with 20% Down

* This Variable Rate Loan (VRM) may be obtained in your local area. The note interest rate is based in the current Treasury bill rates. It is also a Graduated Payment Mortgage (GPM) in which payments increase a fixed amount each year for a set number of years, in addition to the variable interest rate.

There are many variations of variable interest rate loans available (also called ARM's; Adjustable Rate Mortgages), some of them very useful, and others to be avoided at all costs. A loan such as the one shown should be avoided because of the uncertainty of the interest rate and monthly payment, and because Graduated Payment Mortgages often include negative amortization (you pay less than the interest due, so you owe *more* than the initial loan amount). In 1988, you're not likely to see the combination. Instead, you'll see ARM's and GPM's as separate loan offerings. ARM's can be useful to the investor, especially to control title to properties which will be sold quickly. GPM's are aimed at buyers who can expect their income to increase during the graduated payment period, and may be a useful tool when looking for buyers for your properties. If you can find these as assumable loans, you're ahead.

The good thing about GPM's is the low monthly payments in the beginning years of the loan. Buyers are qualified on the basis of being able to afford the payments on a 10-7/8% interest rate, as in our example, or on whatever the rate is at the moment (in 1988 it is much lower).

REAL ESTATE PURCHASE CONTRACT AND RECEIPT FOR DEPOSIT

THIS IS MORE THAN A RECEIPT FOR MONEY. IT IS INTENDED TO BE A LEGALLY BINDING CONTRACT. READ IT CAREFULLY.

CALIFORNIA ASSOCIATION OF REALTORS® (CAR) STANDARD FORM

_______________________________ , California. _______________________ , 19______

Received from _______________________________

herein called Buyer, the sum of ______ -Five Hundred- _______________ Dollars $ 500.00 ______

evidenced by cash ☐, cashier's check ☐, or _______________ ☒, personal check ☐ payable to A Reliable

Title Co. ____________ , to be held uncashed until acceptance of this offer, as deposit on account of purchase price of

______ -Seventy-five Thousand- _______________________ Dollars $ 75,000

for the purchase of property, situated in _______________ , County of _______________ , California,

described as follows: ____ 1729 Applegate Drive

1. Buyer will deposit in escrow with _______________________ the balance of purchase price as follows:

A. Buyer to put 20% cash down payment of $15,000, including above deposit.

*B. Subject to buyer obtaining a new 1st mortgage of $60,000 from Capitol Pacific Mortgage Co. The interest rate will be calculated at 10-7/8% interest with graduated payments of 7.5% for the first 5 years. Note rate will be calculated at 2.575% above average weekly yield of United States Treasury Securities. Any negative interest will accumulate to loan balance and will convert to a straight amortizing adjustable rate mortgage after five years.

C. Seller warrants that all heating, cooling, plumbing and electrical will be in proper working order at close of escrow.

D. Buyer reserves the right to a walk-through inspection and approval before closing escrow.

Set forth above any terms and conditions of a factual nature applicable to this sale, such as financing, prior sale of other property, the matter of structural pest control inspection, repairs and personal property to be included in the sale.

2. Deposit will ☐ will not ☒ be increased by $ _____ --- _____ to $ _____ --- _____ within _____ --- _____ days of acceptance of this offer.

3. Buyer does ☒ does not ☐ intend to occupy subject property as his residence.

4. The following supplements are incorporated as part of this agreement:

Other

☐ Structural Pest Control Certification Agreement   ☐ Occupancy Agreement   ☐ _______________

☐ Special Studies Zone Disclosure   ☐ VA Amendment   ☐ _______________

☐ Flood Insurance Disclosure   ☐ FHA Amendment   ☐ _______________

5. Buyer and Seller shall deliver signed instructions to the escrow holder within _______ days from Seller's acceptance which shall provide for closing within _______ days from Seller's acceptance. Escrow fees to be paid as follows:

6. Buyer and Seller acknowledge receipt of a copy of this page, which constitutes Page 1 of _____ Pages.

Buyer _______________________________   Seller _______________________________

Buyer _______________________________   Seller _______________________________

A REAL ESTATE BROKER IS THE PERSON QUALIFIED TO ADVISE ON REAL ESTATE. IF YOU DESIRE LEGAL ADVICE CONSULT YOUR ATTORNEY.

FOR ILLUSTRATION ONLY - Consult your attorney for legal advice ON CONTRACTS IN YOUR STATE

Reprinted with permission, California Association of Realtors®, Endorsment not implied

(3) FHA - 203-B LOAN - MINIMUM DOWN

* In this contract the deposit is made out to the real estate broker who is handling the transaction, to be kept in his trust account.

** The down payment on an FHA 203 loan is 3% of the first $25,000 and 5% of the balance. The maximum loan is slightly different in various areas.

*** The points charged on an FHA loan are variable depending on the market.

**** An FHA loan requires that the property meet the FHA's structural code. The code includes the electrical system, roof, hot water heaters, and broken glass. This is great for the buyer but may put an unknown selling expense on the seller.

REAL ESTATE PURCHASE CONTRACT AND RECEIPT FOR DEPOSIT

THIS IS MORE THAN A RECEIPT FOR MONEY. IT IS INTENDED TO BE A LEGALLY BINDING CONTRACT. READ IT CAREFULLY.

CALIFORNIA ASSOCIATION OF REALTORS® (CAR) STANDARD FORM

_______________________________________ , California. _________________________ , 19__________

Received from ____

herein called Buyer, the sum of __________ -Five Hundred- __________________ Dollars $____500.00____

evidenced by cash ☐, cashier's check ☐, or _______________________ ☒ personal check ☐ payable to____A Reliable____

____Real Estate Broker*____ , to be held uncashed until acceptance of this offer, as deposit on account of purchase price of

__________ -Seventy-one Thousand- _______________________ Dollars $____71,000____

for the purchase of property, situated in _______________________ , County of_______________________ , California,

described as follows: ______ 1798 Mild Lane ____

1. Buyer will deposit in escrow with _______________________ the balance of purchase price as follows:

**A. Buyer to put $3,500 cash down payment including above deposit.

B. Subject to buyer qualifying for an FHA 203-B loan for approximately $60,000 at current interest rates and terms of market of 10-1/2% interest. Payments to be approximately $548.84 per month principal and interest.

***C. Seller to pay up to but not to exceed 5 loan points of approximately $3,880.

**** D. Seller to make any corrections to property as required by FHA.

Set forth above any terms and conditions of a factual nature applicable to this sale, such as financing, prior sale of other property, the matter of structural pest control inspection, repairs and personal property to be included in the sale.

2. Deposit will ☐ will not ☒ be increased by $ ___ --- ___ to $ ___ --- ___ within ____ --- ____ days of acceptance of this offer.

3. Buyer does ☒ does not ☐ intend to occupy subject property as his residence.

4. The following supplements are incorporated as part of this agreement:

Other

☒ Structural Pest Control Certification Agreement ☐ Occupancy Agreement ☐ ___________________

☐ Special Studies Zone Disclosure ☐ VA Amendment ☐ ___________________

☐ Flood Insurance Disclosure ☒ FHA Amendment ☐ ___________________

5. Buyer and Seller shall deliver signed instructions to the escrow holder within ____________ days from Seller's acceptance which shall provide for closing within ____________ days from Seller's acceptance. Escrow fees to be paid as follows:

6. Buyer and Seller acknowledge receipt of a copy of this page, which constitutes Page 1 of________ Pages.

Buyer_________________________ Seller _________________________

Buyer_________________________ Seller _________________________

A REAL ESTATE BROKER IS THE PERSON QUALIFIED TO ADVISE ON REAL ESTATE. IF YOU DESIRE LEGAL ADVICE CONSULT YOUR ATTORNEY.

(4) FHA - 245 Plan I - Low Down

* To figure the amount of the FHA-245 Plan I loan, you multiply the sales price X .93991. (This factor will change as the interest rate changes. Check with your lender to determine the current factor to use.) This loan is graduated 2-1/2% per year for 5 years and then levels off. Graduated payment programs do not include principle nor all of the interest in the beginning.

REAL ESTATE PURCHASE CONTRACT AND RECEIPT FOR DEPOSIT
THIS IS MORE THAN A RECEIPT FOR MONEY. IT IS INTENDED TO BE A LEGALLY BINDING CONTRACT. READ IT CAREFULLY.
CALIFORNIA ASSOCIATION OF REALTORS* (CAR) STANDARD FORM

____ , California _____________________ , 19________

Received from ____
herein called Buyer, the sum of ___ -One Hundred- ________________________ Dollars $___ 100.00

evidenced by cash ☐, cashier's check ☐, or _______________________ ☒ personal check ☐ payable to ___ A Reliable

___ Title Company ___________ , to be held uncashed until acceptance of this offer, as deposit on account of purchase price of

____________ -Seventy Thousand- ____________________________ Dollars $___ 70,000

for the purchase of property, situated in ___________________________ County of _______________________ , California,

described as follows: _____ 1975 Matthews Circle ____

1.　　Buyer will deposit in escrow with _________________________________ the balance of purchase price as follows:

　　A.　Buyer to put $4,250 down including above deposit.

　*B.　Subject to the buyer qualifying for a new FHA -
　　　　245 Plan I loan for $65,750 payable at 10-1/2% interest
　　　　with graduated interest payments starting at $576.32
　　　　per month including principal and interest.

　　C.　Seller to provide a pest inspection and clearance
　　　　before close of escrow.

　　D.　Seller agrees to pay for all improvements needed for
　　　　FHA approval of the house.

Set forth above any terms and conditions of a factual nature applicable to this sale, such as financing, prior sale of other property, the matter of structural pest control inspection, repairs and personal property to be included in the sale.

2.　　Deposit will ☐ will not ☐ be increased by $ _________________ to $ _________________ within _________________ days of acceptance of this offer.

3.　　Buyer does ☐ does not ☐ intend to occupy subject property as his residence.

4.　　The following supplements are incorporated as part of this agreement.

Other
☐ Structural Pest Control Certification Agreement　☐ Occupancy Agreement　☐ _______________________
☐ Special Studies Zone Disclosure　☐ VA Amendment　☐ _______________________
☐ Flood Insurance Disclosure　☐ FHA Amendment　☐ _______________________

5.　　Buyer and Seller shall deliver signed instructions to the escrow holder within _________ days from Seller's acceptance which shall provide for closing within _________________ days from Seller's acceptance. Escrow fees to be paid as follows:

6.　　Buyer and Seller acknowledge receipt of a copy of this page, which constitutes Page 1 of_________ Pages.

Buyer____　Seller ____

Buyer____　Seller ____

A REAL ESTATE BROKER IS THE PERSON QUALIFIED TO ADVISE ON REAL ESTATE. IF YOU DESIRE LEGAL ADVICE CONSULT YOUR ATTORNEY.

(5) FHA - 245 Plan II

* The down payment on the FHA - 245 Plan II loan is more than the Plan I loan.

** But, you will notice that on a $70,000 house the payments are less per month than the Plan I loan. The loan will also graduate 5% per year for the first 5 years.

*** One of FHA's requirements is that the house have at least a 100 amp service instead of fuses in the electrical panel.

REAL ESTATE PURCHASE CONTRACT AND RECEIPT FOR DEPOSIT

THIS IS MORE THAN A RECEIPT FOR MONEY. IT IS INTENDED TO BE A LEGALLY BINDING CONTRACT. READ IT CAREFULLY.

CALIFORNIA ASSOCIATION OF REALTORS⁺ (CAR) STANDARD FORM

_______________________ , California. _______________________ , 19_______

Received from _______________________

herein called Buyer, the sum of ________ – Five Hundred– _______________________ Dollars $____ 500.00

evidenced by cash ☐, cashier's check ☐, or _______________________ ☒, personal check ☐ payable to____ A Reliable

____ Real Estate Broker , to be held uncashed until acceptance of this offer, as deposit on account of purchase price of

_______________________ –Seventy Thousand– _______________________ Dollars $____ 70,000

for the purchase of property, situated in _______________________ , County of_______________________ , California,

described as follows: ____ 950 Sisk Road _______________________

1.   Buyer will deposit in escrow with _______________________ the balance of purchase price as follows:

*A.   Buyer to put $6,800 cash down payment including above deposit.

**B.   This offer is subject to the buyer qualifying for a new FHA - 245 Plan II loan for $63,200 payable at 10-1/2% interest with graduated interest payments starting at $552.11 per month, including principal and interest.

***C.   Seller agrees to pay for all improvements required by FHA for approval of the loan.

Set forth above any terms and conditions of a factual nature applicable to this sale, such as financing, prior sale of other property, the matter of structural pest control inspection, repairs and personal property to be included in the sale.

2.   Deposit will ☐ will not ☒ be increased by $ ____ – – – ____ to $ ____ – – ____ within____ – – – ____ days of acceptance of this offer.

3.   Buyer does ☒ does not ☐ intend to occupy subject property as his residence.

4.   The following supplements are incorporated as part of this agreement:

☒ Structural Pest Control Certification Agreement   ☐ Occupancy Agreement   Other ☐ _______________

☐ Special Studies Zone Disclosure   ☐ VA Amendment   ☐ _______________

☐ Flood Insurance Disclosure   ☒ FHA Amendment   ☐ _______________

5.   Buyer and Seller shall deliver signed instructions to the escrow holder within _______ days from Seller's acceptance which shall provide for closing within_______ days from Seller's acceptance. Escrow fees to be paid as follows:

6.   Buyer and Seller acknowledge receipt of a copy of this page, which constitutes Page 1 of_______ Pages.

Buyer_______________________   Seller _______________________

Buyer_______________________   Seller _______________________

A REAL ESTATE BROKER IS THE PERSON QUALIFIED TO ADVISE ON REAL ESTATE. IF YOU DESIRE LEGAL ADVICE CONSULT YOUR ATTORNEY.

FOR ILLUSTRATION ONLY - Consult your attorney for legal advice ON CONTRACTS IN YOUR STATE

Reprinted with permission, California Association of Realtors®, Endorsment not implied

(6) FHA - 245 Plan III

*   This type of FHA loan requires the largest down payment.

**   It also graduates at a 7-1/2% per year rate.   The monthly payment is the lowest of the three plans.

***   FHA inspectors are very picky when it comes to roofs. So, if you're selling a house through FHA be sure and check the roof.

Special Note:

There are also FHA - 245 Plans IV and V. They are usually never used by lenders because the payments are graduated over a 10 year period.

REAL ESTATE PURCHASE CONTRACT AND RECEIPT FOR DEPOSIT

THIS IS MORE THAN A RECEIPT FOR MONEY. IT IS INTENDED TO BE A LEGALLY BINDING CONTRACT. READ IT CAREFULLY.

CALIFORNIA ASSOCIATION OF REALTORS® (CAR) STANDARD FORM

_______________________________ , California. _______________ , 19______

Received from __Dave Del Dotto and/or Assignee__

herein called Buyer, the sum of ______-Two Hundred-______________________ Dollars $__200.00__

evidenced by cash ☐, cashier's check ☐, or _________________ ☒, personal check ☐ payable to____ A Reliable

__Title Co.__________ , to be held uncashed until acceptance of this offer, as deposit on account of purchase price of

______-Seventy Thousand-____________________________ Dollars $_70,000_

for the purchase of property, situated in ________________ , County of________________ , California,

described as follows: ________ 7601 Estelle Avenue ________________

1.   Buyer will deposit in escrow with________________________ the balance of purchase price as follows:

    *A.   Buyer to put $9,100 cash down payment including above deposit.

    **B.   Subject to the buyer qualifying and obtaining a new FHA - 245 Plan III loan for $60,900 payable at 10-1/2% interest. Graduated payments to begin at 527.07 per month including principal and interest.

    ***C.   Seller agrees to pay for all improvements required by FHA for approval of the loan.

Set forth above any terms and conditions of a factual nature applicable to this sale, such as financing, prior sale of other property, the matter of structural pest control inspection, repairs and personal property to be included in the sale.

2.   Deposit will ☐ will not ☐ be increased by $________ to $________ within________ days of acceptance of this offer.

3.   Buyer does ☐ does not ☐ intend to occupy subject property as his residence.

4.   The following supplements are incorporated as part of this agreement:

                                                         Other

☐ Structural Pest Control Certification Agreement   ☐ Occupancy Agreement   ☐ ____________________

☐ Special Studies Zone Disclosure   ☐ VA Amendment   ☐ ____________________

☐ Flood Insurance Disclosure   ☐ FHA Amendment   ☐ ____________________

5.   Buyer and Seller shall deliver signed instructions to the escrow holder within __________ days from Seller's acceptance which shall provide for closing within__________ days from Seller's acceptance. Escrow fees to be paid as follows:

6.   Buyer and Seller acknowledge receipt of a copy of this page, which constitutes Page 1 of______ Pages.

Buyer________________________   Seller ________________________

Buyer________________________   Seller ________________________

A REAL ESTATE BROKER IS THE PERSON QUALIFIED TO ADVISE ON REAL ESTATE. IF YOU DESIRE LEGAL ADVICE CONSULT YOUR ATTORNEY.

FOR ILLUSTRATION ONLY - Consult your attorney for legal advice ON CONTRACTS IN YOUR STATE

Reprinted with permission, California Association of Realtors®, Endorsment not implied

(7) FHA - 245-B Loan

* This down payment is 4% to 5%.

** This loan is available only to new homes built under FHA inspection all the way through the construction. It also graduates 7-1/2% for the first 5 years of the loan. It was especially made to help bail out builders from inventory they are holding.

REAL ESTATE PURCHASE CONTRACT AND RECEIPT FOR DEPOSIT

THIS IS MORE THAN A RECEIPT FOR MONEY. IT IS INTENDED TO BE A LEGALLY BINDING CONTRACT. READ IT CAREFULLY.

CALIFORNIA ASSOCIATION OF REALTORS* (CAR) STANDARD FORM

_______________________________________ , California, _____________ , 19______

Received from ____ Mr. and Mrs. Jack Jones and/or Assignee ____

herein called Buyer, the sum of _______ -Three Hundred- _______ Dollars $____ 300.00 ____

evidenced by cash ☐, cashier's check ☐, or ________________ ☒, personal check ☐ payable to____ A Reliable ____ Title Co. ________ , to be held uncashed until acceptance of this offer, as deposit on account of purchase price of

______ -Seventy Thousand- ______ Dollars $__ 70,000 __

for the purchase of property, situated in ________________ , County of ________________ , California,

described as follows: ____ 1709 Idalare Avenue ____

1.   Buyer will deposit in escrow with ____________________________ the balance of purchase price as follows:

*A.   Buyer to put $3,150 cash down payment including the above deposit.

**B.   Subject to the buyer qualifying and obtaining a new FHA - 245-B loan for $66,850. The loan will be payable at 10-1/2% interest with graduated payments to begin at $597.50 per month including principal and interest.

C.   Subject to the builder including drapes and landscaping with the sale of the home.

Set forth above any terms and conditions of a factual nature applicable to this sale, such as financing, prior sale of other property, the matter of structural pest control inspection, repairs and personal property to be included in the sale.

2.   Deposit will ☐ will not ☐ be increased by $____________ to $____________ within____________ days of acceptance of this offer.

3.   Buyer does ☐ does not ☐ intend to occupy subject property as his residence.

4.   The following supplements are incorporated as part of this agreement:

Other

☒ Structural Pest Control Certification Agreement   ☐ Occupancy Agreement   ☐ ____________

☐ Special Studies Zone Disclosure   ☐ VA Amendment   ☐ ____________

☐ Flood Insurance Disclosure   ☒ FHA Amendment   ☐ ____________

5.   Buyer and Seller shall deliver signed instructions to the escrow holder within ____________ days from Seller's acceptance which shall provide for closing within____________ days from Seller's acceptance. Escrow fees to be paid as follows:

6.   Buyer and Seller acknowledge receipt of a copy of this page, which constitutes Page 1 of________ Pages.

Buyer____________________________   Seller ____________________________

Buyer____________________________   Seller ____________________________

A REAL ESTATE BROKER IS THE PERSON QUALIFIED TO ADVISE ON REAL ESTATE. IF YOU DESIRE LEGAL ADVICE CONSULT YOUR ATTORNEY.

FOR ILLUSTRATION ONLY - Consult your attorney for legal advice ON CONTRACTS IN YOUR STATE

Reprinted with permission, California Association of Realtors®, Endorsment not implied

(8) VA Graduated Plan I

* A person must be eligible for a VA loan to obtain this loan. The payment is graduated like the FHA - 245 Plan III loan, over a period of 5 years at 7-1/2% per year. The home must be over 1 year old and lived in before, to qualify.

REAL ESTATE PURCHASE CONTRACT AND RECEIPT FOR DEPOSIT
THIS IS MORE THAN A RECEIPT FOR MONEY. IT IS INTENDED TO BE A LEGALLY BINDING CONTRACT. READ IT CAREFULLY.
CALIFORNIA ASSOCIATION OF REALTORS® (CAR) STANDARD FORM

_____________________________________ , California _________________ , 19_________

Received from ____ Mr. Dave Del Dotto and/or Assignee ____

herein called Buyer, the sum of ______ -Five Hundred- ______ Dollars $ __500.00__

evidenced by cash ☒, cashier's check ☐, or ____________ ☐, personal check ☐ payable to ____ the seller ____

____________________ , to be held uncashed until acceptance of this offer, as deposit on account of purchase price of

______ -Seventy Thousand- ______ Dollars $ __70,000__

for the purchase of property, situated in ________________ County of ________________ , California,

described as follows: ____ 4700 Orangeburg Avenue ____

1.   Buyer will deposit in escrow with ________________ the balance of purchase price as follows:

    A.   Buyer to put $7,200 cash down payment including
       above deposit.

    *B.   Subject to the buyer obtaining a new VA Graduated
       Mortgage Plan I from a lender of buyer's choice.
       The loan amount will be for $62,800 payable at 10-1/2%
       interest with the first years payment to begin at
       approximately $524.45 including principal and interest.

    C.   Buyer is a licensed real estate agent and will use his
       commission as part of the down payment.

Set forth above any terms and conditions of a factual nature applicable to this sale, such as financing, prior sale of other property, the matter of structural pest control inspection, repairs and personal property to be included in the sale.

2.   Deposit will ☐ will not ☐ be increased by $ ____________ to $ ____________ within ____________ days of acceptance of this offer.

3.   Buyer does ☐ does not ☐ intend to occupy subject property as his residence

4.   The following supplements are incorporated as part of this agreement:

☐ Structural Pest Control Certification Agreement   ☐ Occupancy Agreement   Other ☐ ____________
☐ Special Studies Zone Disclosure   ☐ VA Amendment   ☐ ____________
☐ Flood Insurance Disclosure   ☐ FHA Amendment   ☐ ____________

5.   Buyer and Seller shall deliver signed instructions to the escrow holder within ____________ days from Seller's acceptance which shall provide for closing within ____________ days from Seller's acceptance. Escrow fees to be paid as follows:

6.   Buyer and Seller acknowledge receipt of a copy of this page, which constitutes Page 1 of ______ Pages.

Buyer ________________________________   Seller ________________________________

Buyer ________________________________   Seller ________________________________

A REAL ESTATE BROKER IS THE PERSON QUALIFIED TO ADVISE ON REAL ESTATE. IF YOU DESIRE LEGAL ADVICE CONSULT YOUR ATTORNEY.

FOR ILLUSTRATION ONLY - Consult your attorney for legal advice ON CONTRACTS IN YOUR STATE
Reprinted with permission, California Association of Realtors®, Endorsment not implied

(9) VA Graduated Plan II

* Look at this low down payment.

** This loan is for qualified veterans who are purchasing new homes only. The lenders feel they can require less money down on a new home because there will be more appreciation in the early part of the loan. These VA loans with a graduated payment have a maximum loan of $121,000. So, they are quite a bit more than a FHA graduated loan.

*** There are usually more points charged on a graduated payment plan loan. If the seller is unwilling to pay a lot of points, you might try giving him a higher price to make up for the points.

REAL ESTATE PURCHASE CONTRACT AND RECEIPT FOR DEPOSIT
THIS IS MORE THAN A RECEIPT FOR MONEY. IT IS INTENDED TO BE A LEGALLY BINDING CONTRACT. READ IT CAREFULLY.
CALIFORNIA ASSOCIATION OF REALTORS® (CAR) STANDARD FORM

_____________________________ , California. _____________ , 19_____

Received from ____ Dave Del Dotto and/or Assignee ____
herein called Buyer, the sum of _____ -One Hundred- _____ Dollars $ __ 100.00 __
evidenced by cash ☐, cashier's check ☐, or _____________ ☒, personal check ☐ payable to ____ A Reliable __
___ Title Co. ___________ , to be held uncashed until acceptance of this offer, as deposit on account of purchase price of
_____ -Seventy Thousand- _____________ Dollars $ __ 70,000 __
for the purchase of property, situated in ________________ , County of ________________ , California,
described as follows: _____ 5980 Hart Road ________

1.   Buyer will deposit in escrow with __________________ the balance of purchase price as follows:

   *A.   Buyer to put $1,750 cash down including above deposit.

   **B.   Contingent upon the buyer obtaining a new VA Graduated
Mortgage Plan II from Suburban Coastal Corp. The loan
amount to be $68,250 payable at 10-1/2% interest with the
first years payment to begin at approximately $604.30 per
month including principal and interest.

   C.   Contingent upon a final walk-through inspection with the
builder and approval by buyer before the close of escrow.

   ***D.   Seller to pay all loan points.

Set forth above any terms and conditions of a factual nature applicable to this sale, such as financing, prior sale of other property, the matter of structural pest control inspection, repairs and personal property to be included in the sale.

2.   Deposit will ☐ will not ☐ be increased by $ ____________ to $ ____________ within ____________ days of acceptance of this offer.

3.   Buyer does ☐ does not ☐ intend to occupy subject property as his residence.

4.   The following supplements are incorporated as part of this agreement:

Other

☐ Structural Pest Control Certification Agreement   ☐ Occupancy Agreement   ☐ ____________
☐ Special Studies Zone Disclosure   ☐ VA Amendment   ☐ ____________
☐ Flood Insurance Disclosure   ☐ FHA Amendment   ☐ ____________

5.   Buyer and Seller shall deliver signed instructions to the escrow holder within ____________ days from Seller's acceptance which shall provide for closing within ____________ days from Seller's acceptance. Escrow fees to be paid as follows:

6.   Buyer and Seller acknowledge receipt of a copy of this page, which constitutes Page 1 of ____ Pages.

Buyer_____________________   Seller _____________________

Buyer_____________________   Seller _____________________

A REAL ESTATE BROKER IS THE PERSON QUALIFIED TO ADVISE ON REAL ESTATE. IF YOU DESIRE LEGAL ADVICE CONSULT YOUR ATTORNEY.

FOR ILLUSTRATION ONLY - Consult your attorney for legal advice ON CONTRACTS IN YOUR STATE
Reprinted with permission, California Association of Realtors®, Endorsment not implied

(10) FHA - VA

* When obtaining an FHA - VA loan, figure your down payment like the standard 203-B FHA loan. The veteran applying for the loan here must get a copy of his DD214 - Certification of Veteran's Status. This form should not be confused with the Certification of Eligibility form he must have a copy of when obtaining a straight VA loan. The FHA - VA loan is not used much by lenders.

REAL ESTATE PURCHASE CONTRACT AND RECEIPT FOR DEPOSIT

THIS IS MORE THAN A RECEIPT FOR MONEY. IT IS INTENDED TO BE A LEGALLY BINDING CONTRACT. READ IT CAREFULLY.

CALIFORNIA ASSOCIATION OF REALTORS® (CAR) STANDARD FORM

_______________________________ , California, _______________ , 19_______

Received from ____ David Del Dotto and/or Assignee ____

herein called Buyer, the sum of ____ -Five Hundred- ____ Dollars $ ___ 500.00

evidenced by cash [X] cashier's check [ ], or ________________ [ ], personal check [ ] payable to ____ A Reliable Title Co. ____ , to be held uncashed until acceptance of this offer, as deposit on account of purchase price of ____ -Seventy-one Thousand- ____ Dollars $ ___ 71,000

for the purchase of property, situated in ________________ , County of ________________ , California,

described as follows: ____ 897 Westland Way ____

1. Buyer will deposit in escrow with ________________ the balance of purchase price as follows:

   A. This offer is subject to the buyer obtaining a new FHA - VA loan from Suburban Coastal Corp. for $68,000 payable at 10-1/2% interest with monthly payments of approximately $622.02 per month.

   B. The buyer will put $3,500 cash down payment.

   *C. This offer is subject to the buyer obtaining a copy of his DD214 - Certification of Veteran's Status for the lender.

   D. All electrical, plumbing, and mechanical will be in proper working order at the close of escrow.

   E. Seller agrees to pay for all work required by FHA to qualify for the loan.

Set forth above any terms and conditions of a factual nature applicable to this sale, such as financing, prior sale of other property, the matter of structural pest control inspection, repairs and personal property to be included in the sale.

2. Deposit will [ ] will not [ ] be increased by $ ________________ to $ ________________ within ________________ days of acceptance of this offer.

3. Buyer does [ ] does not [ ] intend to occupy subject property as his residence.

4. The following supplements are incorporated as part of this agreement:

Other

[ ] Structural Pest Control Certification Agreement   [ ] Occupancy Agreement   [ ] ________________

[ ] Special Studies Zone Disclosure   [ ] VA Amendment   [ ] ________________

[ ] Flood Insurance Disclosure   [ ] FHA Amendment   [ ] ________________

5. Buyer and Seller shall deliver signed instructions to the escrow holder within ________________ days from Seller's acceptance which shall provide for closing within ________________ days from Seller's acceptance. Escrow fees to be paid as follows:

6. Buyer and Seller acknowledge receipt of a copy of this page, which constitutes Page 1 of ________ Pages.

Buyer ________________________ Seller ________________________

Buyer ________________________ Seller ________________________

A REAL ESTATE BROKER IS THE PERSON QUALIFIED TO ADVISE ON REAL ESTATE. IF YOU DESIRE LEGAL ADVICE CONSULT YOUR ATTORNEY.

(11) VA Loan - No Down

* The VA loan was set up by the Federal Government for all United States War Veterans, except World War I and the Spanish-American War. This loan was the original "100% financing" loan, intended to help these veterans. This loan is generally available at below conventional market rates.

This loan is generally very easy to obtain, because the VA is usually lenient when the borrower is a borderline case.

** VA will not allow the borrower to pay any of the lender's discount points, but will allow him to pay the lender's origination fee, generally 1 or 2% of the loan.

*** A veteran can receive more than one VA loan as long as a qualifying veteran assumes his old loan and restores his eligibility, or the old loan is paid off.

**** Sometimes a seller will balk at selling VA because he may have to pay an excessive amount of discount points. So to ease the pain and help make up for the seller's costs, the buyer may credit the seller for some personal property which in essence assists the seller with the costs.

REAL ESTATE PURCHASE CONTRACT AND RECEIPT FOR DEPOSIT

THIS IS MORE THAN A RECEIPT FOR MONEY. IT IS INTENDED TO BE A LEGALLY BINDING CONTRACT. READ IT CAREFULLY.

CALIFORNIA ASSOCIATION OF REALTORS® (CAR) STANDARD FORM

_______________________________ , California, _______________________ , 19______

Received from _______________________________
herein called Buyer, the sum of ____________ —One Hundred— ________________ Dollars $ ____100.00
evidenced by cash ☐, cashier's check ☐, or ____________________ ☒, personal check ☐ payable to ____ A Reliable Title Company ____________ , to be held uncashed until acceptance of this offer, as deposit on account of purchase price of
—One Hundred Thousand— ________________________________ Dollars $ 100,000

for the purchase of property, situated in ________________________ , County of ____________________ , California,
described as follows: ____ 2676 Caylor Drive

1. Buyer will deposit in escrow with ________________________________ the balance of purchase price as follows:

      A.   Above deposit to be applied to buyer's closing costs.

     *B.   Subject to buyer applying and qualifying for Veterans
           Administration (VA) loan for $100,000 at current interest
           rate of 10.5%. Payments including principal and interest
           are not to exceed $914.74.

    **C.   All loan points to be paid by seller, except loan origination
           fee of $1,000, which will be paid by buyer.

   ***D.   This offer is subject to buyer receiving his full eligibility
           back from sale of his present home located at 202 Willow
           Springs Drive, San Jose, California, which is also being
           financed through the VA Administration.

  ****E.   Buyer to credit seller $3,000 in escrow for drapes.

Set forth above any terms and conditions of a factual nature applicable to this sale, such as financing, prior sale of other property, the matter of structural pest control inspection, repairs and personal property to be included in the sale.

2. Deposit will ☒ will not ☐ be increased by $ ____400.00____ to $ ____500.00____ within ____five (5)____ days of acceptance of this offer.

3. Buyer does ☒ does not ☐ intend to occupy subject property as his residence.

4. The following supplements are incorporated as part of this agreement:

☒ Structural Pest Control Certification Agreement   ☐ Occupancy Agreement   Other ☐ ____________________
☐ Special Studies Zone Disclosure   ☒ VA Amendment   ☐ ____________________
☐ Flood Insurance Disclosure   ☐ FHA Amendment   ☐

5. Buyer and Seller shall deliver signed instructions to the escrow holder within ____________ days from Seller's acceptance which shall provide for closing within ____________ days from Seller's acceptance. Escrow fees to be paid as follows:

6. Buyer and Seller acknowledge receipt of a copy of this page, which constitutes Page 1 of ______ Pages.

Buyer_______________________________   Seller _______________________________

Buyer_______________________________   Seller _______________________________

A REAL ESTATE BROKER IS THE PERSON QUALIFIED TO ADVISE ON REAL ESTATE. IF YOU DESIRE LEGAL ADVICE CONSULT YOUR ATTORNEY.

FOR ILLUSTRATION ONLY - Consult your attorney for legal advice ON CONTRACTS IN YOUR STATE
Reprinted with permission, California Association of Realtors®, Endorsment not implied

(12) Cal-Vet Loan - Low Down

* This loan is applicable to California veterans only. This type of loan has the lowest interest rates available to date. The funding is provided by the sale of bonds by the State of California. You should check your local area for any local or state bond money provided for homes in your area.

There are usually many strings attached to this type of loan. For instance, income requirements are for first time home buyers only.

** One drawback to this loan is the funding time, up to 12 months. Legal title is actually held by the State of California, not the veteran. Therefore, the buyer may have to lease for a time. These loans are not assumable; only to qualified Cal-Vets are they assumable. The houses are not supposed to be used as rental property for investment, even though there are certain conditions where this may be allowed for a time.

Check your local Cal-Vet office for further details.

This kind of loan could be your way to buy a first house when it seems there's no other way you can, or a way to sell an investment property to a buyer who otherwise would not qualify.

REAL ESTATE PURCHASE CONTRACT AND RECEIPT FOR DEPOSIT
THIS IS MORE THAN A RECEIPT FOR MONEY. IT IS INTENDED TO BE A LEGALLY BINDING CONTRACT. READ IT CAREFULLY.
CALIFORNIA ASSOCIATION OF REALTORS® (CAR) STANDARD FORM

____ , California. _____________________ , 19______

Received from ____
herein called Buyer, the sum of __________ -One Hundred- ___________________ Dollars $ 100.00
evidenced by cash ☐, cashier's check ☒, or Upon acceptance ☐, personal check ☐ payable to ___ A Reliable Title Company ___________ , to be held uncashed until acceptance of this offer, as deposit on account of purchase price of _____ -Fifty eight thousand five hundred- _____________ Dollars $ 58,500

for the purchase of property, situated in ___________________ , County of __________________ , California, described as follows: 1549 Groff Road

1. Buyer will deposit in escrow with _________________________ the balance of purchase price as follows:

   A.   Buyer to make a $1,500 cash down payment including above deposit.

  *B.   Subject to buyer obtaining a new 1st mortgage from Cal-Vet for a maximum loan of $57,000 at current interest rate of 8% with monthly payments of approximately $440.00 principal and interest.

  **C.   Seller is aware that Cal-Vet funding may take up to 12 months to obtain. Buyer agrees to lease subject property for $450.00 per month until such loan is funded.

   D.   This offer is subject to Cal-Vet approval of buyer within 45 days of acceptance of this offer. At such time, buyer may take possession of house under a lease agreement.

   E.   Seller to provide a clear pest report as required by Cal-Vet.

Set forth above any terms and conditions of a factual nature applicable to this sale, such as financing, **prior sale of other property, the matter of structural pest control inspection, repairs and personal property to be included in the sale.**

2. Deposit will ☒ will not ☐ be increased by $ 400.00 to $ 500.00 within five (5) days of acceptance of this offer.

3. Buyer does ☒ does not ☐ intend to occupy subject property as his residence.

4. The following supplements are incorporated as part of this agreement:

		Other
☒ Structural Pest Control Certification Agreement	☐ Occupancy Agreement	☐ ___________
☐ Special Studies Zone Disclosure	☒ VA Amendment	☐ ___________
☐ Flood Insurance Disclosure	☐ FHA Amendment	☐ ___________

5. Buyer and Seller shall deliver signed instructions to the escrow holder within __________ days from Seller's acceptance which shall provide for closing within __________ days from Seller's acceptance. Escrow fees to be paid as follows:

6. Buyer and Seller acknowledge receipt of a copy of this page, which constitutes Page 1 of _______ Pages.

Buyer ___________________________   Seller ___________________________

Buyer ___________________________   Seller ___________________________

A REAL ESTATE BROKER IS THE PERSON QUALIFIED TO ADVISE ON REAL ESTATE. IF YOU DESIRE LEGAL ADVICE CONSULT YOUR ATTORNEY.

(13) No Interest Loan - 30% Cash Down

* This is a unique new financing arrangement which has been offered by many builders of new projects throughout the United States. It is a way to sell new houses in a slow or high-interest market, but may also be useful at other times. If the builder doesn't offer the program, try asking for it, if you have the down payment.

The biggest problem is that people just don't have the 30% down payment needed to make the deal. This is more likely to work with high-income buyers who have the equity from a previous home to invest. Or, you might make it work with your profits from previous real estate investment deals.

REAL ESTATE PURCHASE CONTRACT AND RECEIPT FOR DEPOSIT

THIS IS MORE THAN A RECEIPT FOR MONEY. IT IS INTENDED TO BE A LEGALLY BINDING CONTRACT. READ IT CAREFULLY.

CALIFORNIA ASSOCIATION OF REALTORS® (CAR) STANDARD FORM

_______________________________ , California. _______________ , 19______

Received from ____
herein called Buyer, the sum of ______ -One Thousand- ______________ Dollars $___1,000___
evidenced by cash ☐, cashier's check ☐, or _______________ ☐, personal check ☐ payable to______ A reliable builder ______ , to be held uncashed until acceptance of this offer, as deposit on account of purchase price of
______ - Eighty-three Thousand four Hundred- ______ Dollars $___83,400___
for the purchase of property, situated in_______________ , County of_______________ , California,
described as follows: ______ 1010 Senic _______________

1. Buyer will deposit in escrow with _______________ the balance of purchase price as follows:

> A. Buyer to pay $23,400 cash down payment including above deposit.

> *B. This offer is subject to buyer obtaining a zero percent interest rate loan of $60,000 from builder's current lender. Buyer to make 60 equal payments of $1,000.00 per month to be credited to principal only. At the end of 5 years buyer will then own subject property free and clear of any mortgage.

> C. Seller will provide buyer with a 1-year warranty on all appliances, mechanical, electrical, plumbing, heating, and air conditioning.

> D. Seller will also credit buyer with $1,000 for landscaping to be done by buyer.

Set forth above any terms and conditions of a factual nature applicable to this sale, such as financing, prior sale of other property, the matter of structural pest control inspection, repairs and personal property to be included in the sale.

2. Deposit will ☐ will not ☒ be increased by $______ --- ______ to $ ______ --- ______ within______ --- ______ days of acceptance of this offer.

3. Buyer does ☒ does not ☐ intend to occupy subject property as his residence.

4. The following supplements are incorporated as part of this agreement:

Other
☐ Structural Pest Control Certification Agreement   ☐ Occupancy Agreement   ☐ _______________
☐ Special Studies Zone Disclosure   ☐ VA Amendment   ☐ _______________
☐ Flood Insurance Disclosure   ☐ FHA Amendment   ☐ _______________

5. Buyer and Seller shall deliver signed instructions to the escrow holder within _______ days from Seller's acceptance which shall provide for closing within_______________ days from Seller's acceptance. Escrow fees to be paid as follows:

6. Buyer and Seller acknowledge receipt of a copy of this page, which constitutes Page 1 of_______ Pages.

Buyer_______________________   Seller _______________________

Buyer_______________________   Seller _______________________

A REAL ESTATE BROKER IS THE PERSON QUALIFIED TO ADVISE ON REAL ESTATE. IF YOU DESIRE LEGAL ADVICE CONSULT YOUR ATTORNEY.

FOR ILLUSTRATION ONLY - Consult your attorney for legal advice ON CONTRACTS IN YOUR STATE
Reprinted with permission, California Association of Realtors®, Endorsment not implied

(14) 75% Fixed Rate - 15% 2nd - 10% down

* The offer here contains the basic order of cash down, amount of new loan, amount of loan carried by the seller. The cash plus the loans should add up to your sales price.

** In this contract the buyer was a real estate agent, which must be revealed to the seller in California, and should be revealed, even in states where it is not required.

*** This clause for replacing any broken glass may seem a small item, but will save you lots of money in the long run if you buy a lot of houses.

REAL ESTATE PURCHASE CONTRACT AND RECEIPT FOR DEPOSIT

THIS IS MORE THAN A RECEIPT FOR MONEY. IT IS INTENDED TO BE A LEGALLY BINDING CONTRACT. READ IT CAREFULLY.

CALIFORNIA ASSOCIATION OF REALTORS® (CAR) STANDARD FORM

_______________________________________, California, ___________________________, 19_______

Received from _______________________________________
herein called Buyer, the sum of ________ -Three Hundred- ________ Dollars $ __300.00__
evidenced by cash [X], cashier's check [ ], or ____________________ [ ], personal check [ ] payable to __Seller's__
__Title Company__, to be held uncashed until acceptance of this offer, as deposit on account of purchase price of
__-Sixty five Thousand four Hundred-__ Dollars $ __65,400__
for the purchase of property, situated in ______________________, County of ____________________, California,
described as follows: __101 Modesto Court__

1. Buyer will deposit in escrow with ________________________________ the balance of purchase price as follows:

    *A.   Buyer to put $6,550 cash down payment including above deposit.

    B.   Subject to buyer obtaining a new 1st loan in the amount of .$49,050 from Security Pacific Bank at a fixed rate of 10.5% with monthly payments of principal and interest of approximately $448.68 per month.

    C.   Subject to seller carrying back a 2nd note secured by a 2nd deed of trust in the amount of $9,800 at 10% interest amortized over 30 years, but all due and payable in 10 years. Monthly payments to be $87.00 per month.

    **D.   Buyer is a licensed real estate agent and is buying property for his real estate portfolio.

    ***E.   Seller will replace all broken glass prior to close of escrow.

Set forth above any terms and conditions of a factual nature applicable to this sale, such as financing, prior sale of other property, the matter of structural pest control inspection, repairs and personal property to be included in the sale.

2. Deposit will [X] will not [ ] be increased by $ __200.00__ to $ __500.00__ within __five (5)__ days of acceptance of this offer.

3. Buyer does [X] does not [ ] intend to occupy subject property as his residence.

4. The following supplements are incorporated as part of this agreement:

		Other
[X] Structural Pest Control Certification Agreement	[ ] Occupancy Agreement	[ ]
[ ] Special Studies Zone Disclosure	[ ] VA Amendment	[ ]
[ ] Flood Insurance Disclosure	[ ] FHA Amendment	[ ]

5. Buyer and Seller shall deliver signed instructions to the escrow holder within ____________ days from Seller's acceptance which shall provide for closing within ____________ days from Seller's acceptance. Escrow fees to be paid as follows:

6. Buyer and Seller acknowledge receipt of a copy of this page, which constitutes Page 1 of ________ Pages.

Buyer _________________________________   Seller _________________________________

Buyer _________________________________   Seller _________________________________

A REAL ESTATE BROKER IS THE PERSON QUALIFIED TO ADVISE ON REAL ESTATE. IF YOU DESIRE LEGAL ADVICE CONSULT YOUR ATTORNEY.

CREATIVE FINANCING - CONTRACT EXAMPLES   *Page A - 37*

(15) OWNER FINANCE - 20% DOWN

* Here we are using a promissory note as the deposit; it sure looks impressive, but it doesn't tie up our cash.

** The buyer purchased the motor home at an auction for $5,000 and is trying to pick up $5,000 by trading it for part of the down payment on a house owned free and clear by the seller.

** We don't want a prepayment penalty on any of our loans. And we always want to include in our note conditions, the 1st option to buy the note at a discount if the seller needs cash at any time during the future.

REAL ESTATE PURCHASE CONTRACT AND RECEIPT FOR DEPOSIT
THIS IS MORE THAN A RECEIPT FOR MONEY. IT IS INTENDED TO BE A LEGALLY BINDING CONTRACT. READ IT CAREFULLY.
CALIFORNIA ASSOCIATION OF REALTORS® (CAR) STANDARD FORM

____ , California. _________________ , 19__________

Received from ____

herein called Buyer, the sum of _______ -One Thousand- _________________ Dollars $____1,000.00

evidenced by cash ☐, cashier's check ☐, or *personal note ☐, personal check ☐ payable to_____ A Reliable

____Title Company_______ , to be held uncashed until acceptance of this offer, as deposit on account of purchase price of

______ -One Hundred Thousand- ____________________________ Dollars $ 100,000.

for the purchase of property, situated in ___________________ , County of_____________________ , California,

described as follows: _________ 1500 Twainharte Road _____________________________

1.   Buyer will deposit in escrow with_________________________________ the balance of purchase price as follows:

     A.   Buyer to pay $10,000 cash down payment not including
          above deposit.

  **B.   Subject to seller accepting a 1978, 30-foot motor
          home with a value of $10,000 as part of the down
          payment.

     C.   Subject to seller carrying a 1st note secured by a
          deed of trust in the amount of $80,000 payable at 9%
          interest, amortized over 30 years but all due and
          payable in 15 years from close of escrow. Monthly
          payments will be $643.70 including principal and
          interest.

 ***D.   Above 1st loan will have no penalty if prepaid
          before the due date of 15 years. And buyer will
          have first right of refusal if seller decides to sell
          the note at a discount.

     E.   Sale to include all pool equipment and freezer in garage.

Set forth above any terms and conditions of a factual nature applicable to this sale, such as financing, prior sale of other property, the matter of structural pest control inspection, repairs and personal property to be included in the sale.

2.   Deposit will ☐ will not ☐ be increased by $ _____ --- _____ to $ _____ --- _____ within_____ --- _____ days of acceptance of this offer.

3.   Buyer does ☒ does not ☐ intend to occupy subject property as his residence.

4.   The following supplements are incorporated as part of this agreement:

Other
☐ Structural Pest Control Certification Agreement   ☐ Occupancy Agreement   ☐ ______________________
☐ Special Studies Zone Disclosure   ☐ VA Amendment   ☐ ______________________
☐ Flood Insurance Disclosure   ☐ FHA Amendment   ☐ ______________________

5.   Buyer and Seller shall deliver signed instructions to the escrow holder within _________ days from Seller's acceptance which shall provide for closing within_____________ days from Seller's acceptance. Escrow fees to be paid as follows:

6.   Buyer and Seller acknowledge receipt of a copy of this page, which constitutes Page 1 of______ Pages.

Buyer___________________________________   Seller ___________________________________

Buyer___________________________________   Seller ___________________________________

A REAL ESTATE BROKER IS THE PERSON QUALIFIED TO ADVISE ON REAL ESTATE. IF YOU DESIRE LEGAL ADVICE CONSULT YOUR ATTORNEY.

(16) Wrap-Around - All Inclusive Deed of Trust

* In the past few years this type of financing has been used quite extensively in many states. It makes a good tool for the sellers to wrap-around any existing low interest loans and make a profit by charging a higher interest rate than they were paying, thus, providing a good cash flow. But, notice where the buyer is making his payments? To a trust fund. Why? So the underlying 1st loan payments are guaranteed to be made. If you do not insist on this you could possibly lose the house in foreclosure or have to start litigation against the seller to protect your interest.

** Don't take a title company's printed all inclusive deed of trust and assume it covers everything important to your deal. Have your attorney check over the terms and remedies.

Special Note:

Always check the underlying notes for due dates, balloons or acceleration clauses and never accept a wrap-around mortgage where the underlying loans are for more than the wrap-around!

Example:

Existing 1st loan - $ 50,000 wrap to you, $55,000
Existing 2nd loan - $ 10,000
————
$ 60,000 owed

REAL ESTATE PURCHASE CONTRACT AND RECEIPT FOR DEPOSIT
THIS IS MORE THAN A RECEIPT FOR MONEY. IT IS INTENDED TO BE A LEGALLY BINDING CONTRACT. READ IT CAREFULLY.
CALIFORNIA ASSOCIATION OF REALTORS® (CAR) STANDARD FORM

____ , California, ___________________ , 19_____________

Received from ____
herein called Buyer, the sum of __________ -Five Hundred- _____________________ Dollars $ __500.00__
evidenced by cash ⊠ cashier's check ☐, or Upon acceptance ☐, personal check ☐ payable to ____Seller____
_______________________________ to be held uncashed until acceptance of this offer, as deposit on account of purchase price of
____ -Ninety Eight Thousand- ____ Dollars $____98,000__
for the purchase of property, situated in ___________________________ , County of ______________________ , California,
described as follows: _______ 5072 Goldmont Forest Road ____

1.   Buyer will deposit in escrow with ______________________________________ the balance of purchase price as follows:

    A.   Buyer to put a $5,000 cash down payment including
       above deposit.

   *B.   Subject to seller financing $93,000 with an all
       inclusive deed of trust payable at 10% interest for
       15 years with interest only payments of $775.00 payable
       to Bank of America trust account in the seller's name.

    C.   From this trust account the existing 1st loan in the
       amount of $15,000 payable at 6% with monthly payments
       of $200.00 including principal and interest will be paid
       with balance of $575.00 to be credited to the seller.

  **D.   The conditions of the all inclusive deed of trust will
       be drawn by an attorney or a qualified title company,
       acceptable to both parties.

    E.   Buyer to pay for the yearly taxes and insurance separately
       from principal and interest payments.

Set forth above any terms and conditions of a factual nature applicable to this sale, such as financing, prior sale of other property, the matter of structural pest control inspection, repairs and personal property to be included in the sale.

2   Deposit will ☐ will not ⊠ be increased by $ _ _ _ to $ _ _ _ within _ _ _ days of acceptance of this offer.

3.   Buyer does ⊠ does not ☐ intend to occupy subject property as his residence.

4.   The following supplements are incorporated as part of this agreement:

☐ Structural Pest Control Certification Agreement   ☐ Occupancy Agreement   Other ☐ __________________
☐ Special Studies Zone Disclosure   ☐ VA Amendment   ☐ __________________
☐ Flood Insurance Disclosure   ☐ FHA Amendment   ☐ __________________

5.   Buyer and Seller shall deliver signed instructions to the escrow holder within ___________ days from Seller's acceptance which shall provide for closing within ______________ days from Seller's acceptance. Escrow fees to be paid as follows:

6   Buyer and Seller acknowledge receipt of a copy of this page which constitutes Page 1 of _______ Pages.

Buyer ____ Seller ____

Buyer ____ Seller ____

A REAL ESTATE BROKER IS THE PERSON QUALIFIED TO ADVISE ON REAL ESTATE. IF YOU DESIRE LEGAL ADVICE CONSULT YOUR ATTORNEY.

FOR ILLUSTRATION ONLY - Consult your attorney for legal advice ON CONTRACTS IN YOUR STATE
Reprinted with permission, California Association of Realtors®, Endorsment not implied

(17) Contract of Sale

* Again, this type of financing has been used by sellers over the years. But, a buyer should watch this type of financing. First of all, the buyer does not receive a deed to the property and if the seller is a flake and doesn't make the underlying payment it could cost the buyer a lot of money in attorney's fees to get the mess straightened out. That's why the trust account is included in the contract. I suggest you have an attorney give you counsel before going into this.

One reason for going into a transaction like this is to leave any existing non assumable loans on the property.

REAL ESTATE PURCHASE CONTRACT AND RECEIPT FOR DEPOSIT

THIS IS MORE THAN A RECEIPT FOR MONEY. IT IS INTENDED TO BE A LEGALLY BINDING CONTRACT. READ IT CAREFULLY.

CALIFORNIA ASSOCIATION OF REALTORS* (CAR) STANDARD FORM

___________________________________ , California. _________________ , 19________

Received from ____

herein called Buyer, the sum of ________ -Four Hundred- ____________ Dollars $ __400.00__

evidenced by cash ☐, cashier's check ☒, or __Upon acceptance☐__, personal check ☐ payable to __Seller__

_________________________________ , to be held uncashed until acceptance of this offer, as deposit on account of purchase price of

__-Ninety Five Thousand Five Hundred-________________ Dollars $ __95,500__

for the purchase of property, situated in ________________________ , County of __________________________ , California,

described as follows: __________ 824 Hawthorn Avenue __________________________

1. Buyer will deposit in escrow with ____ the balance of purchase price as follows:

   A. Buyer will put a $6,500 cash down payment.

   *B. It is agreed that this transaction will be a contract
        of sale with the deed remaining in the seller's name
        until the debt is paid in full by the buyer.

   C. The contract interest rate on the $89,000 carried by
        the seller will be 10% amortized for 30 years with monthly
        payments of $779.00 per month.

        1. Seller agrees to pay existing 1st loan of $16,000
             with monthly payments of $150.00 per month.

        2. Seller agrees to set up a trust account at a bank
             of his choice to handle the underlying payments.

   D. Subject to buyer's attorney's approval of the contract
        of sale agreement.

   E. Seller will provide a clear pest report.

Set forth above any terms and conditions of a factual nature applicable to this sale, such as financing, prior sale of other property, the matter of structural pest control inspection, repairs and personal property to be included in the sale.

2. Deposit will ☐ will not ☒ be increased by $ ___ - - - ___ to $ ___ - - - ___ within ___ - - - ___ days of acceptance of this offer.

3. Buyer does ☒ does not ☐ intend to occupy subject property as his residence.

4. The following supplements are incorporated as part of this agreement:

		Other
☐ Structural Pest Control Certification Agreement	☐ Occupancy Agreement	☐ ____________
☐ Special Studies Zone Disclosure	☐ VA Amendment	☐ ____________
☐ Flood Insurance Disclosure	☐ FHA Amendment	☐ ____________

5. Buyer and Seller shall deliver signed instructions to the escrow holder within ___________ days from Seller's acceptance which shall provide for closing within ___________ days from Seller's acceptance. Escrow fees to be paid as follows:

6. Buyer and Seller acknowledge receipt of a copy of this page, which constitutes Page 1 of ______ Pages.

Buyer ________________________ Seller ________________________

Buyer ________________________ Seller ________________________

A REAL ESTATE BROKER IS THE PERSON QUALIFIED TO ADVISE ON REAL ESTATE. IF YOU DESIRE LEGAL ADVICE CONSULT YOUR ATTORNEY.

(18) Bond Money Loan -First Time Buyer - 12% loan

* Keep aware of any bond money programs issued by your city for first time home buyers. The loans are generally around 12%, long term and will range from 90% to 95% loan to value of property. Some bond programs require a certain income bracket, usually lower middle income bracket. To get in with no down payment, just use your real estate commission, or a credit back trick or even have the seller agree to carrying a 2nd. Usually, when these bond money programs are available all the money is gobbled up fast, so don't hesitate in getting your fair share. You might consider buying one for each of your friends and relatives too!

REAL ESTATE PURCHASE CONTRACT AND RECEIPT FOR DEPOSIT
THIS IS MORE THAN A RECEIPT FOR MONEY. IT IS INTENDED TO BE A LEGALLY BINDING CONTRACT. READ IT CAREFULLY.
CALIFORNIA ASSOCIATION OF REALTORS® (CAR) STANDARD FORM

_______________________________________ , California. _______________ , 19_______

Received from _____ Dave Del Dotto and/or assignee _____

herein called Buyer, the sum of _____ -One Hundred- _____ Dollars $ __100.00__

evidenced by cash ☐, cashier's check ☐, or _Note in escrow_ ☐, personal check ☐ payable to _____ A Reliable

Title Company , to be held uncashed until acceptance of this offer, as deposit on account of purchase price of

-Fifty Five Thousand- Dollars $ __55,000__

for the purchase of property, situated in _____________________ , County of _____________________ , California,

described as follows: _____ 404 Maple Avenue _____

1.   Buyer will deposit in escrow with _____________________ the balance of purchase price as follows:

    A.   Buyer will put $2,250 cash as down payment.

    *B.   Subject to buyer qualifying for a new bond money loan
        from Capital Pacific Mortgage for $52,250 payable at
        12% interest with payments amortized over 30 years of
        approximately $535.00 per month.

    C.   The buyer is a first time purchaser of a home and meets
        the income requirements set forth by the bond loan
        committee.

    D.   Sale to include freezer in garage.

Set forth above any terms and conditions of a factual nature applicable to this sale, such as financing, prior sale of other property, the matter of structural pest control inspection, repairs and personal property to be included in the sale.

2.   Deposit will ☐ will not ☐ be increased by $_____________ to $_____________ within _____________ days of acceptance of this offer.

3.   Buyer does ☐ does not ☐ intend to occupy subject property as his residence.

4.   The following supplements are incorporated as part of this agreement:

☐ Structural Pest Control Certification Agreement   ☐ Occupancy Agreement   Other ☐ _____________

☐ Special Studies Zone Disclosure   ☐ VA Amendment   ☐ _____________

☐ Flood Insurance Disclosure   ☐ FHA Amendment   ☐ _____________

5.   Buyer and Seller shall deliver signed instructions to the escrow holder within _____________ days from Seller's acceptance which shall provide for closing within _____________ days from Seller's acceptance. Escrow fees to be paid as follows:

6.   Buyer and Seller acknowledge receipt of a copy of this page, which constitutes Page 1 of _____ Pages.

Buyer _____________________   Seller _____________________

Buyer _____________________   Seller _____________________

A REAL ESTATE BROKER IS THE PERSON QUALIFIED TO ADVISE ON REAL ESTATE. IF YOU DESIRE LEGAL ADVICE CONSULT YOUR ATTORNEY.

FOR ILLUSTRATION ONLY - Consult your attorney for legal advice ON CONTRACTS IN YOUR STATE
Reprinted with permission, California Association of Realtors®, Endorsment not implied

(19) Conventional Loan - Second

REAL ESTATE PURCHASE CONTRACT AND RECEIPT FOR DEPOSIT
THIS IS MORE THAN A RECEIPT FOR MONEY. IT IS INTENDED TO BE A LEGALLY BINDING CONTRACT. READ IT CAREFULLY.
CALIFORNIA ASSOCIATION OF REALTORS* (CAR) STANDARD FORM

____ , California, _____________________ , 19________

Received from _________________________________ and/or assignee ________________________

herein called Buyer, the sum of ________ -One Hundred- _______________________ Dollars $____100.00****

evidenced by cash ☐, cashier's check ☐, or Note in escrow ☐, personal check ☐ payable to ________ A Reliable

____ Title Company ____ , to be held uncashed until acceptance of this offer, as deposit on account of purchase price of

____ -Eighty Four Thousand Two Hundred- _____________________ Dollars $____84,200

for the purchase of property, situated in _______________________ , County of _______________________ , California,

described as follows: _______________ 980 Perano Drive _______________________

1. Buyer will deposit in escrow with _________________________________ the balance of purchase price as follows:

    A. Buyer to assist seller in obtaining a new assumable loan
        for $70,000 at current terms and interest of money market.
        Interest rate not to exceed 10% with payments of $614.30
        per month including principal and interest. Buyer to take
        over loan subject to.

    B. All FHA points and buyer's closing cost to be paid out of
        1st loan proceeds.

    C. Buyer to execute a 2nd note secured by a deed of trust
        for $14,200 at 9% interest amortized for 30 years with
        monthly payments of approximately $112.65 per month.

    D. Second note executed by buyer will contain no prepayment
        penalty or alienation clause. Seller agrees to subordinate
        to any new 1st financing at buyer's option in case the
        interest rates drop at any time in the future.

Set forth above any terms and conditions of a factual nature applicable to this sale, such as financing, prior sale of other property,
the matter of structural pest control inspection, repairs and personal property to be included in the sale.

2. Deposit will ☐ will not ☐ be increased by $ _____________ to $ _____________ within _____________ days of
acceptance of this offer.

3. Buyer does ☐ does not ☐ intend to occupy subject property as his residence.

4. The following supplements are incorporated as part of this agreement:

Other

☐ Structural Pest Control Certification Agreement   ☐ Occupancy Agreement   ☐ ___________

☐ Special Studies Zone Disclosure   ☐ VA Amendment   ☐ ___________

☐ Flood Insurance Disclosure   ☐ FHA Amendment   ☐ ___________

5. Buyer and Seller shall deliver signed instructions to the escrow holder within _____________ days from Seller's acceptance which
shall provide for closing within _____________ days from Seller's acceptance. Escrow fees to be paid as follows:

6. Buyer and Seller acknowledge receipt of a copy of this page, which constitutes Page 1 of _______ Pages.

Buyer _________________________________ Seller _________________________________

Buyer _________________________________ Seller _________________________________

A REAL ESTATE BROKER IS THE PERSON QUALIFIED TO ADVISE ON REAL ESTATE. IF YOU DESIRE LEGAL ADVICE CONSULT YOUR ATTORNEY.

FOR ILLUSTRATION ONLY - Consult your attorney for legal advice ON CONTRACTS IN YOUR STATE
Reprinted with permission, California Association of Realtors®, Endorsment not implied

(20) 80% - No payment 2nd

* Not only is this a no payment 2nd loan carried by the seller but the terminology of accumulative interest, actually means simple interest. By not compounding the interest it will save you thousands.

Also, we have maintained the 1st right of refusal on the note if it is ever offered for sale.

** Most houses need carpet so don't be afraid to ask for a credit back. Investors need spending money too!

REAL ESTATE PURCHASE CONTRACT AND RECEIPT FOR DEPOSIT
THIS IS MORE THAN A RECEIPT FOR MONEY. IT IS INTENDED TO BE A LEGALLY BINDING CONTRACT. READ IT CAREFULLY.
CALIFORNIA ASSOCIATION OF REALTORS· (CAR) STANDARD FORM

_______________________________________, California _____________________, 19____

Received from ___________________________ and/or assignee ___________________________

herein called Buyer, the sum of _________________ -Five Hundred- _________________ Dollars $ ___500.00___

evidenced by cash ☐, cashier's check ☐, or Personal Note ☐, personal check ☐ payable to ___A Reliable

Title Company_____, to be held uncashed until acceptance of this offer, as deposit on account of purchase price of

___-Seventy Thousand-____ Dollars $ ___70,000___

for the purchase of property, situated in _______________ County of _______________, California.

described as follows: ________ 300 E. Granger ____

1.   Buyer will deposit in escrow with ____________________________ the balance of purchase price as follows:

    A. Buyer to assist seller in obtaining a new assumable
        1st loan for $56,000 from Bank of America at current
        terms and interest of 10% with payments of approximately
        $491.44 per month including principal and interest.
        Buyer to take over loan subject to.

    *B. Buyer to execute a 2nd note and deed of trust to seller
        for $14,000 payable at 12% accumulative interest all due and
        payable in 5 years from the close of escrow. Seller will
        give buyer 1st option to purchase note if seller decides
        to sell at a discount.

    C. Buyer is a licenced real estate agent.

    **D. Seller to credit buyer $1,200 in escrow for new carpet.

Set forth above any terms and conditions of a factual nature applicable to this sale, such as financing, prior sale of other property, **the matter of structural pest control** inspection, repairs and personal property to be included in the sale.

2.   Deposit will ☐ will not ☐ be increased by $ _____________ to $ _____________ within _____________ days of acceptance of this offer.

3.   Buyer does ☐ does not ☐ intend to occupy subject property as his residence.

4.   The following supplements are incorporated as part of this agreement:

                                                  Other

☐ Structural Pest Control Certification Agreement   ☐ Occupancy Agreement   ☐ _______________

☐ Special Studies Zone Disclosure   ☐ VA Amendment   ☐ _______________

☐ Flood Insurance Disclosure   ☐ FHA Amendment   ☐ _______________

5.   Buyer and Seller shall deliver signed instructions to the escrow holder within _____________ days from Seller's acceptance which shall provide for closing within _____________ days from Seller's acceptance. Escrow fees to be paid as follows:

6.   Buyer and Seller acknowledge receipt of a copy of this page, which constitutes Page 1 of _______ Pages.

Buyer _______________________________________ Seller _______________________________________

Buyer _______________________________________ Seller _______________________________________

A REAL ESTATE BROKER IS THE PERSON QUALIFIED TO ADVISE ON REAL ESTATE. IF YOU DESIRE LEGAL ADVICE CONSULT YOUR ATTORNEY.

(21) 50% Conventional - interest only 2nd

* In this case, during a time of high interest, we had the seller obtain a loan for 50% of the value of the house because the payments would be way too high at a 16% conventional interest rate. We offset some of the payment by getting a 9% interest only second from the seller. Our combined interest rate is around 13%, which isn't too bad.

REAL ESTATE PURCHASE CONTRACT AND RECEIPT FOR DEPOSIT

THIS IS MORE THAN A RECEIPT FOR MONEY. IT IS INTENDED TO BE A LEGALLY BINDING CONTRACT. READ IT CAREFULLY.

CALIFORNIA ASSOCIATION OF REALTORS® (CAR) STANDARD FORM

____ , California. _________________________ , 19____

Received from ________________________ and/or assignee

herein called Buyer, the sum of ________ -Two Hundred- ________ Dollars $ __200.00__

evidenced by cash ☐, cashier's check ☐, or _Personal Note_ ☐, personal check ☐ payable to ____ Seller ____

_______________________ , to be held uncashed until acceptance of this offer, as deposit on account of purchase price of

__ -Eighty Seven Thousand- __________________ Dollars $ _87,000_

for the purchase of property, situated in ___________________ , County of _______________ , California,

described as follows: ______ 7600 Shoemaker Road ___________________________

1.   Buyer will deposit in escrow with ______________________ the balance of purchase price as follows:

    *A. Buyer to assist seller in obtaining a new assumable
         1st loan for $44,000 from Guarantee Savings and Loan
         at current terms and interest of 10% with payments of
         approximately $386.13 per month including principal and
         interest. Buyer to take over loan subject to.

    B. Buyer to execute a 2nd note and deed of trust to seller
        for $43,000 payable at 9% interest with monthly interest
        only payments of $322.05 per month. Loan will be for a
        5-year period from close of escrow, and there will be no
        prepayment penalty.

    C. Seller to provide a pest inspection and clearance.

Set forth above any terms and conditions of a factual nature applicable to this sale, such as financing, prior sale of other property, the matter of structural pest control inspection, repairs and personal property to be included in the sale.

2.   Deposit will ☐ will not ☐ be increased by $ __________ to $ __________ within __________ days of acceptance of this offer.

3.   Buyer does ☐ does not ☐ intend to occupy subject property as his residence.

4   The following supplements are incorporated as part of this agreement:

Other

☒ Structural Pest Control Certification Agreement   ☐ Occupancy Agreement   ☐ ______________

☐ Special Studies Zone Disclosure   ☐ VA Amendment   ☐ ______________

☐ Flood Insurance Disclosure   ☐ FHA Amendment   ☐ ______________

5.   Buyer and Seller shall deliver signed instructions to the escrow holder within __________ days from Seller's acceptance which shall provide for closing within __________ days from Seller's acceptance. Escrow fees to be paid as follows:

6.   Buyer and Seller acknowledge receipt of a copy of this page, which constitutes Page 1 of ______ Pages.

Buyer __________________________   Seller __________________________

Buyer __________________________   Seller __________________________

A REAL ESTATE BROKER IS THE PERSON QUALIFIED TO ADVISE ON REAL ESTATE. IF YOU DESIRE LEGAL ADVICE CONSULT YOUR ATTORNEY.

(22) 60% FHA LOAN - LESS THAN INTEREST 2ND

* Again we borrow only a percentage of the value of the home. This time we are going to assume the impound account, which includes prepaid taxes and insurance. This will save us a bundle.

** To help keep our payments down we're asking the seller to accept less than interest only payments. At 10% interest the $34,500 should be payable at about $285.08. So, the $135.08 is going to accumulate each month and then be added to the principle at the end of 5 years. Again, don't let the unpaid interest be compounded!

Remember that in order to make our profit, the property must appreciate more than the total of the unpaid interest, so pay attention to predicted appreciation rates, as well as your rental or lease income cash flow, in deciding whether this deal will work for you.

REAL ESTATE PURCHASE CONTRACT AND RECEIPT FOR DEPOSIT

THIS IS MORE THAN A RECEIPT FOR MONEY. IT IS INTENDED TO BE A LEGALLY BINDING CONTRACT. READ IT CAREFULLY.
CALIFORNIA ASSOCIATION OF REALTORS® (CAR) STANDARD FORM

_______________________________________ , California. ___________________ , 19_______

Received from _____________________ and/or assignee _________________________

herein called Buyer, the sum of _____________ -Five Hundred- _______________ Dollars $____ 500.00

evidenced by cash ☐, cashier's check ☐, or __Note in escrow__ ☐, personal check ☐ payable to ____ A Reliable

____ Title Company _____ , to be held uncashed until acceptance of this offer, as deposit on account of purchase price of

____ -Eighty Seven Thousand- _________________________ Dollars $___ 87,00

for the purchase of property, situated in ________________________ , County of____________________ , California,

described as follows: _____ 7600 Shoemaker Road _________________________

1.　　Buyer will deposit in escrow with ________________________ the balance of purchase price as follows:

*A.　Buyer to assist seller in obtaining a new assumable
　　　conventional 1st loan for $52,200 at current terms
　　　and interest of money market. Interest rate not to
　　　exceed 10% with payments of approximately $458.09 per
　　　month including principal and interest. Buyer to take
　　　over loan subject to and assume impounds at no cost
　　　buyer.

**B.　Buyer to execute a 2nd note secured by a second deed
　　　of trust with less than interest payments of $750.00 per
　　　month. All accumulated interest will be added on to the
　　　principal when the note becomes due and payable in five
　　　years from the close of escrow.

C.　All electrical and plumbing to be in proper working order
　　　at the close of escrow.

Set forth above any terms and conditions of a factual nature applicable to this sale, such as financing, prior sale of other property, the matter of structural pest control inspection, repairs and personal property to be included in the sale.

2.　　Deposit will ☐ will not ☐ be increased by $ _____________ to $___________ within____________ days of acceptance of this offer.

3.　　Buyer does ☐ does not ☐ intend to occupy subject property as his residence.

4.　　The following supplements are incorporated as part of this agreement:

Other

☐ Structural Pest Control Certification Agreement　　☐ Occupancy Agreement　　☐ _____________

☐ Special Studies Zone Disclosure　　☐ VA Amendment　　☐ _____________

☐ Flood Insurance Disclosure　　☐ FHA Amendment　　☐ _____________

5.　　Buyer and Seller shall deliver signed instructions to the escrow holder within ___________ days from Seller's acceptance which shall provide for closing within____________________ days from Seller's acceptance. Escrow fees to be paid as follows:

6.　　Buyer and Seller acknowledge receipt of a copy of this page, which constitutes Page 1 of _______ Pages.

Buyer_______________________________　　Seller _______________________________

Buyer_______________________________　　Seller _______________________________

A REAL ESTATE BROKER IS THE PERSON QUALIFIED TO ADVISE ON REAL ESTATE. IF YOU DESIRE LEGAL ADVICE CONSULT YOUR ATTORNEY.

(23) 60% CONVENTIONAL - GRADUATED 2ND

* Here we're also graduating the second loan from 10% to 12% over a five year period. This often works well when the seller balks at carrying the loan at a low 10% rate throughout the period of the loan.

REAL ESTATE PURCHASE CONTRACT AND RECEIPT FOR DEPOSIT
THIS IS MORE THAN A RECEIPT FOR MONEY. IT IS INTENDED TO BE A LEGALLY BINDING CONTRACT. READ IT CAREFULLY.
CALIFORNIA ASSOCIATION OF REALTORS® (CAR) STANDARD FORM

____ , California. _____________________ , 19_______

Received from ______ Dave Del Dotto and/or assignee ______

herein called Buyer, the sum of ______ –One Thousand– ______ Dollars $ __1,000.00__

evidenced by cash ☐, cashier's check ☐, or personal note during escrow, personal check ☐ payable to __A Reliable__

__Title Company__ , to be held uncashed until acceptance of this offer, as deposit on account of purchase price of

__–Seventy Seven Thousand–__ Dollars $ __77,000__

for the purchase of property, situated in ______________________ , County of__________________ , California,

described as follows: ______ 1500 Oakdale Road ______

1. Buyer will deposit in escrow with ________________________ the balance of purchase price as follows:

    A. Buyer to assist seller in obtaining a new assumable conventional loan for $46,200 payable at 10-1/2% interest with monthly payments of approximately $422.61 including principal and interest. Buyer agrees to take over loan subject to.

    *B. Seller agrees to carry a second note and deed of trust for $30,800 payable at 10% the first year interest only payments of $256.66 per month, 11% the 2nd year payable at $282.33 per month and 12% the 3rd through 5th year payable at $308.00 per month.

    C. Seller to provide a pest report and clearance on the house before close of escrow.

Set forth above any terms and conditions of a factual nature applicable to this sale, such as financing, prior sale of other property, the matter of structural pest control inspection, repairs and personal property to be included in the sale.

2. Deposit will ☐ will not ☐ be increased by $ ______________ to $ ______________ within______________ days of acceptance of this offer.

3. Buyer does ☐ does not ☐ intend to occupy subject property as his residence.

4. The following supplements are incorporated as part of this agreement:

Other

☐ Structural Pest Control Certification Agreement   ☐ Occupancy Agreement   ☐ ______________

☐ Special Studies Zone Disclosure   ☐ VA Amendment   ☐ ______________

☐ Flood Insurance Disclosure   ☐ FHA Amendment   ☐ ______________

5. Buyer and Seller shall deliver signed instructions to the escrow holder within ______ days from Seller's acceptance which shall provide for closing within______________ days from Seller's acceptance. Escrow fees to be paid as follows:

6. Buyer and Seller acknowledge receipt of a copy of this page, which constitutes Page 1 of______ Pages.

Buyer ____________________________________ Seller ____________________________

Buyer ____________________________________ Seller ____________________________

A REAL ESTATE BROKER IS THE PERSON QUALIFIED TO ADVISE ON REAL ESTATE. IF YOU DESIRE LEGAL ADVICE CONSULT YOUR ATTORNEY.

(24) 60% Variable loan - UNSECURED NOTE

* Having the seller carry an unsecured promissory note is high-lighted here. If there's a reason you don't want the second mortgage showing up, this is an effective way of structuring. But, be careful doing this! An unsecured note will attach your entire net worth if the person has to enforce payment of it. This makes a deed of trust better in most instances, because you can sell the property and get rid of the note.

REAL ESTATE PURCHASE CONTRACT AND RECEIPT FOR DEPOSIT

THIS IS MORE THAN A RECEIPT FOR MONEY. IT IS INTENDED TO BE A LEGALLY BINDING CONTRACT. READ IT CAREFULLY.

CALIFORNIA ASSOCIATION OF REALTORS® (CAR) STANDARD FORM

_________________________, California __________________, 19______

Received from __________ Dave Del Dotto and/or assignee __________

herein called Buyer, the sum of ______ -One Thousand- ______ Dollars $______ 1,000.00

evidenced by cash ☐, cashier's check ☐, or __Note in Escrow__ ☐ personal check ☐ payable to______ Seller

_________________, to be held uncashed until acceptance of this offer, as deposit on account of purchase price of

__-Sixty Four Thousand Dollars-__ Dollars $____ 64,000

for the purchase of property, situated in ______________ County of ________________ , California,

described as follows: ______ 198 Mellow Lane ______

1.   Buyer will deposit in escrow with __________________ the balance of purchase price as follows:

> A.   Buyer to assist seller in obtaining a new variable rate
>   mortgage from Security Pacific Bank for $38,000 at
>   current terms and interest of 10% with payments of
>   approximately 333.47 per month including principal and
>   interest. Buyer to take over loan subject to.
>
> *B.   Seller agrees to carry back a promissory note
>   executed by seller for the balance of $26,000 including
>   the above deposit. The note terms will be 10% accumulative
>   interest, all due and payable in 4 years from close of
>   escrow. Buyer may secure subject note with property at
>   any time.
>
> C.   The buyer reserves the right to a walk-through inspection
>   and acceptance before closing escrow.

Set forth above any terms and conditions of a factual nature applicable to this sale, such as financing, prior sale of other property, the matter of structural pest control inspection, repairs and personal property to be included in the sale.

2.   Deposit will ☐ will not ☐ be increased by $ ______________ to $ ______________ within ______________ days of acceptance of this offer.

3.   Buyer does ☐ does not ☐ intend to occupy subject property as his residence.

4.   The following supplements are incorporated as part of this agreement:

Other

☐ Structural Pest Control Certification Agreement   ☐ Occupancy Agreement   ☐ ______________

☐ Special Studies Zone Disclosure   ☐ VA Amendment   ☐ ______________

☐ Flood Insurance Disclosure   ☐ FHA Amendment   ☐ ______________

5.   Buyer and Seller shall deliver signed instructions to the escrow holder within ______________ days from Seller's acceptance which shall provide for closing within ______________ days from Seller's acceptance. Escrow fees to be paid as follows:

6.   Buyer and Seller acknowledge receipt of a copy of this page, which constitutes Page 1 of ______ Pages.

Buyer _________________________   Seller _________________________

Buyer _________________________   Seller _________________________

A REAL ESTATE BROKER IS THE PERSON QUALIFIED TO ADVISE ON REAL ESTATE. IF YOU DESIRE LEGAL ADVICE CONSULT YOUR ATTORNEY.

FOR ILLUSTRATION ONLY - Consult your attorney for legal advice ON CONTRACTS IN YOUR STATE

Reprinted with permission, California Association of Realtors®, Endorsment not implied

(25A & 25B) 2- ESCROW CONTRACTS

In most states, you can not enter into "side" agreements with the seller on a particular property you want financed by a bank. It is important that you not mislead the financial institution as to the purchase price of the property you have placed before it for financing.

But most states allow more than one transaction between seller and buyer which affect more than the property itself. Two separate contracts, one dealing with the sale of the property or asset, may co-exist.

* The buyer purchased the first property from the seller, then the seller purchases some other property of the buyer at the same time or after the sale of the first property. This allows the seller to return to the buyer some or all of the purchase price of the first property.

Check the details of your two contracts with your real estate attorney. There will also be tax consequences to consider.

In the example here, you have a motivated seller who is willing to take $10,000 down in a note for his $100,000 property without any cash other than the financing from the bank. You also have tax sale land in Arizona, which you can justify is worth between $5,000 and $15,000, though the original price two years ago may have been $1,000.

You enter into the first contract (A) with a down of $10,000 (You borrow from a friend for 90 days). You enter into a second contract (B) with the seller (of A) to purchase your tax sale land for $15,000 ($10,000 cash, $5,000 note). As soon as sale (A) closes, The seller has $10,000 cash to purchase your tax sale land. You sell him the land and get back your $10,000 cash, plus his note for $5,000. You pay back your friend $10,000.

Later on (a month or so) the seller of (A) decides he doesn't want the tax sale land and negotiates for you to take it back for $5,000-his note.

Remember, there are tax consequences to this transaction which you should review with your lawyer and accountant.

Note that in the contract we have used the term, "tax sale land." In an actual contract, you would use the address and/or legal description.

REAL ESTATE PURCHASE CONTRACT AND RECEIPT FOR DEPOSIT
THIS IS MORE THAN A RECEIPT FOR MONEY. IT IS INTENDED TO BE A LEGALLY BINDING CONTRACT. READ IT CAREFULLY.
CALIFORNIA ASSOCIATION OF REALTORS* (CAR) STANDARD FORM

____ , California. ________________ , 19________

Received from ______________ Dave Del Dotto and/or assignee ________________

herein called Buyer, the sum of ____________ -Ten Thousand Dollars- ____________ Dollars $_____ 10,000.00

evidenced by cash ☐, cashier's check ☐, or ___________________ ☐, personal check ☒ payable to________________

________________________________ , to be held uncashed until acceptance of this offer, as deposit on account of purchase price of

_____ -One Hundred Thousand Dollars- ________________________ Dollars $ 100,000.

for the purchase of property, situated in _______________________ , County of__________________________ , California,

described as follows: __________ Beauty Lane ______________________

1.   Buyer will deposit in escrow with ______ Escrow Company ____________ the balance of purchase price as follows:

A.   Subject to buyer securing a conventional loan at
     10% per annum, 30 year term.

B.   (Other terms and escape clauses)

Set forth above any terms and conditions of a factual nature applicable to this sale, such as financing, prior sale of other property, the matter of structural pest control inspection, repairs and personal property to be included in the sale.

2.   Deposit will ☐ will not ☐ be increased by $____________ to $____________ within__________ days of acceptance of this offer.

3.   Buyer does ☐ does not ☐ intend to occupy subject property as his residence.

4.   The following supplements are incorporated as part of this agreement:

Other

☐ Structural Pest Control Certification Agreement   ☐ Occupancy Agreement   ☐ ________________

☐ Special Studies Zone Disclosure   ☐ VA Amendment   ☐ ________________

☐ Flood Insurance Disclosure   ☐ FHA Amendment   ☐ ________________

5.   Buyer and Seller shall deliver signed instructions to the escrow holder within __________ days from Seller's acceptance which shall provide for closing within__________ days from Seller's acceptance. Escrow fees to be paid as follows:

6.   Buyer and Seller acknowledge receipt of a copy of this page, which constitutes Page 1 of ______ Pages.

Buyer _______________________________________   Seller _____________________________

Buyer _______________________________________   Seller _____________________________

A REAL ESTATE BROKER IS THE PERSON QUALIFIED TO ADVISE ON REAL ESTATE. IF YOU DESIRE LEGAL ADVICE CONSULT YOUR ATTORNEY.

REAL ESTATE PURCHASE CONTRACT AND RECEIPT FOR DEPOSIT

THIS IS MORE THAN A RECEIPT FOR MONEY. IT IS INTENDED TO BE A LEGALLY BINDING CONTRACT. READ IT CAREFULLY.

CALIFORNIA ASSOCIATION OF REALTORS® (CAR) STANDARD FORM

_______________________________________ , California. _____________________ , 19_______

Received from ______________ A. Smith __________________________

herein called Buyer, the sum of ______ –Ten Thousand Dollars– _____________ Dollars $_____ 10,000.00

evidenced by cash ☐, cashier's check ☐, or Note for $10,000 ☐, personal check ☐ payable to______ Escrow Company ______________ , to be held uncashed until acceptance of this offer, as deposit on account of purchase price of

______ –Twenty Thousand– _______________________________ Dollars $_____ 20,000.

for the purchase of property, situated in __________________________ , County of________________________ , California,

described as follows: ______ Tax Sale Land in Arizona Valued at $20,000. __________

1. Buyer will deposit in escrow with ________ Escrow Company ________ the balance of purchase price as follows:

     *A. Purchase of this tax sale land is subject to the
          closing of the sale of Smith's Beauty Lane property
          to Dave Del Dotto and/or assignee.

     B. (Other terms and escape clauses)

Set forth above any terms and conditions of a factual nature applicable to this sale, such as financing, prior sale of other property, the matter of structural pest control inspection, repairs and personal property to be included in the sale.

2. Deposit will ☐ will not ☐ be increased by $ ________________ to $ ____________ within_________________ days of acceptance of this offer.

3. Buyer does ☐ does not ☐ intend to occupy subject property as his residence.

4. The following supplements are incorporated as part of this agreement:

		Other
☐ Structural Pest Control Certification Agreement	☐ Occupancy Agreement	☐ ________________
☐ Special Studies Zone Disclosure	☐ VA Amendment	☐ ________________
☐ Flood Insurance Disclosure	☐ FHA Amendment	☐ ________________

5. Buyer and Seller shall deliver signed instructions to the escrow holder within ____________ days from Seller's acceptance which shall provide for closing within___________________ days from Seller's acceptance. Escrow fees to be paid as follows:

6. Buyer and Seller acknowledge receipt of a copy of this page, which constitutes Page 1 of _______ Pages.

Buyer_________________________________   Seller _________________________________

Buyer_________________________________   Seller _________________________________

A REAL ESTATE BROKER IS THE PERSON QUALIFIED TO ADVISE ON REAL ESTATE. IF YOU DESIRE LEGAL ADVICE CONSULT YOUR ATTORNEY.

(26) I.R.A. Account Contract

* Many people have I.R.A accounts, which, under certain circumstances, may be used to invest in real property. Check with your
accountant and attorney for the rules which govern your account.
Don't let the banks have all the fun.

REAL ESTATE PURCHASE CONTRACT AND RECEIPT FOR DEPOSIT
THIS IS MORE THAN A RECEIPT FOR MONEY. IT IS INTENDED TO BE A LEGALLY BINDING CONTRACT. READ IT CAREFULLY.
CALIFORNIA ASSOCIATION OF REALTORS* (CAR) STANDARD FORM

____ , California, _______________________ , 19 _________

Received from ____
herein called Buyer, the sum of ____ -Ten Thousand- __________________________________ Dollars $ __10,000__
evidenced by cash ☐, cashier's check ☐, or __Note in Escrow__ ☐, personal check ☐ payable to __________
________________________________ , to be held uncashed until acceptance of this offer, as deposit on account of purchase price of
____ -One Hundred Thousand- _____________________________________ Dollars $ __100,000__
for the purchase of property, situated in _____________________ , County of _____________________ , California,
described as follows: ____

1. Buyer will deposit in escrow with ______ Escrow Company ______ the balance of purchase price as follows:

    *A.   Buyer's note secured by I.R.A. account, which shall
         be drawn and used as down payment at closing.

    B.   Subject to buyer qualifying for a new first
         mortgage loan for $90,000 at a conventional financial
         institution, 30 year term.

    C. (Other terms and escape clauses)

Set forth above any terms and conditions of a factual nature applicable to this sale, such as financing, prior sale of other property, the matter of structural pest control inspection, repairs and personal property to be included in the sale.

2. Deposit will ☐ will not ☐ be increased by $ _______________ to $ _______________ within _______________ days of acceptance of this offer.

3. Buyer does ☐ does not ☐ intend to occupy subject property as his residence.

4. The following supplements are incorporated as part of this agreement:

Other
☐ Structural Pest Control Certification Agreement   ☐ Occupancy Agreement   ☐ _______________
☐ Special Studies Zone Disclosure   ☐ VA Amendment   ☐ _______________
☐ Flood Insurance Disclosure   ☐ FHA Amendment   ☐ _______________

5. Buyer and Seller shall deliver signed instructions to the escrow holder within _______________ days from Seller's acceptance which shall provide for closing within _______________ days from Seller's acceptance. Escrow fees to be paid as follows:

6. Buyer and Seller acknowledge receipt of a copy of this page, which constitutes Page 1 of _______ Pages.

Buyer _________________________________ Seller _________________________________

Buyer _________________________________ Seller _________________________________

A REAL ESTATE BROKER IS THE PERSON QUALIFIED TO ADVISE ON REAL ESTATE. IF YOU DESIRE LEGAL ADVICE CONSULT YOUR ATTORNEY.

(27) Credit Card Down

* Draw cash from one or more credit cards and deposit it in an interest bearing savings account, then write a personal check to be held by the agent or escrow company, which you will cover with that cash at closing. (Usually the bank giving you a conventional loan for the balance of the purchase price will want to verify the amount of the savings account as part of your qualification for the loan.)

YOUR CREDIT contains a chapter on how to get and use credit cards, and some suggestions where to look for low-rate cards.

REAL ESTATE PURCHASE CONTRACT AND RECEIPT FOR DEPOSIT

THIS IS MORE THAN A RECEIPT FOR MONEY. IT IS INTENDED TO BE A LEGALLY BINDING CONTRACT. READ IT CAREFULLY.

CALIFORNIA ASSOCIATION OF REALTORS® (CAR) STANDARD FORM

_____________________________, California, _____________________, 19_______

Received from ____

herein called Buyer, the sum of _______ –Ten Thousand– _______________ Dollars $ 10,000 ________

evidenced by cash ☐, cashier's check ☐, or ______________ ☒, personal check ☐ payable to________

__________________, to be held uncashed until acceptance of this offer, as deposit on account of purchase price of

____ Dollars $_______________

for the purchase of property, situated in ________________, County of________________, California,

described as follows: ____

1. Buyer will deposit in escrow with ______ Escrow Company ______ the balance of purchase price as follows:

*A. $10,000 check to be held in escrow until seller satisfies all conditions.

B. (Other terms and escape clauses)

Set forth above any terms and conditions of a factual nature applicable to this sale, such as financing, prior sale of other property, the matter of structural pest control inspection, repairs and personal property to be included in the sale.

2. Deposit will ☐ will not ☐ be increased by $ ______________ to $ ______________ within______________ days of acceptance of this offer

3. Buyer does ☐ does not ☐ intend to occupy subject property as his residence.

4. The following supplements are incorporated as part of this agreement:

Other

☐ Structural Pest Control Certification Agreement ☐ Occupancy Agreement ☐ _______________

☐ Special Studies Zone Disclosure ☐ VA Amendment ☐ _______________

☐ Flood Insurance Disclosure ☐ FHA Amendment ☐ _______________

5. Buyer and Seller shall deliver signed instructions to the escrow holder within ______ days from Seller's acceptance which shall provide for closing within______________ days from Seller's acceptance. Escrow fees to be paid as follows:

6. Buyer and Seller acknowledge receipt of a copy of this page, which constitutes Page 1 of______ Pages.

Buyer______   Seller ________________________________

Buyer______   Seller ________________________________

A REAL ESTATE BROKER IS THE PERSON QUALIFIED TO ADVISE ON REAL ESTATE. IF YOU DESIRE LEGAL ADVICE CONSULT YOUR ATTORNEY.

FOR ILLUSTRATION ONLY - Consult your attorney for legal advice ON CONTRACTS IN YOUR STATE

Reprinted with permission, California Association of Realtors®, Endorsment not implied

(28) Diamond Down

* When sellers are very motivated they will take down payments other than cash. Some people buy wholesale diamonds and then trade them in on real estate deals at retail prices.

REAL ESTATE PURCHASE CONTRACT AND RECEIPT FOR DEPOSIT
THIS IS MORE THAN A RECEIPT FOR MONEY. IT IS INTENDED TO BE A LEGALLY BINDING CONTRACT. READ IT CAREFULLY.
CALIFORNIA ASSOCIATION OF REALTORS® (CAR) STANDARD FORM

____ , California. ___________________________ , 19________

Received from ____

herein called Buyer, the sum of ________ -Ten Thousand- _______________________ Dollars $ 10,000 _______

evidenced by cash ☐, cashier's check ☐, or ____ Diamond _______ ☐, personal check ☐ payable to________________

______________________________ , to be held uncashed until acceptance of this offer, as deposit on account of purchase price of

____ Dollars $_______________

for the purchase of property, situated in ______________________________ , County of______________________ , California,

described as follows: ____

1.   Buyer will deposit in escrow with________ Escrow Company _______________ the balance of purchase price as follows:

    *A.   Subject to seller accepting a diamond ring appraised at $10,000 for the down payment.

    B.   (Other terms and escape clauses)

Set forth above any terms and conditions of a factual nature applicable to this sale, such as financing, prior sale of other property, the matter of structural pest control inspection, repairs and personal property to be included in the sale.

2.   Deposit will ☐ will not ☐ be increased by $______________ to $______________ within______________ days of acceptance of this offer.

3.   Buyer does ☐ does not ☐ intend to occupy subject property as his residence.

4.   The following supplements are incorporated as part of this agreement:

Other

☐ Structural Pest Control Certification Agreement   ☐ Occupancy Agreement   ☐ _______________________

☐ Special Studies Zone Disclosure   ☐ VA Amendment   ☐ _______________________

☐ Flood Insurance Disclosure   ☐ FHA Amendment   ☐ _______________________

5.   Buyer and Seller shall deliver signed instructions to the escrow holder within ___________ days from Seller's acceptance which shall provide for closing within______________ days from Seller's acceptance. Escrow fees to be paid as follows:

6.   Buyer and Seller acknowledge receipt of a copy of this page, which constitutes Page 1 of______ Pages.

Buyer____   Seller ____

Buyer____   Seller ____

A REAL ESTATE BROKER IS THE PERSON QUALIFIED TO ADVISE ON REAL ESTATE. IF YOU DESIRE LEGAL ADVICE CONSULT YOUR ATTORNEY.

FOR ILLUSTRATION ONLY - Consult your attorney for legal advice ON CONTRACTS IN YOUR STATE
Reprinted with permission, California Association of Realtors®, Endorsment not implied

(29) Jewelry as Down

You can use jewelry or other "valuable" items for a non-cash down payment, which can be combined with other techniques I've mentioned to make a total creative financing package. The jewelry is held by the escrow company as your down while you get the rest of the deal in place.

REAL ESTATE PURCHASE CONTRACT AND RECEIPT FOR DEPOSIT
THIS IS MORE THAN A RECEIPT FOR MONEY. IT IS INTENDED TO BE A LEGALLY BINDING CONTRACT. READ IT CAREFULLY.
CALIFORNIA ASSOCIATION OF REALTORS* (CAR) STANDARD FORM

________________________________ , California. ____________________ , 19________

Received from ________________ —One Thousand— ________ escrow ________ Dollars $ 1,000
herein called Buyer, the sum of
evidenced by cash ☐, cashier's check ☐, or Jewelry held by ☐, personal check ☐ payable to ________
____________________ , to be held uncashed until acceptance of this offer, as deposit on account of purchase price of
____ —One Hundred Thousand— ________________________ Dollars $ 100,000
for the purchase of property, situated in ____________________ , County of ____________________ , California,
described as follows: ____________________

1.   Buyer will deposit in escrow with ________ Escrow Company ________ the balance of purchase price as follows:

    A. $90,000 at closing, upon approval of buyer for
       conventional loan of that amount from American
       Savings, at not more than 10% yearly interest,
       30 year term.

    B.   (Other terms and escape clauses)

Set forth above any terms and conditions of a factual nature applicable to this sale, such as financing, prior sale of other property,
the matter of structural pest control inspection, repairs and personal property to be included in the sale.

2.   Deposit will ☐ will not ☐ be increased by $ ____________ to $ ____________ within ____________ days of
acceptance of this offer.

3.   Buyer does ☐ does not ☐ intend to occupy subject property as his residence.

4.   The following supplements are incorporated as part of this agreement:

                                                                 Other

☐ Structural Pest Control Certification Agreement   ☐ Occupancy Agreement   ☐ ________

☐ Special Studies Zone Disclosure   ☐ VA Amendment   ☐ ________

☐ Flood Insurance Disclosure   ☐ FHA Amendment   ☐ ________

5.   Buyer and Seller shall deliver signed instructions to the escrow holder within ________ days from Seller's acceptance which
shall provide for closing within ________ days from Seller's acceptance. Escrow fees to be paid as follows:

6.   Buyer and Seller acknowledge receipt of a copy of this page, which constitutes Page 1 of ____ Pages.

Buyer ____________________   Seller ____________________

Buyer ____________________   Seller ____________________

A REAL ESTATE BROKER IS THE PERSON QUALIFIED TO ADVISE ON REAL ESTATE. IF YOU DESIRE LEGAL ADVICE CONSULT YOUR ATTORNEY.

(30) Bonds for Down

* Zero-coupon bonds or other corporate bonds are good negotiable instruments for a down payment. These bonds can be purchased from your local stock broker. We are able to purchase these zero's at a deep discount. Our intention is to have a seller accept these bonds at face value. They will then receive this face value at sometime in the future when the bonds mature. Usually there is no cash flow to the seller on the bonds, just a one lump sum paid at maturity. If the seller wants payments, we can refinance the equity in the house, and buy annuity bonds, which will make payments to the seller. These transactions work best in distressed situations. A sophisticated seller who understands the time value of money will not want an offer like this. But how many people are that smart?

REAL ESTATE PURCHASE CONTRACT AND RECEIPT FOR DEPOSIT

THIS IS MORE THAN A RECEIPT FOR MONEY. IT IS INTENDED TO BE A LEGALLY BINDING CONTRACT. READ IT CAREFULLY.

CALIFORNIA ASSOCIATION OF REALTORS® (CAR) STANDARD FORM

_______________________________, California, _______________________ , 19__________

Received from _______________ Dave Del Dotto and/or assignee _______________

herein called Buyer, the sum of ________ -One Thousand- ________________ Dollars $____1,000____

evidenced by cash ☐, cashier's check ☐, or Bonds* ____________ ☐, personal check ☐ payable to______ Escrow ______

Company ________________ , to be held uncashed until acceptance of this offer, as deposit on account of purchase price of

-One Hundred Thousand- _________________________________ Dollars $____100,000____

for the purchase of property, situated in _____________________ , County of _____________________ , California,

described as follows: ____

1. Buyer will deposit in escrow with _________________________________ the balance of purchase price as follows:

*A. Buyer's down is zero coupon bonds of XYZ
     corporation, which will be held by Reliable
     Escrow Company.

B. $90,000 at closing, upon approval of buyer
    for conventional loan of that amount from
    American Savings, at not more than 10%
    interest, 30 year term.

C. (Other terms and escape clauses)

Set forth above any terms and conditions of a factual nature applicable to this sale, such as financing, prior sale of other property, the matter of structural pest control inspection, repairs and personal property to be included in the sale.

2. Deposit will ☐ will not ☐ be increased by $ _______________ to $ _______________ within _______________ days of acceptance of this offer.

3. Buyer does ☐ does not ☐ intend to occupy subject property as his residence.

4. The following supplements are incorporated as part of this agreement:

		Other
☐ Structural Pest Control Certification Agreement	☐ Occupancy Agreement	☐ _______________
☐ Special Studies Zone Disclosure	☐ VA Amendment	☐ _______________
☐ Flood Insurance Disclosure	☐ FHA Amendment	☐ _______________

5. Buyer and Seller shall deliver signed instructions to the escrow holder within _______________ days from Seller's acceptance which shall provide for closing within _______________ days from Seller's acceptance. Escrow fees to be paid as follows:

6. Buyer and Seller acknowledge receipt of a copy of this page, which constitutes Page 1 of_______ Pages.

Buyer _______________________________   Seller _______________________________

Buyer _______________________________   Seller _______________________________

A REAL ESTATE BROKER IS THE PERSON QUALIFIED TO ADVISE ON REAL ESTATE. IF YOU DESIRE LEGAL ADVICE CONSULT YOUR ATTORNEY.

FOR ILLUSTRATION ONLY - Consult your attorney for legal advice ON CONTRACTS IN YOUR STATE

Reprinted with permission, California Association of Realtors®, Endorsment not implied

(31) Stocks as Down

* Corporate stocks are good "negotiable" instruments for a down payment. The seller may accept stock in a company which is not listed on a stock exchange.

REAL ESTATE PURCHASE CONTRACT AND RECEIPT FOR DEPOSIT

THIS IS MORE THAN A RECEIPT FOR MONEY. IT IS INTENDED TO BE A LEGALLY BINDING CONTRACT. READ IT CAREFULLY.

CALIFORNIA ASSOCIATION OF REALTORS® (CAR) STANDARD FORM

_____________________________________, California, ___________________, 19______

Received from _______________________
herein called Buyer, the sum of _______ −Ten Thousand− _______ Dollars $ 10,000
evidenced by cash ☐, cashier's check ☐, or Stock in XYZ _____ ☐, personal check ☐ payable to __________
________________________________, to be held uncashed until acceptance of this offer, as deposit on account of purchase price of
−One Hundred Thousand− _______ Dollars $ 100,000
for the purchase of property, situated in _______________________, County of _______________________, California,
described as follows _______________________________________

1. Buyer will deposit in escrow with _____ Escrow company _____ the balance of purchase price as follows:

*A.   Buyer's down is stock in XYZ Company, which
       seller accepts as having a $10,000 value.

B.   (Other terms and escape clauses)

Set forth above any terms and conditions of a factual nature applicable to this sale, such as financing, prior sale of other property, the matter of structural pest control inspection, repairs and personal property to be included in the sale.

2. Deposit will ☐ will not ☐ be increased by $ _______ to $ _______ within _______ days of acceptance of this offer

3. Buyer does ☐ does not ☐ intend to occupy subject property as his residence.

4. The following supplements are incorporated as part of this agreement:

☐ Structural Pest Control Certification Agreement ☐ Occupancy Agreement
☐ Special Studies Zone Disclosure ☐ VA Amendment
☐ Flood Insurance Disclosure ☐ FHA Amendment

Other
☐ _______________
☐ _______________
☐ _______________

5. Buyer and Seller shall deliver signed instructions to the escrow holder within _______ days from Seller's acceptance which shall provide for closing within _______ days from Seller's acceptance. Escrow fees to be paid as follows:

6. Buyer and Seller acknowledge receipt of a copy of this page which constitutes Page 1 of _______ Pages.

Buyer _______________________ Seller _______________________

Buyer _______________________ Seller _______________________

A REAL ESTATE BROKER IS THE PERSON QUALIFIED TO ADVISE ON REAL ESTATE. IF YOU DESIRE LEGAL ADVICE CONSULT YOUR ATTORNEY.

(32) R.E. Commission as Down

* If you are a real estate broker or agent, you may be able to use your commission as all or part of your down payment. Since most commissions are 6%, the seller would probably have to have paid this had he sold the property through a broker. Consider obtaining a real estate license to make a commission on things you purchase.

See the discussion of becoming a real estate agent in THE REAL ESTATE PROFIT GUIDE.

REAL ESTATE PURCHASE CONTRACT AND RECEIPT FOR DEPOSIT

THIS IS MORE THAN A RECEIPT FOR MONEY. IT IS INTENDED TO BE A LEGALLY BINDING CONTRACT. READ IT CAREFULLY.

CALIFORNIA ASSOCIATION OF REALTORS® (CAR) STANDARD FORM

____ , California. _____________________________ , 19______

Received from ____

herein called Buyer, the sum of ________ -Six Thousand- ____________________ Dollars $________ 6,000 ______

evidenced by cash ☐, cashier's check ☐, or ____________________ ☐, personal check ☒ payable to________ Escrow ____

________ Company ____________ , to be held uncashed until acceptance of this offer, as deposit on account of purchase price of

________ -One Hundred Thousand Dollars- ____________________________ Dollars $___ 100,000 ______

for the purchase of property, situated in ____________________ , County of____________________ , California,

described as follows: ____

1.   Buyer will deposit in escrow with____________ Escrow Company ____________ the balance of purchase price as follows:

    A.   Buyer is a licensed real estate broker/agent.

    *B.   Check for $6,000 represents buyer's 6% commission on this sale; check to be held until closing.

    C.   Subject to buyer qualifying for owner-occupied 94% loan.

    D.   (Other terms and escape clauses)

Set forth above any terms and conditions of a factual nature applicable to this sale, such as financing, prior sale of other property, the matter of structural pest control inspection, repairs and personal property to be included in the sale.

2.   Deposit will ☐ will not ☐ be increased by $____________ to $____________ within____________ days of acceptance of this offer.

3.   Buyer does ☐ does not ☐ intend to occupy subject property as his residence.

4   The following supplements are incorporated as part of this agreement:

Other

☐ Structural Pest Control Certification Agreement   ☐ Occupancy Agreement   ☐ ____________

☐ Special Studies Zone Disclosure   ☐ VA Amendment   ☐ ____________

☐ Flood Insurance Disclosure   ☐ FHA Amendment   ☐ ____________

5.   Buyer and Seller shall deliver signed instructions to the escrow holder within ____________ days from Seller's acceptance which shall provide for closing within____________ days from Seller's acceptance. Escrow fees to be paid as follows:

6.   Buyer and Seller acknowledge receipt of a copy of this page, which constitutes Page 1 of________ Pages.

Buyer____________ ____________________________ Seller ____________________________

Buyer____________ ____________________________ Seller ____________________________

A REAL ESTATE BROKER IS THE PERSON QUALIFIED TO ADVISE ON REAL ESTATE. IF YOU DESIRE LEGAL ADVICE CONSULT YOUR ATTORNEY.

FOR ILLUSTRATION ONLY - Consult your attorney for legal advice ON CONTRACTS IN YOUR STATE

Reprinted with permission, California Association of Realtors®, Endorsment not implied

(33) Note from Another Property Owner

* Sometimes sellers will not take a note from you secured by the property, but they will take a note from you from some other reputable person, or a note secured by some other property.

* The key to this is creating paper up to 100% or more of the equity of the other property, with no points and a low interest rate.

Example:

Let's say that you have another property worth $100,000 that has a loan of $80,000 on it now. That leaves a $20,000 equity. You couldn't get a second loan from a bank of $20,000 on your equity because of bank policy. But, you could fill out a second mortgage for $20,000 to your friend (but never "deliver it" to your friend) and record it at the courthouse. You now owe your friend $20,000 payable at 6% interest for 7 years. You make the payments for a few months to season the note, then you look for another property to buy. When you find the new property, you offer your friend's note for $20,000 as part of the down payment. Sellers somehow like the idea of a note with an income as part of the down payment. If they accept it, you have created cheap money on a property that couldn't help you otherwise.

REAL ESTATE PURCHASE CONTRACT AND RECEIPT FOR DEPOSIT

THIS IS MORE THAN A RECEIPT FOR MONEY. IT IS INTENDED TO BE A LEGALLY BINDING CONTRACT. READ IT CAREFULLY.

CALIFORNIA ASSOCIATION OF REALTORS® (CAR) STANDARD FORM

____ , California. _____________________ , 19_______

Received from ____

herein called Buyer, the sum of ________ –Twenty Thousand– ________________ Dollars $ 20,000

evidenced by cash ☐, cashier's check ☐, or Note of $20,000 ☐, personal check ☐ payable to_________

_________________________________ , to be held uncashed until acceptance of this offer, as deposit on account of purchase price of

____ Dollars $________________

for the purchase of property, situated in ______________________________ , County of______________________ , California,

described as follows: ____

1.   Buyer will deposit in escrow with_______________ Escrow Company _______________ the balance of purchase price as follows:

```
   *A.   Down is a note from J. Adams to buyer, secured
         by XYZ property, for $20,000 payable over a 5
         year period at 6% interest, payments due at the
         end of 7 years.

    B    (Other terms and escape clauses)
```

Set forth above any terms and conditions of a factual nature applicable to this sale, such as financing, prior sale of other property, the matter of structural pest control inspection, repairs and personal property to be included in the sale.

2.   Deposit will ☐ will not ☐ be increased by $________________ to $________________ within____________ days of acceptance of this offer.

3.   Buyer does ☐ does not ☐ intend to occupy subject property as his residence.

4   The following supplements are incorporated as part of this agreement:

Other

☐ Structural Pest Control Certification Agreement   ☐ Occupancy Agreement   ☐ ________________

☐ Special Studies Zone Disclosure   ☐ VA Amendment   ☐ ________________

☐ Flood Insurance Disclosure   ☐ FHA Amendment   ☐ ________________

5.   Buyer and Seller shall deliver signed instructions to the escrow holder within ___________ days from Seller's acceptance which shall provide for closing within_________________ days from Seller's acceptance. Escrow fees to be paid as follows:

____

6.   Buyer and Seller acknowledge receipt of a copy of this page, which constitutes Page 1 of_______ Pages.

Buyer_________ __________________________________ Seller _____________________________________

Buyer_________ __________________________________ Seller _____________________________________

A REAL ESTATE BROKER IS THE PERSON QUALIFIED TO ADVISE ON REAL ESTATE. IF YOU DESIRE LEGAL ADVICE CONSULT YOUR ATTORNEY.

FOR ILLUSTRATION ONLY - Consult your attorney for legal advice ON CONTRACTS IN YOUR STATE

Reprinted with permission, California Association of Realtors®, Endorsment not implied

(34) Corporate Guarantee

* The seller may accept a large note from you if you back it up with a corporate guarantee, even though the corporation may be small or in financial trouble. You may be able to negotiate a large portion of the total purchase price on such a note, so that the bank loan remains small.

(34) Corporate Guarantee

REAL ESTATE PURCHASE CONTRACT AND RECEIPT FOR DEPOSIT

THIS IS MORE THAN A RECEIPT FOR MONEY. IT IS INTENDED TO BE A LEGALLY BINDING CONTRACT. READ IT CAREFULLY.

CALIFORNIA ASSOCIATION OF REALTORS® (CAR) STANDARD FORM

____ , California. _______________________ , 19_______

Received from ____

herein called Buyer, the sum of _______ -Fifty Thousand Dollars- _____________ Dollars $_____ 50,000

evidenced by cash ☐, cashier's check ☐, or Note for $50,000 ☐, personal check ☐ payable to__________

___________________________ , to be held uncashed until acceptance of this offer, as deposit on account of purchase price of

_______ -One Hundred Thousand- _________________________________ Dollars $____ 100,000

for the purchase of property, situated in ______________________ , County of ____________________ , California,

described as follows: ____

1.   Buyer will deposit in escrow with ______ Escrow Company ______ the balance of purchase price as follows:

____

*A.   Buyer's note is guaranteed by XYZ Corporation, whom
      shall be liable should buyer fail to pay under terms
      of the note.

B.   (Other terms and escape clauses)

Set forth above any terms and conditions of a factual nature applicable to this sale, such as financing, prior sale of other property, the matter of structural pest control inspection, repairs and personal property to be included in the sale.

2.   Deposit will ☐ will not ☐ be increased by $ _____________ to $ ___________ within ___________ days of acceptance of this offer.

3.   Buyer does ☐ does not ☐ intend to occupy subject property as his residence.

4.   The following supplements are incorporated as part of this agreement:

Other

☐ Structural Pest Control Certification Agreement   ☐ Occupancy Agreement   ☐ ___________

☐ Special Studies Zone Disclosure   ☐ VA Amendment   ☐ ___________

☐ Flood Insurance Disclosure   ☐ FHA Amendment   ☐ ___________

5.   Buyer and Seller shall deliver signed instructions to the escrow holder within ___________ days from Seller's acceptance which shall provide for closing within ___________ days from Seller's acceptance. Escrow fees to be paid as follows:

6.   Buyer and Seller acknowledge receipt of a copy of this page, which constitutes Page 1 of ______ Pages.

Buyer _________________________________   Seller _________________________________

Buyer _________________________________   Seller _________________________________

A REAL ESTATE BROKER IS THE PERSON QUALIFIED TO ADVISE ON REAL ESTATE. IF YOU DESIRE LEGAL ADVICE CONSULT YOUR ATTORNEY.

FOR ILLUSTRATION ONLY - Consult your attorney for legal advice ON CONTRACTS IN YOUR STATE

Reprinted with permission, California Association of Realtors®, Endorsment not implied

(35) 75% FNMA Refi - 25% 2nd
WITH ANNUAL PAYMENTS

* I agreed to formally assume the loan within 60 days. During the 60 days the seller would make the loan payments. Before using this method, make sure you will qualify for the formal assumption.

** Making the note payable annually gives the buyer an opportunity to use the return money or some other form of annual income he might have. It would then relieve any pressure of a monthly payment. The no-prepayment clause makes it sound like the note is going to be paid soon.

*** If the pest report shows work that needs to be completed, I usually take the option to take the cash and do it myself. The reason for this is that the pest companies charge about 10 percent too much and I can usually have it done by friends and put money in my pocket.

REAL ESTATE PURCHASE CONTRACT AND RECEIPT FOR DEPOSIT
THIS IS MORE THAN A RECEIPT FOR MONEY. IT IS INTENDED TO BE A LEGALLY BINDING CONTRACT. READ IT CAREFULLY.
CALIFORNIA ASSOCIATION OF REALTORS* (CAR) STANDARD FORM

____, California _________________, 19________

Received from ______________ Dave Del Dotto and/or assignee ________________________

herein called Buyer, the sum of ______ -One Hundred- ____________________ . Dollars $ 100.00

evidenced by cash ☐, cashier's check ☐, or __ Personal note ☐, personal check ☐ payable to ______ A Reliable

____ Title Company ____ , to be held uncashed until acceptance of this offer, as deposit on account of purchase price of

____ -Sixty Four Thousand- ________________________________ Dollars $ 64,000

for the purchase of property, situated in ______________________ County of ____________________ , California,

described as follows: ____________ 1908 "H" Street ____________________________________

1.   Buyer will deposit in escrow with ________________________________ the balance of purchase price as follows:

        *A.   Buyer to assist seller in obtaining a FNMA refinance
              loan from lender of buyer's choice. The new loan will be
              in the amount of $48,000 payable at 12% interest with payments
              not to exceed $500.00 per month. Buyer then agrees to formally
              assume this loan within 60 days of close of escrow.

        **B. Buyer will execute a 2nd note secured by a mortgage
              on a second property for $16,000 payable at 10% interest
              payable annually on one balloon payment of $1,600 in May
              of each year. The loan will be for a 10-year term when
              all principal will be due in one payment of $16,000. There
              will be no prepayment penalty in case buyer wishes to pay
              off entire loan in full before the due date.

        ***C. Seller to provide a pest report and buyer will have
              option to complete any work to be done at buyer's
              discretion.

Set forth above any terms and conditions of a factual nature applicable to this sale, such as financing, prior sale of other property,
the matter of structural pest control inspection, repairs and personal property to be included in the sale.

2.   Deposit will ☐ will not ☐ be increased by $ ______________ to $ ______________ within ______________ days of
acceptance of this offer.

3.   Buyer does ☐ does not ☐ intend to occupy subject property as his residence.

4.   The following supplements are incorporated as part of this agreement

		Other
☐ Structural Pest Control Certification Agreement	☐ Occupancy Agreement	☐ ______________
☐ Special Studies Zone Disclosure	☐ VA Amendment	☐ ______________
☐ Flood Insurance Disclosure	☐ FHA Amendment	☐ ______________

5.   Buyer and Seller shall deliver signed instructions to the escrow holder within ____________ days from Seller's acceptance which
shall provide for closing within ______________ days from Seller's acceptance. Escrow fees to be paid as follows

____

6.   Buyer and Seller acknowledge receipt of a copy of this page, which constitutes Page 1 of ______ Pages.

Buyer_________________________________   Seller_________________________________

Buyer_________________________________   Seller_________________________________

A REAL ESTATE BROKER IS THE PERSON QUALIFIED TO ADVISE ON REAL ESTATE. IF YOU DESIRE LEGAL ADVICE CONSULT YOUR ATTORNEY.

Creative Contracts:
Nothing Down
The Buyer Using Primary Lenders

(36) 80 Percent FNMA Resale Loan - Created Note as Down

(37) 95 Percent FNMA Resale Loan - At Appraised Value

(38) 70 Percent FHA Investor Loan - Interest Only Second

(36) 80% FNMA Resale Loan - Created Note as Down

* Don't let this $3,400 cash down payment fool you. It's actually there to fool you because any FNMA loan must have 5% cash down payment, no matter what else you trade in for the down. I would never let this happen to you; look down in item "D" ; what do you know, our $3,400!

** Folks, believe it or not this note on one of our other properties wasn't even a figment of our imagination the day before our offer. Why not borrow money from ourselves on another property where the existing low equity is going to waste?

REAL ESTATE PURCHASE CONTRACT AND RECEIPT FOR DEPOSIT

THIS IS MORE THAN A RECEIPT FOR MONEY. IT IS INTENDED TO BE A LEGALLY BINDING CONTRACT. READ IT CAREFULLY.

CALIFORNIA ASSOCIATION OF REALTORS* (CAR) STANDARD FORM

_______________________________________ , California. _______________ , 19 __________

Received from ___________ Dave Del Dotto and/or assignee

herein called Buyer, the sum of ___________ -One Hundred- ___________ Dollars $___ 100.00

evidenced by cash ☐, cashier's check ☐, or _Note in Escrow_ ☐, personal check ☐ payable to ___ A Reliable

___ Title Company ___ , to be held uncashed until acceptance of this offer, as deposit on account of purchase price of

___ -Sixty Eight Thousand- ___________________ Dollars $___ 68,000

for the purchase of property, situated in ___________________ , County of ___________________ , California,

described as follows: ___________ 1541 Santa Lucia Court ___________

1. Buyer will deposit in escrow with _______________________________ the balance of purchase price as follows:

*A. Buyer to put $3,400 cash down payment including above deposit.

B. This offer is subject to the buyer obtaining a new FNMA resale
    loan for $54,400 from Suburban Coastal Corporation. The loan
    will be at 12% interest with payments not to exceed $555.00
    per month including principal and interest.

**C. Subject to the seller accepting an existing note secured
    by a deed of trust on property located at 1700 Carver Drive
    for $10,200. Note is payable at 12% interest with payments
    of $102.00 per month. Seller shall accept this note as
    partial down payment.

D. Seller to credit buyer $3,400 in escrow for new carpets.

Set forth above any terms and conditions of a factual nature applicable to this sale, such as financing, prior sale of other property,
the matter of structural pest control inspection, repairs and personal property to be included in the sale.

2. Deposit will ☐ will not ☐ be increased by $_______________ to $_______________ within_______________ days of
acceptance of this offer.

3. Buyer does ☐ does not ☐ intend to occupy subject property as his residence.

4. The following supplements are incorporated as part of this agreement:

		Other
☐ Structural Pest Control Certification Agreement	☐ Occupancy Agreement	☐ _______________
☐ Special Studies Zone Disclosure	☐ VA Amendment	☐ _______________
☐ Flood Insurance Disclosure	☐ FHA Amendment	☐ _______________

5. Buyer and Seller shall deliver signed instructions to the escrow holder within _______________ days from Seller's acceptance which
shall provide for closing within_______________ days from Seller's acceptance. Escrow fees to be paid as follows:

6. Buyer and Seller acknowledge receipt of a copy of this page, which constitutes Page 1 of_______ Pages.

Buyer_______________   _______________________________ Seller _______________________________

Buyer_______________   _______________________________ Seller _______________________________

A REAL ESTATE BROKER IS THE PERSON QUALIFIED TO ADVISE ON REAL ESTATE. IF YOU DESIRE LEGAL ADVICE CONSULT YOUR ATTORNEY.

(37) 95% FNMA Resale loan - AT APPRAISAL VALUE

* Before writing the offer we asked the seller if he would sell at whatever the appraised value would be. If it is different than what we wrote the offer at we will adjust outside escrow.

** Again, we really don't need any cash. But, since we are not exchanging something for the down payment we need to write a check for the closing to the seller. We should have an agreement with the seller for him to carry back the down payment and any closing costs in a second note. (This will cause the seller to pay out of his own pocket to execute the note.)

REAL ESTATE PURCHASE CONTRACT AND RECEIPT FOR DEPOSIT

THIS IS MORE THAN A RECEIPT FOR MONEY. IT IS INTENDED TO BE A LEGALLY BINDING CONTRACT. READ IT CAREFULLY.

CALIFORNIA ASSOCIATION OF REALTORS® (CAR) STANDARD FORM

_____________________________________ , California _________________ , 19____

Received from ________ Dave Del Dotto and/or assignee

herein called Buyer, the sum of ________ -One Hundred- ________ Dollars $ 100.00

evidenced by cash ☐, cashier's check ☐, or Note in escrow ☐, personal check ☐ payable to A Reliable Title Company , to be held uncashed until acceptance of this offer, as deposit on account of purchase price of

-Fifty One Thousand- ________ Dollars $ 51,000*

for the purchase of property, situated in ________ County of ________ , California,

described as follows: ________ 1605 Coffee Road

1. Buyer will deposit in escrow with ________ the balance of purchase price as follows:

*A. Buyer to put $2,500 cash down payment.

**B. Subject to the buyer qualifying and obtaining a new FNMA resale loan for $48,450 from Capitol Pacific Mortgage Company. The interest rate will be at 11-1/2% with payments of approximately $475.00 per month.

C. Seller to provide a clear pest report.

Set forth above any terms and conditions of a factual nature applicable to this sale, such as financing, prior sale of other property, **the matter of structural pest control inspection, repairs and personal property to be included in the sale.**

2. Deposit will ☐ will not ☐ be increased by $ ________ to $ ________ within ________ days of acceptance of this offer.

3. Buyer does ☐ does not ☐ intend to occupy subject property as his residence.

4. The following supplements are incorporated as part of this agreement:

Other

☐ Structural Pest Control Certification Agreement   ☐ Occupancy Agreement   ☐ ________

☐ Special Studies Zone Disclosure   ☐ VA Amendment   ☐ ________

☐ Flood Insurance Disclosure   ☐ FHA Amendment   ☐ ________

5. Buyer and Seller shall deliver signed instructions to the escrow holder within ________ days from Seller's acceptance which shall provide for closing within ________ days from Seller's acceptance. Escrow fees to be paid as follows:

6. Buyer and Seller acknowledge receipt of a copy of this page, which constitutes Page 1 of ________ Pages.

Buyer ________   Seller ________

Buyer ________   Seller ________

A REAL ESTATE BROKER IS THE PERSON QUALIFIED TO ADVISE ON REAL ESTATE. IF YOU DESIRE LEGAL ADVICE CONSULT YOUR ATTORNEY.

FOR ILLUSTRATION ONLY - Consult your attorney for legal advice ON CONTRACTS IN YOUR STATE

Reprinted with permission, California Association of Realtors®, Endorsment not implied

(38) 70% FHA Investor Loan - Interest Only 2nd

* This looks like we need cash for the down payment, right? It is supposed to.

** You will notice that we are credited $2,200 for deferred maintenance and we will be getting a 6% real estate commission of $3,300 (if we are licensed real estate agents) which will take care of our down payment. If the seller will agree to increase his 2nd note after the close of escrow, we will actually have money in our pocket from the deal.

REAL ESTATE PURCHASE CONTRACT AND RECEIPT FOR DEPOSIT

THIS IS MORE THAN A RECEIPT FOR MONEY. IT IS INTENDED TO BE A LEGALLY BINDING CONTRACT. READ IT CAREFULLY.
CALIFORNIA ASSOCIATION OF REALTORS® (CAR) STANDARD FORM

_______________________________, California, ___________________ , 19________

Received from __________ Dave Del Dotto and/or assignee ______________

herein called Buyer, the sum of __________ -One Hundred- __________ Dollars $ 100.00

evidenced by cash ☐, cashier's check ☐, or Note in escrow ☐, personal check ☐ payable to __________ A Reliable Title Company __________ , to be held uncashed until acceptance of this offer, as deposit on account of purchase price of

__________ -Fifty Five Thousand- __________ Dollars $ 55,000

for the purchase of property, situated in __________________ , County of ________________ , California,

described as follows: __________ 1402 Desiree Avenue __________

1.   Buyer will deposit in escrow with ________________________________ the balance of purchase price as follows:

    *A.   Buyer to put $5,500 cash down payment.

    **B.   Subject to the buyer obtaining a non-owner FHA loan for $38,500 at current interest rate of 10% payable at approximately $337.86 per month principal and interest.

    C.   Subject to the buyer executing a second note secured by a deed of trust for $11,000 payable at 10% interest with monthly interest only payments of $91.66 per month for five years.

    D.   Seller to credit buyer $2,200 in escrow for deferred maintenance.

    ***E.   The buyer is a licensed real estate agent.

Set forth above any terms and conditions of a factual nature applicable to this sale, such as financing, prior sale of other property, the matter of structural pest control inspection, repairs and personal property to be included in the sale.

2.   Deposit will ☐ will not ☐ be increased by $ __________ to $ __________ within __________ days of acceptance of this offer

3.   Buyer does ☐ does not ☐ intend to occupy subject property as his residence.

4.   The following supplements are incorporated as part of this agreement:

		Other	
☐ Structural Pest Control Certification Agreement	☐ Occupancy Agreement	☐	
☐ Special Studies Zone Disclosure	☐ VA Amendment	☐	
☐ Flood Insurance Disclosure	☐ FHA Amendment	☐	

5.   Buyer and Seller shall deliver signed instructions to the escrow holder within __________ days from Seller's acceptance which shall provide for closing within __________ days from Seller's acceptance. Escrow fees to be paid as follows:

6.   Buyer and Seller acknowledge receipt of a copy of this page, which constitutes Page 1 of _____ Pages.

Buyer __________________________   Seller __________________________

Buyer __________________________   Seller __________________________

A REAL ESTATE BROKER IS THE PERSON QUALIFIED TO ADVISE ON REAL ESTATE. IF YOU DESIRE LEGAL ADVICE CONSULT YOUR ATTORNEY.

(39) Land-Trust Purchases

* Some due-on-sale provisions in mortgages or trust deed can be circumvented by a simple document, by which the Seller places the property in a trust managed by a trustee who holds the property either for the Seller or for you as the beneficiary until you are ready to refinance the property.

** You will need to consult with a real estate attorney in your state to see if this technique will work in your situation.

REAL ESTATE PURCHASE CONTRACT AND RECEIPT FOR DEPOSIT

THIS IS MORE THAN A RECEIPT FOR MONEY. IT IS INTENDED TO BE A LEGALLY BINDING CONTRACT. READ IT CAREFULLY.

CALIFORNIA ASSOCIATION OF REALTORS® (CAR) STANDARD FORM

_______________________________________ , California. _______________________ , 19_________

Received from ____

herein called Buyer, the sum of _______ -One Thousand- ____________________ Dollars $_____ 1,000.00

evidenced by cash ☐, cashier's check ☐, or ___________________ ☐, personal check ☒ payable to_______ Escrow

_______ Company _______ , to be held uncashed until acceptance of this offer, as deposit on account of purchase price of

____ Dollars $_____________

for the purchase of property, situated in _______________________ , County of_______________________ , California,

described as follows: ____

1.   Buyer will deposit in escrow with ___________________________ the balance of purchase price as follows:

*A.   Subject to the property being placed in a land-trust
       and the benificial interest being transferred to buyer
       in such a way that the due-on-sale clause governing the
       American First mortgage cannot be exercised by American
       Savings.

**B.   Subject to a favorable legal opinion from a lawyer selected
        by the buyer which confirms the legal effect of "A" above.

C.   (Other terms and escape clauses)

Set forth above any terms and conditions of a factual nature applicable to this sale, such as financing, prior sale of other property, the matter of structural pest control inspection, repairs and personal property to be included in the sale.

2.   Deposit will ☐ will not ☐ be increased by $ _______________ to $ _______________ within_______________ days of acceptance of this offer.

3.   Buyer does ☐ does not ☐ intend to occupy subject property as his residence.

4.   The following supplements are incorporated as part of this agreement:

		Other
☐ Structural Pest Control Certification Agreement	☐ Occupancy Agreement	☐ _______________
☐ Special Studies Zone Disclosure	☐ VA Amendment	☐ _______________
☐ Flood Insurance Disclosure	☐ FHA Amendment	☐ _______________

5.   Buyer and Seller shall deliver signed instructions to the escrow holder within _______________ days from Seller's acceptance which shall provide for closing within_______________ days from Seller's acceptance. Escrow fees to be paid as follows:

6.   Buyer and Seller acknowledge receipt of a copy of this page, which constitutes Page 1 of_______ Pages.

Buyer_______ _______________________________ Seller _______________________________

Buyer_______________________________ Seller _______________________________

A REAL ESTATE BROKER IS THE PERSON QUALIFIED TO ADVISE ON REAL ESTATE. IF YOU DESIRE LEGAL ADVICE CONSULT YOUR ATTORNEY.

FOR ILLUSTRATION ONLY - Consult your attorney for legal advice ON CONTRACTS IN YOUR STATE
Reprinted with permission, California Association of Realtors®, Endorsment not implied

(40) Wrap-Around 2nd - Seller 3rd

* This is a great loan program! What the wrap-around second loan does is make use of a nice low interest rate first with a long due date. The new second money will be loaned a 17-3/4% interest that is adjusted to the current money market, and is combined with the existing first loan interest rate. It then makes a nice blended interest rate that is usually affordable.
And the term of the loan is the exact term of your existing first loan. Here is the formula:

     $ 67,000 sale price
     30,000 existing 1st @ 8% - $2,400 per year payment
     90% Loan = 30,300 new money at 12% - $3,636 per year payment
     ____

     $ 60,300 new wrap loan

     $ 6,036 payment + $ 60,300 new loan amount = 10% interest rate per year.

     This loan is available at 95% of the value of the property!

REAL ESTATE PURCHASE CONTRACT AND RECEIPT FOR DEPOSIT
THIS IS MORE THAN A RECEIPT FOR MONEY. IT IS INTENDED TO BE A LEGALLY BINDING CONTRACT. READ IT CAREFULLY.
CALIFORNIA ASSOCIATION OF REALTORS® (CAR) STANDARD FORM

_______________________ , California _______________________ , 19____

Received from ___ Dave Del Dotto and/or assignee ___

herein called Buyer, the sum of ___ -One Hundred- ___ Dollars $___ 100.00

evidenced by cash ☐, cashier's check ☐, or ___ Note in escrow ☐, personal check ☐ payable to ___ A Reliable Title Company ___ , to be held uncashed until acceptance of this offer, as deposit on account of purchase price of

___ -Sixty Seven Thousand- ___ Dollars $___ 67,000

for the purchase of property, situated in _______________________ , County of _______________________ , California,

described as follows: ___ 427 Sierra Drive ___

1. Buyer will deposit in escrow with _______________________ the balance of purchase price as follows:

*A. This offer is to the buyer assisting the seller in obtaining a new wrap-around second loan from Suburban Coastal and taking over $60,300 payable at 13% interest with payments of approximately $664.00 per month. This loan will wrap-around the existing first loan of $30,000 payable at 8% interest and will be due at the same time the existing first is due. The new second loan will be for approximately $30,300 and will yield approximately 12% interest to the lender.

B. Seller agrees to carry the balance of approximately $6,700 back in a note payable at 10% interest with one balloon payment of principal and interest at the end of seven years from close of escrow.

C. Seller to provide a clear pest report.

Set forth above any terms and conditions of a factual nature applicable to this sale, such as financing, prior sale of other property, the matter of structural pest control inspection, repairs and personal property to be included in the sale.

2. Deposit will ☐ will not ☐ be increased by $ _______________ to $ _______________ within _______________ days of acceptance of this offer.

3. Buyer does ☐ does not ☐ intend to occupy subject property as his residence.

4. The following supplements are incorporated as part of this agreement:

☐ Structural Pest Control Certification Agreement ☐ Occupancy Agreement Other ☐ _______________
☐ Special Studies Zone Disclosure ☐ VA Amendment ☐ _______________
☐ Flood Insurance Disclosure ☐ FHA Amendment ☐ _______________

5. Buyer and Seller shall deliver signed instructions to the escrow holder within _______________ days from Seller's acceptance which shall provide for closing within _______________ days from Seller's acceptance. Escrow fees to be paid as follows:

6. Buyer and Seller acknowledge receipt of a copy of this page, which constitutes Page 1 of ___ Pages.

Buyer _______________________ Seller _______________________

Buyer _______________________ Seller _______________________

A REAL ESTATE BROKER IS THE PERSON QUALIFIED TO ADVISE ON REAL ESTATE. IF YOU DESIRE LEGAL ADVICE CONSULT YOUR ATTORNEY.

(41) Take Over 1st - Seller creates 2nd and sells in escrow - carries 3rd

* Here is a slick way to get a 12% second loan. You have the seller create it at terms that you can afford and then advertise for a private person to buy the note. You can do this with a long escrow period. This would even be a good way to place a nice loan for one of your rich relatives. With a 20% discount on a 12% note, due in eight years, the yield is not bad for a passive investor.

Note that the 1986 tax law changed the rules and limits for passive *loss* investments. While this deal creates a passive *profit* for your investor, keep in mind that it, too, will have tax consequences for your investor friend, who should have proper advice from a qualified accountant. You should make your own inquiries so you know what kind of deal you are offering the person who purchases the note, especially if it is a friend or relative. Also, you might find a case where a deal could be used to create a passive loss, and you or the person seeking tax benefits from the loss should be certain you have had accurate advice before proceeding.

REAL ESTATE PURCHASE CONTRACT AND RECEIPT FOR DEPOSIT   3rd
THIS IS MORE THAN A RECEIPT FOR MONEY. IT IS INTENDED TO BE A LEGALLY BINDING CONTRACT. READ IT CAREFULLY.
CALIFORNIA ASSOCIATION OF REALTORS® (CAR) STANDARD FORM

_______________________________________ , California _______________ , 19______

Received from ______________________ Dave Del Dotto and/or assignee

herein called Buyer, the sum of ______ -One Hundred- ______________ Dollars $ ___ 100.00

evidenced by cash ☐, cashier's check ☐, or __ Note in Escrow ☐, personal check ☐ payable to______ A Reliable

Title Company ______ , to be held uncashed until acceptance of this offer, as deposit on account of purchase price of

_____ -Sixty Three Thousand- _____________________________ Dollars $_____ 63,000

for the purchase of property, situated in ______________________ , County of______________________ , California,

described as follows: ____________ 898 Crank Avenue

1.   Buyer will deposit in escrow with ______________________________________ the balance of purchase price as follows:

   A.   Subject to the buyer qualifying for and taking over
the existing first loan of $21,000 from El Dorado
Savings and Loan. The payments are $180.00 per month
including principal and interest.

  *B.   Subject to the seller creating a second note secured by
a deed of trust on subject property for $25,000 payable
at 12% interest with monthly interest only payments of
$250.00 per month all due and payable in eight years from
close of escrow. Buyer will then assist seller in selling
this note at a discount of 20% to a private party during
the escrow period.

   C.   Subject to the buyer executing a third note and deed of
trust to the seller for $16,500 payable at 12% interest
with interest only payments of $165.00 per month, all due
and payable in 10 years form the close of escrow.

   D.   Buyer will take house in "as is" condition.

Set forth above any terms and conditions of a factual nature applicable to this sale, such as financing, prior sale of other property, the matter of structural pest control inspection, repairs and personal property to be included in the sale.

2.   Deposit will ☐ will not ☐ be increased by $ _______________ to $ _____________ within ____________ days of acceptance of this offer.

3.   Buyer does ☐ does not ☐ intend to occupy subject property as his residence.

4.   The following supplements are incorporated as part of this agreement:

☐ Structural Pest Control Certification Agreement   ☐ Occupancy Agreement   Other ☐ ____________

☐ Special Studies Zone Disclosure   ☐ VA Amendment   ☐ ____________

☐ Flood Insurance Disclosure   ☐ FHA Amendment   ☐ ____________

5.   Buyer and Seller shall deliver signed instructions to the escrow holder within ___________ days from Seller's acceptance which shall provide for closing within_____________ days from Seller's acceptance. Escrow fees to be paid as follows:

6.   Buyer and Seller acknowledge receipt of a copy of this page. which constitutes Page 1 of _______ Pages

Buyer _____________________________   Seller _____________________________

Buyer _____________________________   Seller _____________________________

A REAL ESTATE BROKER IS THE PERSON QUALIFIED TO ADVISE ON REAL ESTATE. IF YOU DESIRE LEGAL ADVICE CONSULT YOUR ATTORNEY.

FOR ILLUSTRATION ONLY - Consult your attorney for legal advice ON CONTRACTS IN YOUR STATE
Reprinted with permission, California Association of Realtors®, Endorsment not implied

(42) Seller gets 1st for 50% - seller caries 50% 2nd

* On this free and clear property the owner wanted at least $25,000 cash. So we suggested he get a new FHA loan for 50% of the value of the house and we would take that loan over. We must wait two years before we can take over the loan without qualifying. If we can qualify, we can take it over at once. If this was an existing loan which was two years or more old, we could assume it without qualifying. Then we asked him to carry the $25,000 balance at only 10% with less than interest payments. So, our total payment would be $476.00 plus taxes and insurance.

REAL ESTATE PURCHASE CONTRACT AND RECEIPT FOR DEPOSIT

THIS IS MORE THAN A RECEIPT FOR MONEY. IT IS INTENDED TO BE A LEGALLY BINDING CONTRACT. READ IT CAREFULLY.

CALIFORNIA ASSOCIATION OF REALTORS® (CAR) STANDARD FORM

_____________________________ , California, _____________ , 19______

Received from _______ Dave Del Dotto and/or assignee _______

herein called Buyer, the sum of ________ -Two Hundred- ________ Dollars $ ______ 200.00

evidenced by cash ☐, cashier's check ☐, or Note in Escrow ☐, personal check ☐ payable to ______ A Reliable Title Company ______ , to be held uncashed until acceptance of this offer, as deposit on account of purchase price of

______ -Fifty Thousand- ______________________ Dollars $ ______ 50,000

for the purchase of property, situated in ______________ , County of ______________ , California, described as follows:

1. Buyer will deposit in escrow with ______________ the balance of purchase price as follows:

*A. Subject to the seller qualifying for and obtaining a new 1st loan from State Savings for $25,000. This loan will be an FHA loan with an interest rate of 10% with payments of approximately $219.39 per month. Buyer will then take over this loan - only after two years.

**B. Subject to the seller taking back a 2nd mortgage for $25,000 secured by a deed of trust on the subject property. The interest rate will be at 10% with less than interest payments of $150.00 per month. All unpaid principal and interest will be due and payable 7 years from the close of escrow.

C. Sale to include the refrigerator, washer, and dryer.

Set forth above any terms and conditions of a factual nature applicable to this sale, such as financing, prior sale of other property, the matter of structural pest control inspection, repairs and personal property to be included in the sale.

2. Deposit will ☐ will not ☐ be increased by $ ______ to $ ______ within ______ days of acceptance of this offer.

3. Buyer does ☐ does not ☐ intend to occupy subject property as his residence.

4. The following supplements are incorporated as part of this agreement:

☐ Structural Pest Control Certification Agreement   ☐ Occupancy Agreement   Other ☐ ______

☐ Special Studies Zone Disclosure   ☐ VA Amendment   ☐ ______

☐ Flood Insurance Disclosure   ☐ FHA Amendment   ☐ ______

5. Buyer and Seller shall deliver signed instructions to the escrow holder within ______ days from Seller's acceptance which shall provide for closing within ______ days from Seller's acceptance. Escrow fees to be paid as follows:

6. Buyer and Seller acknowledge receipt of a copy of this page, which constitutes Page 1 of ______ Pages.

Buyer ______________ Seller ______________

Buyer ______________ Seller ______________

A REAL ESTATE BROKER IS THE PERSON QUALIFIED TO ADVISE ON REAL ESTATE. IF YOU DESIRE LEGAL ADVICE CONSULT YOUR ATTORNEY.

(43) Buyer obtains 1st for 60% - seller caries 40% 2nd - annual payments

Many times a seller will want as much cash as possible when he sells and a cash flow on his note. But we always want to borrow the least amount the seller needs so our monthly payments will be as low as possible. We couldn't get him to accept no payments on his note, but we got him to accept annual interest only payments, which isn't too bad. We expect to sell the property before the second note becomes due, and expect appreciation and tax benefits to cover the interest payments.

REAL ESTATE PURCHASE CONTRACT AND RECEIPT FOR DEPOSIT Annual
THIS IS MORE THAN A RECEIPT FOR MONEY. IT IS INTENDED TO BE A LEGALLY BINDING CONTRACT. READ IT CAREFULLY. Pmts.
CALIFORNIA ASSOCIATION OF REALTORS® (CAR) STANDARD FORM

______________________________ , California. _______________ , 19__________

Received from ________ Dave Del Dotto and/or assignee ________

herein called Buyer, the sum of ________ -Five Hundred- ________ Dollars $________ 500.00

evidenced by cash ☐, cashier's check ☐, or Note in Escrow ☐, personal check ☐ payable to________ A Reliable Title Company ________ , to be held uncashed until acceptance of this offer, as deposit on account of purchase price of

________ -Fifty Six Thousand Five Hundred- ________ Dollars $________ 56,500

for the purchase of property, situated in ________________ , County of________________ , California, described as follows: ________ 1600 Robbie Avenue ________

1.   Buyer will deposit in escrow with ________________________ the balance of purchase price as follows:

A.   Subject to buyer obtaining a new 1st loan for $33,900 from a lender of his choice with interest not to exceed 10% including taxes and insurance. Payment is not to exceed $297.50 per month.

B.   The buyer agrees to execute a 2nd note secured by a deed of trust to the seller for $22,600 payable at 10% interest with annual interest only payments of $2,260 per year due each May 1st for a period of 7 years.

C.   Seller agrees to provide a clear pest report.

Set forth above any terms and conditions of a factual nature applicable to this sale, such as financing, prior sale of other property, the matter of structural pest control inspection, repairs and personal property to be included in the sale.

2.   Deposit will ☐ will not ☐ be increased by $________________ to $________________ within________________ days of acceptance of this offer.

3.   Buyer does ☐ does not ☐ intend to occupy subject property as his residence.

4.   The following supplements are incorporated as part of this agreement:

☐ Structural Pest Control Certification Agreement   ☐ Occupancy Agreement   ☐ Other ________

☐ Special Studies Zone Disclosure   ☐ VA Amendment   ☐ ________

☐ Flood Insurance Disclosure   ☐ FHA Amendment   ☐ ________

5.   Buyer and Seller shall deliver signed instructions to the escrow holder within ________________ days from Seller's acceptance which shall provide for closing within________________ days from Seller's acceptance. Escrow fees to be paid as follows:

6.   Buyer and Seller acknowledge receipt of a copy of this page, which constitutes Page 1 of________ Pages.

Buyer________________________   Seller ________________________

Buyer________________________   Seller ________________________

A REAL ESTATE BROKER IS THE PERSON QUALIFIED TO ADVISE ON REAL ESTATE. IF YOU DESIRE LEGAL ADVICE CONSULT YOUR ATTORNEY.

FOR ILLUSTRATION ONLY - Consult your attorney for legal advice ON CONTRACTS IN YOUR STATE
Reprinted with permission, California Association of Realtors®, Endorsment not implied

(44) Seller creates 1st for 60% - Buyer gets 20% 2nd - Seller carries 20% 3rd

* This seller was looking for a long term cash flow and we gave it to him.

** But this time the seller expected us to go get our own loan, he didn't want to hassle with the paper work. He ended up paying the loan fees because we stated he would receive the net loan. You will find most sellers will make you get the loan, but not always.

REAL ESTATE PURCHASE CONTRACT AND RECEIPT FOR DEPOSIT   20% 3rd
THIS IS MORE THAN A RECEIPT FOR MONEY. IT IS INTENDED TO BE A LEGALLY BINDING CONTRACT. READ IT CAREFULLY.
CALIFORNIA ASSOCIATION OF REALTORS® (CAR) STANDARD FORM

_____________________________, California ___________________, 19_______

Received from _______________ Dave Del Dotto and/or assignee _______________

herein called Buyer, the sum of ________ -One Thousand- ________________ Dollars $ __1,000.00__

evidenced by cash ☐, cashier's check ☐, or _Personal note_ ☐, personal check ☐ payable to ______ Seller ______

________________________, to be held uncashed until acceptance of this offer, as deposit on account of purchase price of

____ -Eighty Two Thousand- ___________________________ Dollars $ __82,000__

for the purchase of property, situated in ___________________, County of _____________________, California,

described as follows: ____________ 509 Riverbank Road ________________________

1.   Buyer will deposit in escrow with ____________________________________ the balance of purchase price as follows:

   *A.   Seller agrees to record a 1st note and deed of trust in
his favor executed by buyer for $49,200 payable at 12%
interest with payments of $514.00 per month amortized
over 30 years.

   *B.   Buyer agrees to apply for a new 2nd loan from Beneficial
Finance Corp. for $16,400 payable at 12% with payments
of approximately 196.83 per month amortized over 15 years.
Seller to receive the net proceeds from this loan.

   C.   Buyer will execute a 3rd note and deed of trust for
$16,400 to the seller payable at 10% interest with all
principal and interest due in one balloon payment 5
years from close of escrow.

Set forth above any terms and conditions of a factual nature applicable to this sale, such as financing, prior sale of other property, the matter of structural pest control inspection, repairs and personal property to be included in the sale.

2.   Deposit will ☐ will not ☐ be increased by $ __________ to $ __________ within __________ days of acceptance of this offer.

3.   Buyer does ☐ does not ☐ intend to occupy subject property as his residence

4   The following supplements are incorporated as part of this agreement.

Other
☐ Structural Pest Control Certification Agreement   ☐ Occupancy Agreement   ☐ ___________
☐ Special Studies Zone Disclosure   ☐ VA Amendment   ☐ ___________
☐ Flood Insurance Disclosure   ☐ FHA Amendment   ☐ ___________

5.   Buyer and Seller shall deliver signed instructions to the escrow holder within __________ days from Seller's acceptance which shall provide for closing within __________ days from Seller's acceptance. Escrow fees to be paid as follows:

6   Buyer and Seller acknowledge receipt of a copy of this page, which constitutes Page 1 of _______ Pages.

Buyer _________________________________   Seller _________________________________

Buyer _________________________________   Seller _________________________________

A REAL ESTATE BROKER IS THE PERSON QUALIFIED TO ADVISE ON REAL ESTATE. IF YOU DESIRE LEGAL ADVICE CONSULT YOUR ATTORNEY.

(45) Sell the Option while in Escrow

The idea here is to tie up a good deal, even if you do not have the means to close it yourself, and then "sell" the deal to someone else who takes your place. You can structure your offer with an escape clause to protect yourself, and then substitute the actual buyer as your "assignee" when time comes to close.

* You can wait until closing to designate the actual buyer who takes title, as long as you have included "and/or assignee" next to your name.

You will have a separate deal with the person you assign the purchase to, and charge him an "assignment fee" (not a commission).

This is a good method to get started when you don't have any cash or assets. All you need is a good deal and some imagination.

REAL ESTATE PURCHASE CONTRACT AND RECEIPT FOR DEPOSIT
THIS IS MORE THAN A RECEIPT FOR MONEY. IT IS INTENDED TO BE A LEGALLY BINDING CONTRACT. READ IT CAREFULLY.
CALIFORNIA ASSOCIATION OF REALTORS* (CAR) STANDARD FORM

_______________________________________ California, _______, 19_____

Received from _____ Dave Del Lotto and/or assignee _____

herein called Buyer, the sum of _____ -One Thousand- _____ Dollars $_____ 1,000.00

evidenced by cash ☐, cashier's check ☐, or _______________ ☐, personal check ☒ payable to_____ Escrow

Company ___________________ , to be held uncashed until acceptance of this offer, as deposit on account of purchase price of

-One Hundred Thousand- ___________________ Dollars $_____ 100,000

for the purchase of property, situated in _______________ , County of_______________ , California,

described as follows: _______________

1. Buyer will deposit in escrow with _____ Escrow Company _____ the balance of purchase price as follows:

*A. Buyer to designate at closing how title is
     to be taken.

B. (Other terms and escape clauses)

Set forth above any terms and conditions of a factual nature applicable to this sale, such as financing, prior sale of other property, the matter of structural pest control inspection, repairs and personal property to be included in the sale.

2. Deposit will ☐ will not ☐ be increased by $_______________ to $_______________ within_______________ days of acceptance of this offer.

3. Buyer does ☐ does not ☐ intend to occupy subject property as his residence.

4. The following supplements are incorporated as part of this agreement:

Other

☐ Structural Pest Control Certification Agreement ☐ Occupancy Agreement ☐ _______________

☐ Special Studies Zone Disclosure ☐ VA Amendment ☐ _______________

☐ Flood Insurance Disclosure ☐ FHA Amendment ☐ _______________

5. Buyer and Seller shall deliver signed instructions to the escrow holder within _______________ days from Seller's acceptance which shall provide for closing within_______________ days from Seller's acceptance. Escrow fees to be paid as follows:

6. Buyer and Seller acknowledge receipt of a copy of this page, which constitutes Page 1 of_______ Pages.

Buyer_______________ Seller _______________

Buyer_______________ Seller _______________

A REAL ESTATE BROKER IS THE PERSON QUALIFIED TO ADVISE ON REAL ESTATE. IF YOU DESIRE LEGAL ADVICE CONSULT YOUR ATTORNEY.

(46) Contingent on Dividing into Multi-Units

You may be able to take a property which is not worth much as a single family home and divide it into several separate dwelling units.

The division may be governed by local zoning regulations which usually take time to work through. You may have to request and receive a zoning change or variance.

You may have to do some alterations in the floor plan or access to water and other utilities, which costs you must calculate in your plan to purchase the property.

* Give yourself plenty of time to solve the unexpected governmental and legal problems that will arise. If at all possible, don't agree to a deadline, but instead tie the closing to when government approves the division. Make sure you get your deposit back if governmental approvals can not be obtained.

REAL ESTATE PURCHASE CONTRACT AND RECEIPT FOR DEPOSIT

THIS IS MORE THAN A RECEIPT FOR MONEY. IT IS INTENDED TO BE A LEGALLY BINDING CONTRACT. READ IT CAREFULLY.

CALIFORNIA ASSOCIATION OF REALTORS® (CAR) STANDARD FORM

____ , California, _________________ , 19_________

Received from ____

herein called Buyer, the sum of ________ -One Thousand-- ________________ Dollars $ __ 1,000.00

evidenced by cash ☐, cashier's check ☐, or ___________________ ☐, personal check ☒ payable to ______ Escrow

______ Company ________ , to be held uncashed until acceptance of this offer, as deposit on account of purchase price of

____ Dollars $_______________

for the purchase of property, situated in _______________________ , County of __________________ , California,

described as follows: ____

1.   Buyer will deposit in escrow with ________ Escrow Company ________ the balance of purchase price as follows:

*A.   Subject to buyer receiving all governmental
       approvals and securing necessary legal documents
       to divide property into 3 separate dwelling units.

B.   (Other terms and escape clauses)

Set forth above any terms and conditions of a factual nature applicable to this sale, such as financing, prior sale of other property, the matter of structural pest control inspection, repairs and personal property to be included in the sale.

2.   Deposit will ☐ will not ☐ be increased by $ ___________ to $ ___________ within ___________ days of acceptance of this offer.

3.   Buyer does ☐ does not ☐ intend to occupy subject property as his residence.

4.   The following supplements are incorporated as part of this agreement:

Other

☐ Structural Pest Control Certification Agreement   ☐ Occupancy Agreement   ☐ ___________

☐ Special Studies Zone Disclosure   ☐ VA Amendment   ☐ ___________

☐ Flood Insurance Disclosure   ☐ FHA Amendment   ☐ ___________

5.   Buyer and Seller shall deliver signed instructions to the escrow holder within ___________ days from Seller's acceptance which shall provide for closing within ___________ days from Seller's acceptance. Escrow fees to be paid as follows:

6.   Buyer and Seller acknowledge receipt of a copy of this page, which constitutes Page 1 of ___ Pages.

Buyer _______________________________   Seller _______________________________

Buyer _______________________________   Seller _______________________________

A REAL ESTATE BROKER IS THE PERSON QUALIFIED TO ADVISE ON REAL ESTATE. IF YOU DESIRE LEGAL ADVICE CONSULT YOUR ATTORNEY.

FOR ILLUSTRATION ONLY - Consult your attorney for legal advice ON CONTRACTS IN YOUR STATE

Reprinted with permission, California Association of Realtors®, Endorsment not implied

(47) Contingent on Approval for Shared Use

In vacation areas, you may be able to sell 2-month "shared owner-ships" to 6 people who use the property as a vacation home.

Shared use may be governed by local zoning regulations, which usually take time to work through. You may have to request and receive a zoning change or variance.

While you are working out the governmental approvals, use the time to market the 2-month ownerships. Divide the purchase price by 5. That way, you get to keep one of the six interests for your compensation. If you can get the other 5 purchasers lined up before closing, you will not have to come up with your own money for the actual purchase of the property.

* Give yourself plenty of time to solve the unexpected governmental and legal problems that will arise. If at all possible, don't agree to a deadline. Make sure you get your deposit back if governmental approvals cannot be obtained.

REAL ESTATE PURCHASE CONTRACT AND RECEIPT FOR DEPOSIT

THIS IS MORE THAN A RECEIPT FOR MONEY. IT IS INTENDED TO BE A LEGALLY BINDING CONTRACT. READ IT CAREFULLY.

CALIFORNIA ASSOCIATION OF REALTORS® (CAR) STANDARD FORM

___________________________________ , California. _______________________ , 19________

Received from ____

herein called Buyer, the sum of ____ -One Thousand- ________________ Dollars $____ 1,000.00

evidenced by cash ☐, cashier's check ☐, or ____________________ ☐, personal check ☐ payable to______ Escrow

______ Company ____________ , to be held uncashed until acceptance of this offer. as deposit on account of purchase price of

______ -One Hundred Thousand- __________________________________ Dollars $____ 100,000

for the purchase of property, situated in ________________________ , County of____________________ , California,

described as follows: ____

1.　　Buyer will deposit in escrow with ______ Escrow Company ______ the balance of purchase price as follows:

　　　　*A.　　Subject to buyer receiving all governmental
　　　　　　　approvals and securing necessary documents
　　　　　　　to utilize the property for 1/6 shared
　　　　　　　ownership plan.

　　　　 B.　　(Other terms and escape clauses)

Set forth above any terms and conditions of a factual nature applicable to this sale, such as financing, prior sale of other property, the matter of structural pest control inspection, repairs and personal property to be included in the sale.

2.　　Deposit will ☐ will not ☐ be increased by $ ________________ to $ ______________ within______________ days of acceptance of this offer.

3.　　Buyer does ☐ does not ☐ intend to occupy subject property as his residence.

4.　　The following supplements are incorporated as part of this agreement:

Other

☐ Structural Pest Control Certification Agreement　　☐ Occupancy Agreement　　☐ _______________

☐ Special Studies Zone Disclosure　　☐ VA Amendment　　☐ _______________

☐ Flood Insurance Disclosure　　☐ FHA Amendment　　☐ _______________

5.　　Buyer and Seller shall deliver signed instructions to the escrow holder within ________ days from Seller's acceptance which shall provide for closing within______________ days from Seller's acceptance. Escrow fees to be paid as follows

6.　　Buyer and Seller acknowledge receipt of a copy of this page. which constitutes Page 1 of ______ Pages.

Buyer ____________________________　　Seller ____________________________

Buyer ____________________________　　Seller ____________________________

A REAL ESTATE BROKER IS THE PERSON QUALIFIED TO ADVISE ON REAL ESTATE. IF YOU DESIRE LEGAL ADVICE CONSULT YOUR ATTORNEY.

CREATIVE FINANCING - CONTRACT EXAMPLES　　　　　　*Page A - 107*

(48) Contingent on Seller Assisted Subdividing

You may be able to take a property which is not worth much as a single family home and divide the land itself into separate lots, one or more of which can be sold or built upon. You may leave an existing single-family home or not, depending on its condition. This deal also works for raw land, where there are no improvements on the property, and the land is more valuable as several lots than as one.

Sub-division is governed by local zoning regulations which usually take time to work through. You may have to request and receive a zoning change or variance.

* Give yourself plenty of time to solve the unexpected governmental and legal problems that will arise, If at all possible, don't agree to a deadline. Make sure you get your deposit back if governmental approvals cannot be obtained.

REAL ESTATE PURCHASE CONTRACT AND RECEIPT FOR DEPOSIT

THIS IS MORE THAN A RECEIPT FOR MONEY. IT IS INTENDED TO BE A LEGALLY BINDING CONTRACT. READ IT CAREFULLY.

CALIFORNIA ASSOCIATION OF REALTORS® (CAR) STANDARD FORM

____ , California. ____________________ , 19______

Received from ____

herein called Buyer, the sum of ____ Dollars $ 1,000

evidenced by cash ☐, cashier's check ☐, or ____________________ ☐, personal check ☒ payable to ____ Escrow

______ Company ______ , to be held uncashed until acceptance of this offer, as deposit on account of purchase price of

____ Dollars $______________

for the purchase of property, situated in ____________________ , County of____________________ , California,

described as follows: ____

1.   Buyer will deposit in escrow with__________ Escrow Company __________ the balance of purchase price as follows:

*A.   Subject to lot being approved for subdivision into a
         seperate building lot for single family homes.

B.   Seller agrees to assist buyer in all matters
        necessary to receiving governmental approval
        for subdivision.

C.   (Other terms and escape clauses)

Set forth above any terms and conditions of a factual nature applicable to this sale, such as financing, prior sale of other property, the matter of structural pest control inspection, repairs and personal property to be included in the sale.

2.   Deposit will ☐ will not ☐ be increased by $ ____________ to $ ____________ within____________ days of acceptance of this offer.

3.   Buyer does ☐ does not ☐ intend to occupy subject property as his residence.

4.   The following supplements are incorporated as part of this agreement:

Other

☐ Structural Pest Control Certification Agreement   ☐ Occupancy Agreement   ☐ ________________

☐ Special Studies Zone Disclosure   ☐ VA Amendment   ☐ ________________

☐ Flood Insurance Disclosure   ☐ FHA Amendment   ☐ ________________

5.   Buyer and Seller shall deliver signed instructions to the escrow holder within ____________ days from Seller's acceptance which shall provide for closing within____________ days from Seller's acceptance. Escrow fees to be paid as follows:

6.   Buyer and Seller acknowledge receipt of a copy of this page. which constitutes Page 1 of ______ Pages.

Buyer ____________________________   Seller ____________________________

Buyer ____________________________   Seller ____________________________

A REAL ESTATE BROKER IS THE PERSON QUALIFIED TO ADVISE ON REAL ESTATE. IF YOU DESIRE LEGAL ADVICE CONSULT YOUR ATTORNEY

(49) Offer to Trustee in Bankruptcy

Bankruptcy Court is a fertile ground for offers. There are few people who know about the bankruptcy process, and fewer who understand that you can meet with the trustee of a bankrupt's Estate and negotiate a deal directly. The trustee has little time to check your financial status and is usually simply glad to see someone paying attention to the case. You can get basic information about cases from the clerk of the court, and details from the trustee assigned to each case. The court must approve every sale, but you may be the only one making an offer.

Once sale is approved by the court, you have time to raise the funds. These deals are usually all cash, but you should get a substantial discount, which can attract a financial partner who will put up the money for a percent of the profit or equity. A solution to a bankruptcy can be intriguing and profitable. (Try contacting all the creditors and have them discount for cash.)

* You can probably get the escrow company and trustee to hold your check without depositing it, until the sale is approved by the court (which may take some time, and you do not want your money tied up). You should argue that your offer really hasn't been accepted until the court approves it.

** You can also argue that since the property is usually unoccupied, you will have to inspect it just before closing. After all, it could be vandalized. This will allow you a final escape should you not want to proceed with the sale.

REAL ESTATE PURCHASE CONTRACT AND RECEIPT FOR DEPOSIT
THIS IS MORE THAN A RECEIPT FOR MONEY. IT IS INTENDED TO BE A LEGALLY BINDING CONTRACT. READ IT CAREFULLY.
CALIFORNIA ASSOCIATION OF REALTORS* (CAR) STANDARD FORM

_______________________________________ , California _________________________ , 19______

Received from ____ Dave Del Dotto and/or assignee ________________________________

herein called Buyer, the sum of ____ -One Thousand- ____________________ Dollars $____ 1,000 ____

evidenced by cash ☐, cashier's check ☐, or ________________ ☒, personal check ☐ payable to ____ Escrow ____

____ Company ____ , to be held uncashed until acceptance of this offer, as deposit on account of purchase price of

____ Dollars $________________

for the purchase of property, situated in ________________________ , County of ________________ , California,

described as follows: ____

1.   Buyer will deposit in escrow with __ Federal Bankruptcy Court __ the balance of purchase price as follows:

    *A.   Escrow shall hold check and not deposit such until
         sale is approved by Bankruptcy Court.

    B.   Trustee for Bankrupt shall give buyer full access
         to the property for inspection at reasonable times.

    **C.   Subject to final inspection and approval by buyer
         before closing.

    D.   Subject to approval of sale by Bankruptcy Court.

Set forth above any terms and conditions of a factual nature applicable to this sale, such as financing, prior sale of other property, the matter of structural pest control inspection, repairs and personal property to be included in the sale.

2.   Deposit will ☐ will not ☐ be increased by $ ________ to $ ________ within ________ days of acceptance of this offer.

3.   Buyer does ☐ does not ☐ intend to occupy subject property as his residence.

4.   The following supplements are incorporated as part of this agreement:

☐ Structural Pest Control Certification Agreement   ☐ Occupancy Agreement   Other ☐ ________________

☐ Special Studies Zone Disclosure   ☐ VA Amendment   ☐ ________________

☐ Flood Insurance Disclosure   ☐ FHA Amendment   ☐ ________________

5.   Buyer and Seller shall deliver signed instructions to the escrow holder within ________ days from Seller's acceptance which shall provide for closing within ________ days from Seller's acceptance. Escrow fees to be paid as follows:

6.   Buyer and Seller acknowledge receipt of a copy of this page, which constitutes Page 1 of ____ Pages.

Buyer ________________________________   Seller ________________________________

Buyer ________________________________   Seller ________________________________

A REAL ESTATE BROKER IS THE PERSON QUALIFIED TO ADVISE ON REAL ESTATE. IF YOU DESIRE LEGAL ADVICE CONSULT YOUR ATTORNEY.

(50) I.R.S. Seized Property Bid

The I.R.S. in your jurisdiction periodically holds sealed bid or open bid auctions of seized property. Check with my directory of U.S. Government Auctions, call up the I.R.S. and ask for information and get the name of the person who can help you. Get on the auction mailing list.

* You will have to abide by the bidding process established in your jurisdiction, which may include a form other than the standard purchase offer form I use here for illustration. But this form will get a dialogue started between you and the proper people at the agency, and they will quickly know you are serious.

* Get ready to pay cash for these deals. Line up your investors, so they will be ready to act at your call.

* When you purchase an I.R.S. property, you should get a deep discount on the price. There is a 6 month right of redemption on an I.R.S. property. If the owner redeems, you still get 18% interest on your money. After six months, if he doesn't redeem, you will probably have to create a friendly sale to someone you know at the real market value-then refinance the property at the then-established higher price. (Remember, a lender will only loan 70-90% of the property's appraised value, or what you paid for it—whichever is lower. So, if you bought a property at 50% of value, and then try to refinance, they may only give you 70- 90% of that 50%, unless you create a higher sale at the actual appraised value.)

REAL ESTATE PURCHASE CONTRACT AND RECEIPT FOR DEPOSIT
THIS IS MORE THAN A RECEIPT FOR MONEY. IT IS INTENDED TO BE A LEGALLY BINDING CONTRACT. READ IT CAREFULLY.
CALIFORNIA ASSOCIATION OF REALTORS® (CAR) STANDARD FORM

____ , California _________________________ , 19 __________

Received from ____
herein called Buyer, the sum of -Ten Thousand Dollars- _______________________ Dollars $ ___10,000____
evidenced by cash ☐, cashier's check ☒, or ___________________ ☐, personal check ☐ payable to _______________
_______________________________ , to be held uncashed until acceptance of this offer, as deposit on account of purchase price of
_____________________ -One Hundred Thousand - _____________________ Dollars $ ___100,000____
for the purchase of property, situated in _______________________ County of _______________________ , California,
described as follows: ____

1.　　Buyer will deposit in escrow with　　Escrow Company　　　　the balance of purchase price as follows:

_____*A.　Buyer agrees to follow established bid proceedure
_________prescribed by I.R.S.

_____ B.　(Other terms and escape clauses)

Set forth above any terms and conditions of a factual nature applicable to this sale, such as financing, prior sale of other property,
the matter of structural pest control inspection, repairs and personal property to be included in the sale.

2.　　Deposit will ☐ will not ☐ be increased by $ _______________ to $ _______________ within _______________ days of
acceptance of this offer.

3.　　Buyer does ☐ does not ☐ intend to occupy subject property as his residence.

4.　　The following supplements are incorporated as part of this agreement:

☐ Structural Pest Control Certification Agreement　　☐ Occupancy Agreement　Other ☐ _______________
☐ Special Studies Zone Disclosure　　　　　　　　☐ VA Amendment　　　　　☐ _______________
☐ Flood Insurance Disclosure　　　　　　　　　　☐ FHA Amendment　　　　　☐ _______________

5.　　Buyer and Seller shall deliver signed instructions to the escrow holder within _______________ days from Seller's acceptance which
shall provide for closing within _______________ days from Seller's acceptance. Escrow fees to be paid as follows:

6.　　Buyer and Seller acknowledge receipt of a copy of this page, which constitutes Page 1 of _______ Pages.

Buyer _______________________________ Seller _______________________________

Buyer _______________________________ Seller _______________________________

A REAL ESTATE BROKER IS THE PERSON QUALIFIED TO ADVISE ON REAL ESTATE. IF YOU DESIRE LEGAL ADVICE CONSULT YOUR ATTORNEY.

FOR ILLUSTRATION ONLY - Consult your attorney for legal advice ON CONTRACTS IN YOUR STATE
Reprinted with permission, California Association of Realtors®, Endorsment not implied

(51) Probate Sale

"Probate" is the legal term for the process by which a court settles the affairs of someone who has passed away. The assets of the deceased are called the "estate" and the person in charge of selling or distributing the estate is called the "personal representative" or "executor". Many pieces of real property from such estates are being sold all the time at bargain prices without the public actually being aware. A small public notice of the opening of a probate is usually posted in the legal notices in the newspaper (near the foreclosure sales) which names the executor (and sometimes the attorney who filed the papers). Then you can normally find that person listed in the phone book. Call them up and find out the details. If you act early you can make some good deals.

* Most probate sales are subject to approval by the Probate court, which usually gives approval without question unless the price is extremely low.

* Since the property is probably unoccupied during the time of probate, you may wish to include this clause to allow you to back out if the property is damaged before closing.

REAL ESTATE PURCHASE CONTRACT AND RECEIPT FOR DEPOSIT

THIS IS MORE THAN A RECEIPT FOR MONEY. IT IS INTENDED TO BE A LEGALLY BINDING CONTRACT. READ IT CAREFULLY.

CALIFORNIA ASSOCIATION OF REALTORS® (CAR) STANDARD FORM

_________________________ , California. _________________________ , 19 _________

Received from _________________________

herein called Buyer, the sum of _________________ —Ten Thousand— _______________ Dollars $ 10,000

evidenced by cash ☐, cashier's check ☐, or _________________ ☐, personal check ☒ payable to _______ Escrow

_____ Company _____ , to be held uncashed until acceptance of this offer, as deposit on account of purchase price of

_________________________ Dollars $ _________________

for the purchase of property, situated in _________________ , County of _________________ , California.

described as follows: _________________

1.   Buyer will deposit in escrow with _________ Escrow Company _________ the balance of purchase price as follows:

*A.   Seller is executor (personal representative) of X
estate. Sale is subject to approval of Probate
Court on or before 30 August, 19--

**B.   Subject to buyer's final inspection and approval
before close of escrow.

C.   Subject to buyer qualifying for conventional loan
of $90,000 at 10% annual interest, 30 year term
by close of escrow.

D.   (Other terms and escape clauses)

Set forth above any terms and conditions of a factual nature applicable to this sale, such as financing, prior sale of other property, the matter of structural pest control inspection, repairs and personal property to be included in the sale.

2.   Deposit will ☐ will not ☐ be increased by $ _________________ to $ _________________ within _________________ days of acceptance of this offer.

3.   Buyer does ☐ does not ☐ intend to occupy subject property as his residence.

4   The following supplements are incorporated as part of this agreement:

Other

☐ Structural Pest Control Certification Agreement   ☐ Occupancy Agreement   ☐ _________________

☐ Special Studies Zone Disclosure   ☐ VA Amendment   ☐ _________________

☐ Flood Insurance Disclosure   ☐ FHA Amendment   ☐ _________________

5   Buyer and Seller shall deliver signed instructions to the escrow holder within _________________ days from Seller's acceptance which shall provide for closing within _________________ days from Seller's acceptance. Escrow fees to be paid as follows:

6.   Buyer and Seller acknowledge receipt of a copy of this page, which constitutes Page 1 of _________ Pages.

Buyer _________________________   Seller _________________________

Buyer _________________________   Seller _________________________

A REAL ESTATE BROKER IS THE PERSON QUALIFIED TO ADVISE ON REAL ESTATE. IF YOU DESIRE LEGAL ADVICE CONSULT YOUR ATTORNEY.

CREATIVE FINANCING - CONTRACT EXAMPLES   *PAGE A - 115*

(52) 30% REFI - HOUSE FOR DOWN
- NO PAYMENT SECOND

* This time we have a few houses we bought a few years back that we purchased with no money down and have packaged them up for a trade. We have created an equity in the trade and have ended up with a low monthly holding cost on the land. It may be easier to sell the land with easy terms to generate some cash than to try and sell our houses.

REAL ESTATE PURCHASE CONTRACT AND RECEIPT FOR DEPOSIT
THIS IS MORE THAN A RECEIPT FOR MONEY. IT IS INTENDED TO BE A LEGALLY BINDING CONTRACT. READ IT CAREFULLY.
CALIFORNIA ASSOCIATION OF REALTORS® (CAR) STANDARD FORM

_______________________________, California, _____________, 19____

Received from ___ Dave Del Dotto and/or assignee ___
herein called Buyer, the sum of ___ -One Hundred- ___ Dollars $___ 100.00 ___
evidenced by cash ☐, cashier's check ☐, or ___ Note in Escrow ☐, personal check ☐ payable to ___ A Reliable Title Company ___, to be held uncashed until acceptance of this offer, as deposit on account of purchase price of
___ -One Hundred Sixty Thousand- ___ Dollars $ ___ 160,000 ___
for the purchase of property, situated in _____________________, County of _________________ California,
described as follows: ___ 1600 Mapes Road ___

1.   Buyer will deposit in escrow with _________________________ the balance of purchase price as follows:

   A.   Buyer will trade three houses located at 1402, 1404, 1406
       Torado Avenue, Modesto with an equity of $60,000 to the
       seller upon the following conditions:

       1.   The seller will agree to refinance his land with Farmer's
          Home 13-1/4% money for $48,000 with annual payments of no
          more than $6,600 per year, amortized over 30 years. The
          seller will then keep this money as part of the down payment.

       2.   The seller agrees to finance the remaining $52,000 for the
          buyer at 9% interest with all principal and interest due in
          one balloon payment seven years from close of escrow.

       3.   Buyer may pay entire second note owed to seller off at
          any time with the annual crop with no prepayment penalty
          to the buyer.

Set forth above any terms and conditions of a factual nature applicable to this sale, such as financing, prior sale of other property, the matter of structural pest control inspection, repairs and personal property to be included in the sale.

2.   Deposit will ☐ will not ☐ be increased by $ ___________ to $ ___________ within ___________ days of acceptance of this offer

3.   Buyer does ☐ does not ☐ intend to occupy subject property as his residence.

4.   The following supplements are incorporated as part of this agreement:

Other
☐ Structural Pest Control Certification Agreement   ☐ Occupancy Agreement   ☐ _______________
☐ Special Studies Zone Disclosure   ☐ VA Amendment   ☐ _______________
☐ Flood Insurance Disclosure   ☐ FHA Amendment   ☐ _______________

5.   Buyer and Seller shall deliver signed instructions to the escrow holder within ___________ days from Seller's acceptance which shall provide for closing within ___________ days from Seller's acceptance. Escrow fees to be paid as follows:

6.   Buyer and Seller acknowledge receipt of a copy of this page, which constitutes Page 1 of _______ Pages

Buyer _________________________   Seller _________________________

Buyer _________________________   Seller _________________________

A REAL ESTATE BROKER IS THE PERSON QUALIFIED TO ADVISE ON REAL ESTATE. IF YOU DESIRE LEGAL ADVICE CONSULT YOUR ATTORNEY

(53) 50% Refi - prepay 1st - 50% 2nd

* Where else can you get annual payments at 13-3/4% interest at a time when most interest is 16-18 percent?

** We are having the seller borrow $10,000 more than he needed so we could pay the first payment a year in advance. That way we have no payments until the second year. And what do you think we do with the crop and rental money for two years? If you guessed go to the Caribbean, you are right!

REAL ESTATE PURCHASE CONTRACT AND RECEIPT FOR DEPOSIT

THIS IS MORE THAN A RECEIPT FOR MONEY. IT IS INTENDED TO BE A LEGALLY BINDING CONTRACT. READ IT CAREFULLY.

CALIFORNIA ASSOCIATION OF REALTORS* (CAR) STANDARD FORM

____ , California. ____________________ , 19_______

Received from _________ Dave Del Dotto and/or assignee _______________

herein called Buyer, the sum of __________ -One Thousand- __________ Dollars $___ 1,000 ____

evidenced by cash ☐, cashier's check ☐, or Note in Escrow ☐, personal check ☐ payable to ___ A Reliable

___ Title Company _______ , to be held uncashed until acceptance of this offer, as deposit on account of purchase price of

___ -One Hundred Forty Thousand- ___________________ Dollars $_____ 140,000

for the purchase of property, situated in _______________________ , County of _______________ , California,

described as follows: ___________ 1100 Hugerson Road ___________

1. Buyer will deposit in escrow with ________________________________ the balance of purchase price as follows:

    *A. This offer is subject to the buyer assisting the seller
        in obtaining a new first loan from Farmer's Home for
        $70,000. This loan will be payable at 13-3/4% interest
        and amortized over 40 years with annual payments of
        $9,322.92 per year.

    ** The loan proceeds will be distributed as follows:

        1. Buyer to be credited $10,000 for the first year's
           payment on the first loan.

        2. Seller shall receive all proceeds less the loan
           origination costs and the first year's interest
           on the first loan.

    B. The seller agrees to finance a total of $80,000 for the
        buyer secured by a second note and deed of trust payable
        at 10% interest with less than interest payments of $4,000
        per year. All unpaid principal and interest will be due and
        payable 10 years from close of escrow.

Set forth above any terms and conditions of a factual nature applicable to this sale, such as financing, prior sale of other property,
the matter of structural pest control inspection, repairs and personal property to be included in the sale.

2. Deposit will ☐ will not ☐ be increased by $ ________________ to $ ______________ within _______________ days of
acceptance of this offer.

3. Buyer does ☐ does not ☐ intend to occupy subject property as his residence.

4. The following supplements are incorporated as part of this agreement:

                                        Other

☐ Structural Pest Control Certification Agreement   ☐ Occupancy Agreement   ☐ ________________

☐ Special Studies Zone Disclosure   ☐ VA Amendment   ☐ ________________

☐ Flood Insurance Disclosure   ☐ FHA Amendment   ☐ ________________

5. Buyer and Seller shall deliver signed instructions to the escrow holder within ___________ days from Seller's acceptance which
shall provide for closing within ______________ days from Seller's acceptance. Escrow fees to be paid as follows:

6. Buyer and Seller acknowledge receipt of a copy of this page, which constitutes Page 1 of ______ Pages.

Buyer ___________________________________ Seller ___________________________________

Buyer ___________________________________ Seller ___________________________________

A REAL ESTATE BROKER IS THE PERSON QUALIFIED TO ADVISE ON REAL ESTATE. IF YOU DESIRE LEGAL ADVICE CONSULT YOUR ATTORNEY

FOR ILLUSTRATION ONLY - Consult your attorney for legal advice ON CONTRACTS IN YOUR STATE
Reprinted with permission, California Association of Realtors®, Endorsement not implied

(54) Buyer obtains New Farmer's Home 1st for 40% - 60% 2nd - Pocket Crop

* To qualify for one of these farm loans you must have farming experience. So if you are a city slicker, either forget it, or find a farmer to front for you or go in partnership with you.

** It is always smart to ask for personal property with the sale. And when it comes to farm land, there is always a lot of equipment you can ask for with the house. If you are not into farming, you can sell the equipment for cash.

REAL ESTATE PURCHASE CONTRACT AND RECEIPT FOR DEPOSIT   pocket
THIS IS MORE THAN A RECEIPT FOR MONEY. IT IS INTENDED TO BE A LEGALLY BINDING CONTRACT. READ IT CAREFULLY.   crop
CALIFORNIA ASSOCIATION OF REALTORS" (CAR) STANDARD FORM

_______________ , California. _______________ , 19_______

Received from _______________ Dave Del Dotto and/or assignee _______________

herein called Buyer, the sum of _______ -One Thousand- _______ Dollars $ 1,000.00

evidenced by cash ☐, cashier s check ☐, or _____ Note in Escrow ☑, personal check ☐ payable to _______ A Reliable

Title Company _______ , to be held uncashed until acceptance of this offer, as deposit on account of purchase price of

-One Hundred Twenty-Seven Thousand- Dollars $ 127,000

for the purchase of property, situated in _______________ , County of _______________ , California,

described as follows: _______ 2900 Estle Road _______

1   Buyer will deposit in escrow with _______________ the balance of purchase price as follows:

*A.   Subject to the buyer applying and qualifying for a
new first loan with Farmer's Home for $50,000 with
an interest rate of 13-1/2% with payments of
approximately $575.00 per month.

B.   Subject to the buyer executing a second note and deed
of trust to the seller for $77,000 payable at 10%
interest with annual payments of $7,700 of interest
only for 10 years.

C.   Seller agrees to allow the buyer to harvest the crop
at seller's expense.

**D.   Sale to include the tractor, disc, rake, and shop equipment.

Set forth above any terms and conditions of a factual nature applicable to this sale, such as financing, prior sale of other property,
the matter of structural pest control inspection, repairs and personal property to be included in the sale.

2   Deposit will ☐ will not ☐ be increased by $ _______ to $ _______ within _______ days of
acceptance of this offer

3   Buyer does ☐ does not ☐ intend to occupy subject property as his residence

4   The following supplements are incorporated as part of this agreement:

☐ Structural Pest Control Certification Agreement   ☐ Occupancy Agreement   Other ☐ _______
☐ Special Studies Zone Disclosure   ☐ VA Amendment   ☐ _______
☐ Flood Insurance Disclosure   ☐ FHA Amendment   ☐ _______

5   Buyer and Seller shall deliver signed instructions to the escrow holder within _______ days from Seller s acceptance which
shall provide for closing within _______ days from Seller's acceptance. Escrow fees to be paid as follows.

6   Buyer and Seller acknowledge receipt of a copy of this page, which constitutes Page 1 of _______ Pages

Buyer _______________   Seller _______________

Buyer _______________   Seller _______________

A REAL ESTATE BROKER IS THE PERSON QUALIFIED TO ADVISE ON REAL ESTATE IF YOU DESIRE LEGAL ADVICE CONSULT YOUR ATTORNEY.

(55) ASSUME 1ST - NEW 2ND - 3RD
WITH PRINCIPAL BALLOONS

* If you apply for this loan be sure to create a down payment for the amount the seller is willing to carry back and then record the third later. If you show a contract like this to a lender, where you are getting 100% financing, he will probably have a heart attack.

** This guy was hard to deal with. He came form the old school that stated a buyer must always pay down the principal on a loan. So instead of paying him monthly we agreed to make principal reduction payments every five years.

REAL ESTATE PURCHASE CONTRACT AND RECEIPT FOR DEPOSIT

THIS IS MORE THAN A RECEIPT FOR MONEY. IT IS INTENDED TO BE A LEGALLY BINDING CONTRACT. READ IT CAREFULLY.

CALIFORNIA ASSOCIATION OF REALTORS® (CAR) STANDARD FORM

_______________________________ , California. _______________________ , 19_______

Received from ________ David Del Dotto and/or assignee ________

herein called Buyer, the sum of ________ -One Thousand- ________ Dollars $ 1,000.00

evidenced by cash ☐, cashier's check ☐, or _Note in Escrow_ ☐, personal check ☐ payable to ____ A Reliable

____ Title Company ____ , to be held uncashed until acceptance of this offer, as deposit on account of purchase price of

____ -One Hundred Nineteen Thousand- ____ Dollars $ 119,000

for the purchase of property, situated in _______________________ , County of _______________________ , California,

described as follows: ________ 7800 Gates Road ________

1.   Buyer will deposit in escrow with _______________________ the balance of purchase price as follows:

A.   Buyer to qualify for and assume existing loan of $40,000
      payable at 7% interest with payments of $250.00 per month

*B.   Subject to the buyer obtaining a new second loan from
      Farmer's Home for $40,000 payable at 13-1/4% interest
      with annual payments of $5,400 per year. This loan will
      be amortized over 30 years.

**C. Subject to the buyer executing a third note and deed
      of trust for $39,000 to the seller payable at 9%
      interest with monthly interest only payments of
      $292.50 per month. Buyer agrees to make principal
      reduction payments of $5,000 each five years until
      note is paid in full.

Set forth above any terms and conditions of a factual nature applicable to this sale, such as financing, prior sale of other property, the matter of structural pest control inspection, repairs and personal property to be included in the sale.

2.   Deposit will ☐ will not ☐ be increased by $_______________ to $_______________ within_______________ days of acceptance of this offer.

3.   Buyer does ☐ does not ☐ intend to occupy subject property as his residence.

4.   The following supplements are incorporated as part of this agreement.

Other

☐ Structural Pest Control Certification Agreement   ☐ Occupancy Agreement   ☐ _______________

☐ Special Studies Zone Disclosure   ☐ VA Amendment   ☐ _______________

☐ Flood Insurance Disclosure   ☐ FHA Amendment   ☐ _______________

5.   Buyer and Seller shall deliver signed instructions to the escrow holder within __________ days from Seller's acceptance which shall provide for closing within_______________ days from Seller's acceptance. Escrow fees to be paid as follows:

6.   Buyer and Seller acknowledge receipt of a copy of this page, which constitutes Page 1 of________ Pages.

Buyer_______________________   Seller _______________________

Buyer_______________________   Seller _______________________

A REAL ESTATE BROKER IS THE PERSON QUALIFIED TO ADVISE ON REAL ESTATE. IF YOU DESIRE LEGAL ADVICE CONSULT YOUR ATTORNEY.

(56) REFI 1ST 50% - WRAP-AROUND ANNUAL PAYMENT

* This time the owner gets a new first loan for $73,000 and puts the cash in his pocket. He then wraps the loan and finances the place for the new buyer. Since the seller's payments are annual, he can pass annual payments on to the buyer.

** Always check the well or water system when buying small acreages. They can be quite costly to dig later if they fail.

REAL ESTATE PURCHASE CONTRACT AND RECEIPT FOR DEPOSIT

THIS IS MORE THAN A RECEIPT FOR MONEY. IT IS INTENDED TO BE A LEGALLY BINDING CONTRACT. READ IT CAREFULLY.

CALIFORNIA ASSOCIATION OF REALTORS® (CAR) STANDARD FORM

_________________________, California, _____________, 19____

Received from _____ Dave Del Dotto and/or assignee _____

herein called Buyer, the sum of _____ -One Thousand- _____ Dollars $ 1,000.00

evidenced by cash ☐, cashier's check ☐, or Note in Escrow ☐, personal check ☐ payable to _____ A Reliable Title Company _____, to be held uncashed until acceptance of this offer, as deposit on account of purchase price of

_____ -One Hundred Forty-Five Thousand- _____ Dollars $ 145,000

for the purchase of property, situated in _____, County of _____, California,

described as follows: _____ 7500 Edsel Lane _____

1. Buyer will deposit in escrow with _____ the balance of purchase price as follows:

    A. Seller will obtain a new first loan from Farmer's
        Home Loans for $73,000 payable at 13-3/4% interest
        with annual payments of $9,600 amortized over 30 years.

    *B. Seller agrees to finance $145,000 on an all inclusive
         deed of trust for the buyer with 10% interest. The
         buyer agrees to pay $15,264 per year annually for
         15 years, then loan will be due and payable.

    **C. Subject to inspection of the well by a professional
          and approved by buyer.

Set forth above any terms and conditions of a factual nature applicable to this sale, such as financing, prior sale of other property, the matter of structural pest control inspection, repairs and personal property to be included in the sale.

2. Deposit will ☐ will not ☐ be increased by $ _____ to $ _____ within _____ days of acceptance of this offer.

3. Buyer does ☐ does not ☐ intend to occupy subject property as his residence.

4. The following supplements are incorporated as part of this agreement:

		Other
☐ Structural Pest Control Certification Agreement	☐ Occupancy Agreement	☐ _____
☐ Special Studies Zone Disclosure	☐ VA Amendment	☐ _____
☐ Flood Insurance Disclosure	☐ FHA Amendment	☐ _____

5. Buyer and Seller shall deliver signed instructions to the escrow holder within _____ days from Seller's acceptance which shall provide for closing within _____ days from Seller's acceptance. Escrow fees to be paid as follows:

6. Buyer and Seller acknowledge receipt of a copy of this page, which constitutes Page 1 of _____ Pages.

Buyer _____________________ Seller _____________________

Buyer _____________________ Seller _____________________

A REAL ESTATE BROKER IS THE PERSON QUALIFIED TO ADVISE ON REAL ESTATE. IF YOU DESIRE LEGAL ADVICE CONSULT YOUR ATTORNEY.

CREATIVE FINANCING - CONTRACT EXAMPLES   *PAGE A - 125*

(57) LEASE - OPTION ON FORECLOSURE

* This particular ranchette was foreclosed on by Farmer's Home Administration. They agreed to a lease-option for one year if just the first loan of $400.00 per month was paid. Then at the end of the year they would put a new second loan on the property with $10,000 down. The property was below market value, so by agreeing to lease-option the property we can control the property for one year and then sell it if we want. Now is the time to call Farmer's Home Administration for properties they have taken back. Believe me, there are many.

REAL ESTATE PURCHASE CONTRACT AND RECEIPT FOR DEPOSIT
THIS IS MORE THAN A RECEIPT FOR MONEY. IT IS INTENDED TO BE A LEGALLY BINDING CONTRACT. READ IT CAREFULLY.
CALIFORNIA ASSOCIATION OF REALTORS' (CAR) STANDARD FORM

_____________________________________ , California. _______________ , 19______

Received from _______ Dave Del Dotto and/or assignee _______

herein called Buyer, the sum of _____ -One Hundred- _____ Dollars $ 100.00

evidenced by cash ☐, cashier's check ☐, or Note in Escrow ☐, personal check ☐ payable to _____ A Reliable Title Company _____ , to be held uncashed until acceptance of this offer, as deposit on account of purchase price of

_____ -One Hundred Twenty Thousand- _____ Dollars $ 120,000

for the purchase of property, situated in _________________ , County of _________________ , California, described as follows: _____ 7800 Teirnan Road _____

1. Buyer will deposit in escrow with _________________ the balance of purchase price as follows:

   *A. Buyer agrees to lease this 10-acre ranchette paying all underlying loans for one year with the option of purchase for the above stated price.

   B. The existing first loan is for $60,000 payable at 6% interest with payments of $300.00 per month. This loan is a private loan with 15 years left to pay.

   C. Farmer's Home Administration agrees to put a new $50,000 second loan on the property at the end of one year when the option is taken. This loan will include 13-3/4% interest amortized over 30 years with annual payments.

   D. Buyer will put $10,000 cash down at the end of the year.

Set forth above any terms and conditions of a factual nature applicable to this sale, such as financing, prior sale of other property, the matter of structural pest control inspection, repairs and personal property to be included in the sale.

2. Deposit will ☐ will not ☐ be increased by $_________ to $_________ within _________ days of acceptance of this offer.

3. Buyer does ☐ does not ☐ intend to occupy subject property as his residence.

4. The following supplements are incorporated as part of this agreement:

☐ Structural Pest Control Certification Agreement   ☐ Occupancy Agreement   Other ☐ _________
☐ Special Studies Zone Disclosure   ☐ VA Amendment   ☐ _________
☐ Flood Insurance Disclosure   ☐ FHA Amendment   ☐ _________

5. Buyer and Seller shall deliver signed instructions to the escrow holder within _________ days from Seller's acceptance which shall provide for closing within _________ days from Seller's acceptance. Escrow fees to be paid as follows:

6. Buyer and Seller acknowledge receipt of a copy of this page, which constitutes Page 1 of _____ Pages.

Buyer _____________________________ Seller _____________________________

Buyer _____________________________ Seller _____________________________

A REAL ESTATE BROKER IS THE PERSON QUALIFIED TO ADVISE ON REAL ESTATE. IF YOU DESIRE LEGAL ADVICE CONSULT YOUR ATTORNEY

(58) Farmer's Home - Low Income Loan

* This is a maximum loan on a new house in California's Central Valley. In other areas the price will be different.

** The Farmer's Home program makes an effort to provide new low income housing. If new units are unavailable they will loan on other low income units. They have income qualifications, usually the lower end of the scale, and will subsidize a person's payments in accordance with his income. It is a nothing down program to low income applicants. If you don't qualify for the program, you may be able to use it to sell a property by telling a qualified buyer about it and helping him or her contact the right people.

*** Qualified applicants can usually work with the contractor to finish his house, or get his existing house upgraded over the standard Farmer's Home house.

REAL ESTATE PURCHASE CONTRACT AND RECEIPT FOR DEPOSIT
THIS IS MORE THAN A RECEIPT FOR MONEY. IT IS INTENDED TO BE A LEGALLY BINDING CONTRACT. READ IT CAREFULLY.
CALIFORNIA ASSOCIATION OF REALTORS® (CAR) STANDARD FORM

_______________________________________ , California, _____________ , 19________

Received from ____ Dave Del Dotto and/or assignee

herein called Buyer, the sum of -One Hundred- ___________________________ Dollars $ 100.00

evidenced by cash ☐, cashier's check ☐, or Note in Escrow ☐, personal check ☐ payable to____ A Reliable

Title Company ______ , to be held uncashed until acceptance of this offer, as deposit on account of purchase price of

-Forty Five Thousand- _______________________ Dollars $ 45,000*

for the purchase of property, situated in ________________________ , County of_______________________ , California,

described as follows: ____

1. Buyer will deposit in escrow with ___________________________________ the balance of purchase price as follows:

    A. This offer is subject to the buyer qualifying
       for a new first loan of $45,000 from the Farmer's
       Home Administration. The payments will be determined
       by Farmer's Home qualifications.

    B. The buyer is qualified for the program with a yearly
       gross income of $15,000 per year.

    *****C.** The builder agrees to allow the buyer to finish plumbing,
       painting, and sheetrocking with a credit for alloted bids
       going to the buyer.

Set forth above any terms and conditions of a factual nature applicable to this sale, such as financing, prior sale of other property, the matter of structural pest control inspection, repairs and personal property to be included in the sale.

2. Deposit will ☐ will not ☐ be increased by $ _______________ to $ ______________ within______________ days of acceptance of this offer.

3. Buyer does ☐ does not ☐ intend to occupy subject property as his residence.

4. The following supplements are incorporated as part of this agreement:

                                    Other

☐ Structural Pest Control Certification Agreement   ☐ Occupancy Agreement   ☐ _________________

☐ Special Studies Zone Disclosure   ☐ VA Amendment   ☐ _________________

☐ Flood Insurance Disclosure   ☐ FHA Amendment   ☐ _________________

5. Buyer and Seller shall deliver signed instructions to the escrow holder within _________ days from Seller's acceptance which shall provide for closing within______________ days from Seller's acceptance. Escrow fees to be paid as follows:

____

6. Buyer and Seller acknowledge receipt of a copy of this page, which constitutes Page 1 of______ Pages.

Buyer ___________________________   Seller ___________________________

Buyer ___________________________   Seller ___________________________

A REAL ESTATE BROKER IS THE PERSON QUALIFIED TO ADVISE ON REAL ESTATE. IF YOU DESIRE LEGAL ADVICE CONSULT YOUR ATTORNEY.

Creative Contracts:
Land Bank Loans

(59) Land Bank 70% First - 30% Second

(60) New Income Property Exchange - 60% Refinance

(61) Land Bank 40% Refinance - Annual Payments - Split Second and Third

(62) Land Bank 30% Created First - 40% Second - Wrap-Around

(59) LAND BANK 70% FIRST - 30% SECOND

* The Land Bank loans are probably the best interest rates and terms a farmer can get. The rate is subject to change in your area. One drawback of this loan is that not only are there loan origination fees, but also they require that you purchase stock in their corporation. In this particular offer we asked for all the stock to be credited to us when we purchase, which would be worth around 10% of the gross loan amount.

REAL ESTATE PURCHASE CONTRACT AND RECEIPT FOR DEPOSIT

THIS IS MORE THAN A RECEIPT FOR MONEY. IT IS INTENDED TO BE A LEGALLY BINDING CONTRACT. READ IT CAREFULLY.

CALIFORNIA ASSOCIATION OF REALTORS® (CAR) STANDARD FORM

_______________________________________, California _______________, 19______

Received from _____ David Del Dotto and/or assignee _____

herein called Buyer, the sum of _____ -One Hundred- _____ Dollars $_____ 100.00 _____

evidenced by cash ☐, cashier's check ☐, or _Note in Escrow_ ☐, personal check ☐ payable to _A Reliable_

Title Company, to be held uncashed until acceptance of this offer, as deposit on account of purchase price of

-One Hundred Twenty-Five Thousand- Dollars $_____ 125,000 _____

for the purchase of property, situated in _______________________, County of _________________, California,

described as follows: _____ 2700 Hammett Road _____

1.   Buyer will deposit in escrow with _______________________ the balance of purchase price as follows:

*A.   Seller agrees to obtain a new first loan from the
      Land Bank for $87,500 with 11-3/4% interest with
      monthly payments of approximately $880.00 per month.
      Buyer will then qualify for and assume this loan.

      1.   Any stock purchased will be credited to the buyer.

B.   The buyer will execute a second note and deed of trust
      to the seller for $37,500 payable at 10% interest with
      monthly payments of $312.50 per month interest only payable
      for 10 years.

C.   Sale to include all farm equipment.

Set forth above any terms and conditions of a factual nature applicable to this sale, such as financing, prior sale of other property, the matter of structural pest control inspection, repairs and personal property to be included in the sale.

2.   Deposit will ☐ will not ☐ be increased by $ _______________ to $ _______________ within _____________ days of acceptance of this offer.

3.   Buyer does ☐ does not ☐ intend to occupy subject property as his residence.

4.   The following supplements are incorporated as part of this agreement:

☐ Structural Pest Control Certification Agreement   ☐ Occupancy Agreement   Other
☐ Special Studies Zone Disclosure   ☐ VA Amendment   ☐ _______________
☐ Flood Insurance Disclosure   ☐ FHA Amendment   ☐ _______________
                                                                              ☐ _______________

5.   Buyer and Seller shall deliver signed instructions to the escrow holder within _____________ days from Seller's acceptance which shall provide for closing within _____________ days from Seller's acceptance. Escrow fees to be paid as follows:

6.   Buyer and Seller acknowledge receipt of a copy of this page, which constitutes Page 1 of _____ Pages.

Buyer _______________________________   Seller _______________________________

Buyer _______________________________   Seller _______________________________

A REAL ESTATE BROKER IS THE PERSON QUALIFIED TO ADVISE ON REAL ESTATE. IF YOU DESIRE LEGAL ADVICE CONSULT YOUR ATTORNEY.

FOR ILLUSTRATION ONLY - Consult your attorney for legal advice ON CONTRACTS IN YOUR STATE

Reprinted with permission, California Association of Realtors®, Endorsement not implied

CREATIVE FINANCING - CONTRACT EXAMPLES   PAGE A - 133

(60) New Income Property Exchange - 60% Refinance

* Here again builders should take a second look. We are trading in a new home, which must be free and clear, for the full market value and putting it down on a small farm that we can have refinanced at 11-3/4% interest. If we have a loan for the construction, we can ask the seller to borrow enough to pay off our construction loan. Then he can carry the difference in a second.

REAL ESTATE PURCHASE CONTRACT AND RECEIPT FOR DEPOSIT

THIS IS MORE THAN A RECEIPT FOR MONEY. IT IS INTENDED TO BE A LEGALLY BINDING CONTRACT. READ IT CAREFULLY.

CALIFORNIA ASSOCIATION OF REALTORS® (CAR) STANDARD FORM

_____________________, California. _______________, 19_______

Received from ____________ David Del Dotto and/or assignee ____________

herein called Buyer, the sum of ________ -One Thousand- ________ Dollars $____ 1,000.00

evidenced by cash ☐, cashier's check ☐, or Note in Escrow ☐, personal check ☐ payable to____ A Reliable

Title Company ____, to be held uncashed until acceptance of this offer, as deposit on account of purchase price of

-One Hundred Sixty-Five Thousand- ____________ Dollars $____ 165,000

for the purchase of property, situated in __________________, County of__________________, California,

described as follows: ________ 6871 Dunn Road __________________

1.   Buyer will deposit in escrow with __________________ the balance of purchase price as follows:

*A.   Buyer will trade a new house located at 2709 Wesson
       Ranch Road presently under construction and valued
       at $66,000 to the seller upon the following terms:

       1.   Seller agrees to obtain a new Land Bank loan on
             his ranch for $99,000 payable at 11-3/4% with
             payments of approximately $12,000 per year
             amortized over 30 years.

       2.   Buyer will then take over this loan subject to.

       3.   Buyer will take over any corporate stock at no
             cost to buyer.

 B.   Sale to include all shop equipment and tractor.

Set forth above any terms and conditions of a factual nature applicable to this sale, such as financing, prior sale of other property, the matter of structural pest control inspection, repairs and personal property to be included in the sale.

2.   Deposit will ☐ will not ☐ be increased by $____________ to $____________ within____________ days of acceptance of this offer.

3.   Buyer does ☐ does not ☐ intend to occupy subject property as his residence.

4.   The following supplements are incorporated as part of this agreement:

		Other
☐ Structural Pest Control Certification Agreement	☐ Occupancy Agreement	☐ ____________
☐ Special Studies Zone Disclosure	☐ VA Amendment	☐ ____________
☐ Flood Insurance Disclosure	☐ FHA Amendment	☐ ____________

5.   Buyer and Seller shall deliver signed instructions to the escrow holder within ____________ days from Seller's acceptance which shall provide for closing within____________ days from Seller's acceptance. Escrow fees to be paid as follows:

6.   Buyer and Seller acknowledge receipt of a copy of this page, which constitutes Page 1 of ________ Pages.

Buyer __________________   Seller __________________

Buyer __________________   Seller __________________

A REAL ESTATE BROKER IS THE PERSON QUALIFIED TO ADVISE ON REAL ESTATE. IF YOU DESIRE LEGAL ADVICE CONSULT YOUR ATTORNEY.

(61) LAND BANK 40% REFINANCE - ANNUAL PAYMENTS - SPLIT SECOND AND THIRD

* The name of the game is real estate control with a minimum cash flow investment. Here we are splitting the seller's equity of $111,000 into a second and third. With payments of annual interest only on $55,000 and no payments on the third we should be able to get some farm income off the land to come out really well.

REAL ESTATE PURCHASE CONTRACT AND RECEIPT FOR DEPOSIT

THIS IS MORE THAN A RECEIPT FOR MONEY. IT IS INTENDED TO BE A LEGALLY BINDING CONTRACT. READ IT CAREFULLY.

CALIFORNIA ASSOCIATION OF REALTORS® (CAR) STANDARD FORM

____ , California, _________________ , 19______

Received from ______ David Del Dotto and/or assignee

herein called Buyer, the sum of ______ -One Thousand- ______ Dollars $ 1,000.00

evidenced by cash ☐, cashier's check ☐, or Note in Escrow ☐, personal check ☐ payable to ______ A Reliable Title Company ______ , to be held uncashed until acceptance of this offer, as deposit on account of purchase price of -One Hundred Eight-Five Thousand- ______ Dollars $ 185,000

for the purchase of property, situated in _________________ , County of _________________ , California,

described as follows: ______ 2507 Wine Road

1. Buyer will deposit in escrow with _________________________________ the balance of purchase price as follows:

    A. Buyer will assist seller in obtaining a new first loan for $74,000 from the Land Bank. This loan will include 11-3/4% interest with payments of $9,000 per year amortized over 30 years. Buyer agrees to qualify for and assume this loan.

    *B. Buyer will execute a second note and deed of trust in favor of the seller for $55,000 payable at 9% interest with annual interest only payments of $4,950. This loan will be for a period of 15 years then all principal and interest will be due and payable.

    C. Buyer will execute a third note and deed of trust in favor of the seller for $56,000 payable at 10% interest with all principal and interest due in one balloon payment five years from the close of escrow. Buyer has the option to pay entire balance off at any time with no prepayment penalty.

Set forth above any terms and conditions of a factual nature applicable to this sale, such as financing, prior sale of other property, the matter of structural pest control inspection, repairs and personal property to be included in the sale.

2. Deposit will ☐ will not ☐ be increased by $ _________________ to $ _________________ within _________________ days of acceptance of this offer.

3. Buyer does ☐ does not ☐ intend to occupy subject property as his residence.

4. The following supplements are incorporated as part of this agreement:

Other

☐ Structural Pest Control Certification Agreement   ☐ Occupancy Agreement   ☐ _________________

☐ Special Studies Zone Disclosure   ☐ VA Amendment   ☐ _________________

☐ Flood Insurance Disclosure   ☐ FHA Amendment   ☐ _________________

5. Buyer and Seller shall deliver signed instructions to the escrow holder within _________________ days from Seller's acceptance which shall provide for closing within _________________ days from Seller's acceptance. Escrow fees to be paid as follows:

6. Buyer and Seller acknowledge receipt of a copy of this page, which constitutes Page 1 of ______ Pages.

Buyer ____ _________________________________ Seller _________________________________

Buyer ____ _________________________________ Seller _________________________________

A REAL ESTATE BROKER IS THE PERSON QUALIFIED TO ADVISE ON REAL ESTATE. IF YOU DESIRE LEGAL ADVICE CONSULT YOUR ATTORNEY.

(62) Land Bank 30% Created First - 40% Second - Wrap-Around

* You are going to run across a conservative seller sometimes who won't trust you to make the payments. In this contract the seller wanted first position for 30% of his equity. He then agreed to borrow $63,600 from the Land Bank to put in his pocket. But instead of carrying a third he decided he would wrap the existing loans and be the bank. This way he could make sure the payments were being made. Having the seller wrap loans puts him or her in a better position, psychologically.

REAL ESTATE PURCHASE CONTRACT AND RECEIPT FOR DEPOSIT
THIS IS MORE THAN A RECEIPT FOR MONEY. IT IS INTENDED TO BE A LEGALLY BINDING CONTRACT. READ IT CAREFULLY.
CALIFORNIA ASSOCIATION OF REALTORS® (CAR) STANDARD FORM

_______________________________________ , California, _______________________ , 19_________

Received from ________ David Del Dotto and/or assignee ________________

herein called Buyer, the sum of ________ -One Thousand- ________ Dollars $ 1,000.00

evidenced by cash ☐, cashier's check ☐, or Note in Escrow ☐, personal check ☐ payable to A Reliable Title Company , to be held uncashed until acceptance of this offer, as deposit on account of purchase price of -One Hundred Fifty-Nine Thousand- ____________ Dollars $ 159,000

for the purchase of property, situated in __________________________ , County of ____________________ , California,

described as follows: ________ 2917 Vintage Road ________

1.   Buyer will deposit in escrow with _________________________ the balance of purchase price as follows:

*A.   Buyer agrees to execute a note secured by a first
      deed of trust for $47,700 payable to the seller at
      10% interest with annual interest only payments of
      $4,770 per year. This loan will be for a period of
      20 years, then will be all due and payable.

B.   Subject to the seller obtaining a new Land Bank
      loan in the amount of $63,000 payable at 11-3/4%
      interest with annual payments of $7,500 per year
      amortized over 30 years.

C.   The seller then agrees to finance the entire balance
      of $159,000 on an all inclusive wrap-around note and
      deed of trust payable at 10% interest with annual
      interst payments of $15,900 per year for a period
      of 15 years. All payments to seller will be sent
      to Security Pacific Bank and then all underlying
      loans will be disbursed from there.

Set forth above any terms and conditions of a factual nature applicable to this sale, such as financing, prior sale of other property, the matter of structural pest control inspection, repairs and personal property to be included in the sale.

2.   Deposit will ☐ will not ☐ be increased by $ ____________ to $ ____________ within ____________ days of acceptance of this offer.

3.   Buyer does ☐ does not ☐ intend to occupy subject property as his residence.

4.   The following supplements are incorporated as part of this agreement:

Other
☐ Structural Pest Control Certification Agreement   ☐ Occupancy Agreement   ☐ ____________
☐ Special Studies Zone Disclosure   ☐ VA Amendment   ☐ ____________
☐ Flood Insurance Disclosure   ☐ FHA Amendment   ☐ ____________

5.   Buyer and Seller shall deliver signed instructions to the escrow holder within ____________ days from Seller's acceptance which shall provide for closing within ____________ days from Seller's acceptance. Escrow fees to be paid as follows:

6.   Buyer and Seller acknowledge receipt of a copy of this page, which constitutes Page 1 of ______ Pages.

Buyer _________________________________   Seller _________________________________

Buyer _________________________________   Seller _________________________________

A REAL ESTATE BROKER IS THE PERSON QUALIFIED TO ADVISE ON REAL ESTATE. IF YOU DESIRE LEGAL ADVICE CONSULT YOUR ATTORNEY.

CREATIVE CONTRACTS:
FORECLOSURES

(63) Take Over First - Take Over Second - Lender Advances Payments - $2,000 Down Prepaid Payments

(64) Take Over First - New Second from Another Second Lender - Discount on Price

(65) Take Over First - New Second by Existing Lender at Less Interest - No Points

(66) Foreclosure - Create New 50 Percent First at a Discount over Former Loan - New 50 Percent Second - Prepay First

(67) Foreclosure - Create New First at lower rate- New Second with Construction Draws

(68) Take Over First - New Second - Larger than Previous Second - Construction Loan to Finish in Second

(69) Take Over First - Renegotiate First to Waive Interest - Second Lender Waives Second Interest

(70) Lease Option from Lender - Rehabilitate at Set Price

(71) Equity Share with Lender

(63) Take Over First - Take Over Second - Lender Advances Payments - $2,000 Down Prepaid Payments

* What lenders won't do these days with their foreclosed on properties! If you have any inhibitions about asking lenders to finance in ways you wouldn't believe possible, get rid of them. The lenders will very often deal! By the way, this first loan was available for a 95% refinance from FNMA, which the second lender didn't pay attention to, and by spending $5,000 on remodeling this unit was turned into a triplex with a positive cash flow and $30,000 in equity. Are you still wondering where money can be made in real estate in tight times? (This deal was made in 1982, but you'll find cooperative lenders any time.)

REAL ESTATE PURCHASE CONTRACT AND RECEIPT FOR DEPOSIT $2,000

THIS IS MORE THAN A RECEIPT FOR MONEY. IT IS INTENDED TO BE A LEGALLY BINDING CONTRACT. READ IT CAREFULLY. down

CALIFORNIA ASSOCIATION OF REALTORS® (CAR) STANDARD FORM

prepaid

________________________________ , California. _____________________ , 19__________

Received from _________________ David Del Dotto and/or assignee

herein called Buyer, the sum of ____________ -One Hundred- ____________ Dollars $ _____ 100.00

evidenced by cash ☐, cashier's check ☐, or Note in Escrow ☐, personal check ☐ payable to _____ A Reliable Title Company _____ , to be held uncashed until acceptance of this offer, as deposit on account of purchase price of ____ -Fifty One Thousand- ____ Dollars $ _____ 51,000

for the purchase of property, situated in ____________________ , County of ____________________ , California,

described as follows: _______ 127 Lane Street _______

1. Buyer will deposit in escrow with ____________________ the balance of purchase price as follows:

   *A. This offer is subject to the buyer qualifying for and
       taking over the existing first loan of $41,000 from
       Capitol Pacific Mortgage. This loan is payable at
       11-3/4% interest with payments of $420.00 per month
       including taxes and insurance.

   B. The present second lender, Transamerica Financial,
       agrees to the following:

      1. will make up all back payments on the first loan

      2. will waive all back interest due on the second loan

      3. will rewrite a new second loan for $10,000 to the
         buyer at 12% with no loan fees

   C. Buyer agrees to advance $2,000 to prepay the payments
      on the first and second loans at close of escrow.

Set forth above any terms and conditions of a factual nature applicable to this sale, such as financing, prior sale of other property, the matter of structural pest control inspection, repairs and personal property to be included in the sale.

2. Deposit will ☐ will not ☐ be increased by $ ____________ to $ ____________ within ____________ days of acceptance of this offer.

3. Buyer does ☐ does not ☐ intend to occupy subject property as his residence.

4. The following supplements are incorporated as part of this agreement:

Other

☐ Structural Pest Control Certification Agreement   ☐ Occupancy Agreement   ☐ ____________________

☐ Special Studies Zone Disclosure   ☐ VA Amendment   ☐ ____________________

☐ Flood Insurance Disclosure   ☐ FHA Amendment   ☐ ____________________

5. Buyer and Seller shall deliver signed instructions to the escrow holder within ____________ days from Seller's acceptance which shall provide for closing within ____________ days from Seller's acceptance. Escrow fees to be paid as follows:

6. Buyer and Seller acknowledge receipt of a copy of this page, which constitutes Page 1 of ______ Pages.

Buyer ____________________________________ Seller ____________________________________

Buyer ____________________________________ Seller ____________________________________

A REAL ESTATE BROKER IS THE PERSON QUALIFIED TO ADVISE ON REAL ESTATE. IF YOU DESIRE LEGAL ADVICE CONSULT YOUR ATTORNEY.

(64) Take Over First - New Second from Another Second Lender - Discount on Price

* In this particular contract the existing second lender was willing to discount his note $7,000 to get his loan paid off. You see, a second lender in a foreclosure is very motivated to get *something* out of his or her loan, so you can often negotiate profitable concessions. This can work even if the foreclosed property is over-encumbered—the lender knows the property won't support the existing loan, and will negotiate. This house was worth $72,000, and not over-encumbered, so a new second could be arranged to pay off the old one. Sometimes the lender holding the second will both discount the old loan and give you a new loan to pay off the discounted balance.

REAL ESTATE PURCHASE CONTRACT AND RECEIPT FOR DEPOSIT

THIS IS MORE THAN A RECEIPT FOR MONEY. IT IS INTENDED TO BE A LEGALLY BINDING CONTRACT. READ IT CAREFULLY.

CALIFORNIA ASSOCIATION OF REALTORS™ (CAR) STANDARD FORM

_______________________________, California _______________, 19____

Received from _______ David Del Dotto and/or assignee _______

herein called Buyer, the sum of _______ -One Hundred- _______ Dollars $ 100.00

evidenced by cash ☐, cashier's check ☐, or Note in Escrow ☐, personal check ☐ payable to _____ A Reliable

Title Company _____, to be held uncashed until acceptance of this offer, as deposit on account of purchase price of

_____ -Sixty Thousand- _____ Dollars $ $60,000

for the purchase of property, situated in _____________, County of _____________, California,

described as follows: _______ 1259 Mine Shaft Road _______

1. Buyer will deposit in escrow with _____________ the balance of purchase price as follows:

   A. Buyer to qualify for and take over existing 1st loan of
      $27,000 payable at 8% interest. This loan is with Colonial
      Mortgage with payments of $245.00 per month.

   *B. Subject to buyer receiving a new 2nd loan from Beneficial
      Finance of $33,000 payable at 17% interest with payments
      of $507.88 per month amortized over 15 years.

   C. This new 2nd loan will pay off the existing loan of
      $40,000 payable to Household Finance Corp., which the
      lender is discounting due to foreclosure action.

Set forth above any terms and conditions of a factual nature applicable to this sale, such as financing, prior sale of other property, the matter of structural pest control inspection, repairs and personal property to be included in the sale.

2. Deposit will ☐ will not ☐ be increased by $ _____________ to $ _____________ within _____________ days of acceptance of this offer.

3. Buyer does ☐ does not ☐ intend to occupy subject property as his residence.

4. The following supplements are incorporated as part of this agreement:

☐ Structural Pest Control Certification Agreement ☐ Occupancy Agreement Other ☐ _____________

☐ Special Studies Zone Disclosure ☐ VA Amendment ☐ _____________

☐ Flood Insurance Disclosure ☐ FHA Amendment ☐ _____________

5. Buyer and Seller shall deliver signed instructions to the escrow holder within _____________ days from Seller's acceptance which shall provide for closing within _____________ days from Seller's acceptance. Escrow fees to be paid as follows:

6. Buyer and Seller acknowledge receipt of a copy of this page, which constitutes Page 1 of _____ Pages.

Buyer _____________ Seller _____________

Buyer _____________ Seller _____________

A REAL ESTATE BROKER IS THE PERSON QUALIFIED TO ADVISE ON REAL ESTATE. IF YOU DESIRE LEGAL ADVICE CONSULT YOUR ATTORNEY

FOR ILLUSTRATION ONLY - Consult your attorney for legal advice ON CONTRACTS IN YOUR STATE
Reprinted with permission, California Association of Realtors®, Endorsement not implied

(65) Take Over First - New Second by Existing Lender at Less Interest - No Points

* Lenders who take properties back in lieu of foreclosure will often help investors with lower than the market interest rates, especially if the market is slow and interest is high. In distressed areas, they'll almost beg people to take on the loans, just to help them get something out of the property—especially if they are second lenders, as in this example. There is always good money to be made from distressed property, and more than ever when times are tough.

REAL ESTATE PURCHASE CONTRACT AND RECEIPT FOR DEPOSIT and no
THIS IS MORE THAN A RECEIPT FOR MONEY. IT IS INTENDED TO BE A LEGALLY BINDING CONTRACT. READ IT CAREFULLY. points
CALIFORNIA ASSOCIATION OF REALTORS® (CAR) STANDARD FORM

_______________________________________ , California, _______________ , 19_______

Received from ________________ David Del Dotto and/or assignee

herein called Buyer, the sum of ____________ -One Hundred- ____________ Dollars $____ 100.00

evidenced by cash ☐, cashier's check ☐, or Note in Escrow ☐, personal check ☐ payable to____ A Reliable

Title Company ____, to be held uncashed until acceptance of this offer, as deposit on account of purchase price of

____ -Fifty Eight Thousand- ____________________ Dollars $ 58,000

for the purchase of property, situated in ________________________ , County of ________________ , California,

described as follows: ________ 1105 Groveland Trail

1.   Buyer will deposit in escrow with ________________________________ the balance of purchase price as follows:

A.   Subject to the buyer qualifying for and taking over
     the existing 1st loan in the amount of $32,000 from
     Continental Mortgage Co. This loan, payable at 9%
     interest, is payable at $285.00 per month.

*B.   Existing 2nd lender, Granite Home Loans, agrees to rewrite
      the existing 2nd loan of $22,000 to $26,000 to pay all
      interest advances that have been made on loans that were
      in arrears. The lender agrees to provide the loan at 14%
      interest, with interest only payments for 3 years of $303.33
      per month. Also, there will be no loan fees charged the buyer.

C.   The buyer is a licensed real estate agent.

Set forth above any terms and conditions of a factual nature applicable to this sale, such as financing, prior sale of other property, the matter of structural pest control inspection, repairs and personal property to be included in the sale.

2.   Deposit will ☐ will not ☐ be increased by $________________ to $________________ within________________ days of acceptance of this offer.

3.   Buyer does ☐ does not ☐ intend to occupy subject property as his residence.

4.   The following supplements are incorporated as part of this agreement:

☐ Structural Pest Control Certification Agreement ☐ Occupancy Agreement Other ☐ ________________

☐ Special Studies Zone Disclosure ☐ VA Amendment ☐ ________________

☐ Flood Insurance Disclosure ☐ FHA Amendment ☐ ________________

5.   Buyer and Seller shall deliver signed instructions to the escrow holder within ________ days from Seller's acceptance which shall provide for closing within________________ days from Seller's acceptance. Escrow fees to be paid as follows:

6.   Buyer and Seller acknowledge receipt of a copy of this page, which constitutes Page 1 of________ Pages.

Buyer________________________________ Seller________________________________

Buyer________________________________ Seller________________________________

A REAL ESTATE BROKER IS THE PERSON QUALIFIED TO ADVISE ON REAL ESTATE. IF YOU DESIRE LEGAL ADVICE CONSULT YOUR ATTORNEY.

FOR ILLUSTRATION ONLY - Consult your attorney for legal advice ON CONTRACTS IN YOUR STATE
Reprinted with permission, California Association of Realtors®, Endorsement not implied

(66) Foreclosure - Create New 50 Percent First at a Discount over Former Loan - New 50 Percent Second - Prepay First

* The seller here was a group of people who had invested money in a mortgage company that had filed bankruptcy. The investors were put together as beneficiaries on a 1st note and deed of trust. They had to foreclose on the property and take it back. They didn't want it, so they offered to discount their original note of $80,000 down to $37,000 in cash and a $37,000 note all due in 3 years. By borrowing a new second loan we could leverage into the property with 100% financing and get a discount on the 1st. We even got 1 year's interest free. Does this give you any ideas of what people will do if faced with a property received in foreclosure that they don't want?

REAL ESTATE PURCHASE CONTRACT AND RECEIPT FOR DEPOSIT new 50%

THIS IS MORE THAN A RECEIPT FOR MONEY. IT IS INTENDED TO BE A LEGALLY BINDING CONTRACT. READ IT CAREFULLY. 2nd-
CALIFORNIA ASSOCIATION OF REALTORS* (CAR) STANDARD FORM

prepay 1st

_____________________________ , California. _____________________ , 19_________

Received from _______ David Del Dotto and/or assignee

herein called Buyer, the sum of _______ -One Hundred- _______ Dollars $____ 100.00

evidenced by cash ☐, cashier's check ☐, or Note in Escrow ☐, personal check ☐ payable to________

___________________ , to be held uncashed until acceptance of this offer, as deposit on account of purchase price of

_______ -Seventy Four Thousand- _______ Dollars $____ 74,000

for the purchase of property, situated in _______________ , County of_______________ , California.

described as follows: _______ 1400 N. Highland Blvd.

1. Buyer will deposit in escrow with _________________ the balance of purchase price as follows:

*A. The sellers agree to discount the existing 1st loan of
$80,000 they are carrying as beneficiaries to $74,000,
providing the following terms are made:

1. Buyer will obtain a new 2nd loan from a lender of
buyer's choice at terms agreeable to the buyer for
$37,000 and pay down the existing 1st loan to sellers.

2. Sellers remaining discounted balance of $37,000 secured
by a 1st deed of trust will be payable at 10% interest
with monthly payments of $308.33 interest only for 3
years. There will be no prepayment penalty to the buyer.

a. The remaining balance of $37,000 will include the
first year's interest of approximately $4,000 on
the balance so that buyer will have no payment
during the first year from the close of escrow.

B. Sellers to provide a clean pest report.

Set forth above any terms and conditions of a factual nature applicable to this sale, such as financing, prior sale of other property, the matter of structural pest control inspection, repairs and personal property to be included in the sale.

2. Deposit will ☐ will not ☐ be increased by $ _____________ to $ _____________ within_____________ days of acceptance of this offer.

3. Buyer does ☐ does not ☐ intend to occupy subject property as his residence.

4. The following supplements are incorporated as part of this agreement:

Other

☐ Structural Pest Control Certification Agreement ☐ Occupancy Agreement ☐ ___________

☐ Special Studies Zone Disclosure ☐ VA Amendment ☐ ___________

☐ Flood Insurance Disclosure ☐ FHA Amendment ☐ ___________

5. Buyer and Seller shall deliver signed instructions to the escrow holder within ___________ days from Seller's acceptance which shall provide for closing within_____________ days from Seller's acceptance. Escrow fees to be paid as follows:

6. Buyer and Seller acknowledge receipt of a copy of this page, which constitutes Page 1 of_______ Pages.

Buyer_________________________ Seller _________________________

Buyer_________________________ Seller _________________________

A REAL ESTATE BROKER IS THE PERSON QUALIFIED TO ADVISE ON REAL ESTATE. IF YOU DESIRE LEGAL ADVICE CONSULT YOUR ATTORNEY.

(67) Foreclosure - Create New First at lower rate - New Second with Construction Draws

* In this case the first lender had to foreclose on a new building that was unfinished. They had no idea what it would take to finish the construction. It just looked like a big mess to them. So, saviors that we are, we offered to borrow on a new second and finish the construction. Of course, we asked the 1st lender to discount the note and discount the interest rate. The second lender wanted to protect his money by loaning in allotments of $5,000. After the building is done it will be worth $50,000 more than we paid. Not bad!

REAL ESTATE PURCHASE CONTRACT AND RECEIPT FOR DEPOSIT

THIS IS MORE THAN A RECEIPT FOR MONEY. IT IS INTENDED TO BE A LEGALLY BINDING CONTRACT. READ IT CAREFULLY.

CALIFORNIA ASSOCIATION OF REALTORS® (CAR) STANDARD FORM

____ , California. _______________ , 19________

Received from ______ David Del Dotto and/or assignee _______

herein called Buyer, the sum of ______ -One Hundred- ______ Dollars $__ 100.00 __

evidenced by cash ☐, cashier's check ☐, or _Note in Escrow_ ☐, personal check ☐ payable to______ A Reliable

______ Title Company ______ , to be held uncashed until acceptance of this offer, as deposit on account of purchase price of

______ -Seventy Seven Thousand- ______ Dollars $____ 77,000 ____

for the purchase of property, situated in_________________________ , County of___________________________ , California,

described as follows: ______ 8900 Sonora Road ______

1. Buyer will deposit in escrow with_________________________ the balance of purchase price as follows:

______ *A. Sellers agree to rewite the terms of the existing
______ 1st loan they have foreclosed on to the following:

______ 1. A new 1st loan of $57,000 secured by a deed of
______ trust executed by seller at 12% interest with
______ monthly payments of $570.00 per month for 5 years.
______ Loan will not include a prepayment penalty.

______ B. Subject to the buyer obtaining a new 2nd loan of $20,000
______ from Beneficial Finance Co. upon the following terms:

______ 1. Buyer will receive draws of $5,000 per draw during
______ course of construction of the building as inspected
______ by the lender. Buyer agrees to finish the building
______ within 90 days from close of this escrow. The note
______ interest rate will be at 12% interest with payments
______ of 200.00 interest only for 5 years.

Set forth above any terms and conditions of a factual nature applicable to this sale, such as financing, prior sale of other property, the matter of structural pest control inspection, repairs and personal property to be included in the sale.

2. Deposit will ☐ will not ☐ be increased by $_______________ to $______________ within______________ days of acceptance of this offer.

3. Buyer does ☐ does not ☐ intend to occupy subject property as his residence.

4. The following supplements are incorporated as part of this agreement:

Other

☐ Structural Pest Control Certification Agreement   ☐ Occupancy Agreement   ☐ _______________

☐ Special Studies Zone Disclosure   ☐ VA Amendment   ☐ _______________

☐ Flood Insurance Disclosure   ☐ FHA Amendment   ☐ _______________

5. Buyer and Seller shall deliver signed instructions to the escrow holder within ___________ days from Seller's acceptance which shall provide for closing within_______________ days from Seller's acceptance. Escrow fees to be paid as follows:

6. Buyer and Seller acknowledge receipt of a copy of this page, which constitutes Page 1 of_______ Pages.

Buyer___________________________________   Seller ___________________________________

Buyer___________________________________   Seller ___________________________________

A REAL ESTATE BROKER IS THE PERSON QUALIFIED TO ADVISE ON REAL ESTATE. IF YOU DESIRE LEGAL ADVICE CONSULT YOUR ATTORNEY.

CREATIVE FINANCING - CONTRACT EXAMPLES   *PAGE A - 151*

(68) Take Over First - New Second - Larger than Previous Second - Construction Loan to Finish

* This time the buyer has agreed to finish up the remodelling of a home with his own funds. Then the lender will put a new 2nd loan on the property and give back the money the buyer spent. Thus, your typical nothing down deal. Believe it or not, there are a lot of people who have started to remodel and then gone broke. When the lenders get it back they've got a problem, and they're likely to be real happy when we offer to solve it.

REAL ESTATE PURCHASE CONTRACT AND RECEIPT FOR DEPOSIT to

THIS IS MORE THAN A RECEIPT FOR MONEY. IT IS INTENDED TO BE A LEGALLY BINDING CONTRACT. READ IT CAREFULLY. finish

CALIFORNIA ASSOCIATION OF REALTORS® (CAR) STANDARD FORM

_______________________________ , California, _______________________ , 19_______

Received from ___________________ David Del Dotto and/or assignee ___________________

herein called Buyer, the sum of _____________ -One Hundred- _____________ Dollars $ _____ 100.00

evidenced by cash ☐, cashier's check ☐, or Note in Escrow ☐, personal check ☐ payable to______ A Reliable

Title Company ______ , to be held uncashed until acceptance of this offer, as deposit on account of purchase price of

_____________ -Sixty five Thousand- _____________ Dollars $ ___ 65,000

for the purchase of property, situated in _________________________ , County of_________________ , California,

described as follows: _____________ 999 Mellow Lane _____________

1.   Buyer will deposit in escrow with_________________________________ the balance of purchase price as follows:

    A.   Buyer agrees to take over 1st loan of $40,000 from
        Colonial Mortgage Co. This loan is payable at 10%
        interest with payments of $380.00 per month.

    *B.   The seller who has acquired the property through
        foreclosure and holds title agrees to the following:

        1.   The seller representing Beneficial Finance Corporation
            will rewrite a new 2nd loan in the amount of $25,000
            payable at 15% interest with payments of $349.90 per
            month amortized for 15 years.

        2.   Buyer agrees to finish the construction with his own
            funds and then be reimbursed by the new 2nd loan.

    C.   The buyer is a licensed real estate agent.

Set forth above any terms and conditions of a factual nature applicable to this sale, such as financing, prior sale of other property, the matter of structural pest control inspection, repairs and personal property to be included in the sale.

2.   Deposit will ☐ will not ☐ be increased by $ _____________ to $ _____________ within_______________ days of acceptance of this offer.

3.   Buyer does ☐ does not ☐ intend to occupy subject property as his residence.

4.   The following supplements are incorporated as part of this agreement:

Other

☐ Structural Pest Control Certification Agreement   ☐ Occupancy Agreement   ☐ _______________

☐ Special Studies Zone Disclosure   ☐ VA Amendment   ☐ _______________

☐ Flood Insurance Disclosure   ☐ FHA Amendment   ☐ _______________

5.   Buyer and Seller shall deliver signed instructions to the escrow holder within _____________ days from Seller's acceptance which shall provide for closing within_______________ days from Seller's acceptance. Escrow fees to be paid as follows:

6.   Buyer and Seller acknowledge receipt of a copy of this page, which constitutes Page 1 of______ Pages.

Buyer_____________________________________ Seller_____________________________________

Buyer_____________________________________ Seller_____________________________________

A REAL ESTATE BROKER IS THE PERSON QUALIFIED TO ADVISE ON REAL ESTATE. IF YOU DESIRE LEGAL ADVICE CONSULT YOUR ATTORNEY.

FOR ILLUSTRATION ONLY - Consult your attorney for legal advice ON CONTRACTS IN YOUR STATE

Reprinted with permission, California Association of Realtors®, Endorsement not implied

CREATIVE FINANCING - CONTRACT EXAMPLES   *PAGE A - 153*

(69) Take Over First - Renegotiate First to Waive Interest - Second Lender Waives Second Interest

* Usually when lenders get in a spot they will write off any existing interest that's been accumulating on the property during the foreclosure. Always try and kick the terms around with them, but always play dumb. It's not good to act too smart with the lenders. Act dumb, and always take them to lunch and cocktails. Express to them how conservative you are and that you wouldn't make a bad deal to put anybody in jeopardy. Tell them you want to help them market their property but that if you're going to be around to help them in the future, you can't afford a bad investment. Thus they have to bend a little to make your investment pencil out. If you help them, they'll help you.

REAL ESTATE PURCHASE CONTRACT AND RECEIPT FOR DEPOSIT waives
THIS IS MORE THAN A RECEIPT FOR MONEY. IT IS INTENDED TO BE A LEGALLY BINDING CONTRACT. READ IT CAREFULLY. 2nd
CALIFORNIA ASSOCIATION OF REALTORS® (CAR) STANDARD FORM
interest

_______________________________________ , California, __________ , 19 _______

Received from ___________ David Del Dotto and/or assignee ___________

herein called Buyer, the sum of __________ -One Hundred- __________ , Dollars $ ___ 100.00

evidenced by cash ☐, cashier's check ☐, or Note in Escrow ☐, personal check ☐ payable to Seller

_______________________ , to be held uncashed until acceptance of this offer, as deposit on account of purchase price of

_____ -Fifty Nine Thousand- _________________________ Dollars $ 59,000

for the purchase of property, situated in _______________ , County of _______________ , California,

described as follows: ________ 1229-1231 5th Street

1.   Buyer will deposit in escrow with_________________________ the balance of purchase price as follows:

A.   The buyer agrees to qualify for and take over 1st loan of
approximately $39,000 payable at 10% interest with payments
of $380.00 per month. The loan will be taken over from
Medallion Mortgage upon the following conditions:

*1.   All back interest payments totaling $3,800 plus late
charges of $125.00 will be waived by the 1st lender
before buyer will take over the loan.

B.   The buyer will take over the existing 2nd loan with
Transamerica Financial of $20,000 payable at 18% interest
payable at $360.00 per month amortized over 10 years, subject
to. Also, upon the following conditions:

1.   All back unpaid interest totaling $1,440.00 plus late
charges of $80.00 will be waived by the 2nd lender.

2.   Buyer will provide a financial statement and credit
report to show qualifications for purchase.

Set forth above any terms and conditions of a factual nature applicable to this sale, such as financing, prior sale of other property, the matter of structural pest control inspection, repairs and personal property to be included in the sale.

2.   Deposit will ☐ will not ☐ be increased by $ _____________ to $ _____________ within _____________ days of acceptance of this offer.

3.   Buyer does ☐ does not ☐ intend to occupy subject property as his residence.

4.   The following supplements are incorporated as part of this agreement:

		Other
☐ Structural Pest Control Certification Agreement	☐ Occupancy Agreement	☐ _________
☐ Special Studies Zone Disclosure	☐ VA Amendment	☐ _________
☐ Flood Insurance Disclosure	☐ FHA Amendment	☐ _________

5.   Buyer and Seller shall deliver signed instructions to the escrow holder within _____________ days from Seller's acceptance which shall provide for closing within_____________ days from Seller's acceptance. Escrow fees to be paid as follows:

6.   Buyer and Seller acknowledge receipt of a copy of this page, which constitutes Page 1 of _____ Pages

Buyer_________________________________ Seller _______________________________

Buyer_________________________________ Seller _______________________________

A REAL ESTATE BROKER IS THE PERSON QUALIFIED TO ADVISE ON REAL ESTATE. IF YOU DESIRE LEGAL ADVICE CONSULT YOUR ATTORNEY.

FOR ILLUSTRATION ONLY - Consult your attorney for legal advice ON CONTRACTS IN YOUR STATE
Reprinted with permission, California Association of Realtors®. Endorsement not implied

(70) Lease Option from Lender - Rehabilitate at Set Price

* This is a unique way to control an expensive property that has been taken back in foreclosure. We have offered to lease the property with the option to buy it in 1 year. First of all, we are only paying $450 per month to lease it.

Why would a lender do this? Because this lender is sitting on a $1,200-a-month payment on a house that is empty, unfinished and unsalable. So, if they could get someone to live in the house, clean it up, and are guaranteed a sale at the end of the year, they can afford to write off $750 a month or $9,000 over the year's period. It's either that or write off $14,000 of negative cash flow over a year and have the house deteriorate.

REAL ESTATE PURCHASE CONTRACT AND RECEIPT FOR DEPOSIT

THIS IS MORE THAN A RECEIPT FOR MONEY. IT IS INTENDED TO BE A LEGALLY BINDING CONTRACT. READ IT CAREFULLY.

CALIFORNIA ASSOCIATION OF REALTORS® (CAR) STANDARD FORM

_____________________________________ , California. ________________ , 19____

Received from ________ David Del Dotto and/or assignee ________

herein called Buyer, the sum of _________________________________ Dollars $________

evidenced by cash ☐, cashier's check ☐, or Note upon acceptance personal check ☐ payable to____ A Reliable Title Company ____ , to be held uncashed until acceptance of this offer, as deposit on account of purchase price of

____ -One Hundred Thirty Thousand- ____ Dollars $__ 130,000

for the purchase of property, situated in ___________________ , County of______________ , California,

described as follows: ____ 1500 Escalon Street ________

1. Buyer will deposit in escrow with ________________________ the balance of purchase price as follows:

   *A. The buyer agrees to lease the house located at the above address upon the following terms:

   1. The lease will be for 1 year, then the buyer will have the option to buy the property at the above stated price. The monthly lease payment will be for $450.00 per month with no credit towards the purchase at the end of the year.

   2. The buyer will take over the existing 1st loan of $100,000 payable at 14% interest with monthly payments of $1,200 per month, subject to, at the end of 1 year.

   3. The buyer will execute a 2nd note and deed of trust to the seller for $30,000 payable at 12% interest with interest only payments of $300.00 per month for 7 years.

   4. The second lender and seller will subsidize the monthly payment of the buyer for the 1 year lease period, with no cost to the buyer.

   5. Buyer agrees to keep the house clean and do minor repairs and landscaping at no cost to the seller.

Set forth above any terms and conditions of a factual nature applicable to this sale, such as financing, prior sale of other property, the matter of structural pest control inspection, repairs and personal property to be included in the sale.

2. Deposit will ☐ will not ☐ be increased by $____________ to $____________ within____________ days of acceptance of this offer.

3. Buyer does ☐ does not ☐ intend to occupy subject property as his residence.

4. The following supplements are incorporated as part of this agreement:

Other

☐ Structural Pest Control Certification Agreement   ☐ Occupancy Agreement   ☐ ____________

☐ Special Studies Zone Disclosure   ☐ VA Amendment   ☐ ____________

☐ Flood Insurance Disclosure   ☐ FHA Amendment   ☐ ____________

5. Buyer and Seller shall deliver signed instructions to the escrow holder within __________ days from Seller's acceptance which shall provide for closing within____________ days from Seller's acceptance. Escrow fees to be paid as follows:

____

6. Buyer and Seller acknowledge receipt of a copy of this page, which constitutes Page 1 of______ Pages.

Buyer _____________________________   Seller _____________________________

Buyer _____________________________   Seller _____________________________

A REAL ESTATE BROKER IS THE PERSON QUALIFIED TO ADVISE ON REAL ESTATE. IF YOU DESIRE LEGAL ADVICE CONSULT YOUR ATTORNEY.

CREATIVE CONTRACTS:
EQUITY SHARING

(71) Equity Share with Lender

(72) Buyer Takes Over Existing First - Seller Obtains New Second - Buyer Makes Payments on First - Seller Makes Payments on Second (50/50 Ownership) - Duplex - Live Together

(73) Buyer Assumes Existing First - Seller Lives Free

(74) Seller Refinances Existing First - Seller Keeps 50% Ownership in Lieu of Note

(75) Partnership Makes Down Payment - Occupant Owns 50% with no Down

(76) Co-Mortgage Helps get New First for 25% Ownership

(77) Private Lender Loans on Second for Lower Interest and 20% Ownership

(78) Trust Funds Provide Low Interest Loan and 20% down Payment for 33% Ownership

(71) Equity Share with Lender

* Here is another way to obtain ownership with no money down. We could use an equity sharing arrangement with a lender who has taken back a property in foreclosure. As was the case on the previous offer, many lenders would like to have someone living in the homes they've taken back and are unable to sell. So, we're offering to make all or part of the monthly payments for 80% ownership of the property for a 3-year period. The lender can keep 20% ownership and have someone taking care of the property, and making all or most of the payments. It's a good deal for everyone!

REAL ESTATE PURCHASE CONTRACT AND RECEIPT FOR DEPOSIT
THIS IS MORE THAN A RECEIPT FOR MONEY. IT IS INTENDED TO BE A LEGALLY BINDING CONTRACT. READ IT CAREFULLY.
CALIFORNIA ASSOCIATION OF REALTORS® (CAR) STANDARD FORM

_______________ , California, _______________ , 19_______

Received from _______________ David Del Dotto and/or assignee

herein called Buyer, the sum of _______________ -One Hundred- _______________ Dollars $ 100.00

evidenced by cash ☐, cashier's check ☐, or _______________ Personal note ☐, personal check ☐ payable to _______________ A Reliable Title Company _______________ , to be held uncashed until acceptance of this offer, as deposit on account of purchase price of

_______________ -One Hundred Ten Thousand- _______________ Dollars $ 110,000

for the purchase of property, situated in _______________ , County of _______________ , California,

described as follows: _______________ 1601 Applegate Drive _______________

1.   Buyer will deposit in escrow with _______________ the balance of purchase price as follows:

*A.   It is agreed by the buyer and seller that they will
enter into an equity sharing agreement on the house
indicated above. Both parties are aware of the
following conditions:

1.   That the seller has acquired ownership of the
property by a foreclosure action.

2.   The above offered price will be the starting price
of the equity sharing agreement and the agreement
will be for 3 years.

3.   The buyer will have an 80% share in the agreement.

4.   That the parties will have their attorneys prepare
the equity share agreement before close of escrow,
stating all terms and conditions.

5.   There will be a final walk-through inspection by
the buyer before the close of escrow.

Set forth above any terms and conditions of a factual nature applicable to this sale, such as financing, prior sale of other property, the matter of structural pest control inspection, repairs and personal property to be included in the sale.

2.   Deposit will ☐ will not ☐ be increased by $ _______________ to $ _______________ within _______________ days of acceptance of this offer.

3.   Buyer does ☐ does not ☐ intend to occupy subject property as his residence.

4.   The following supplements are incorporated as part of this agreement:

Other
☐ Structural Pest Control Certification Agreement   ☐ Occupancy Agreement   ☐ _______________
☐ Special Studies Zone Disclosure   ☐ VA Amendment   ☐ _______________
☐ Flood Insurance Disclosure   ☐ FHA Amendment   ☐ _______________

5.   Buyer and Seller shall deliver signed instructions to the escrow holder within _______________ days from Seller's acceptance which shall provide for closing within _______________ days from Seller's acceptance. Escrow fees to be paid as follows:

6.   Buyer and Seller acknowledge receipt of a copy of this page, which constitutes Page 1 of _______________ Pages.

Buyer _______________   Seller _______________

Buyer _______________   Seller _______________

A REAL ESTATE BROKER IS THE PERSON QUALIFIED TO ADVISE ON REAL ESTATE. IF YOU DESIRE LEGAL ADVICE CONSULT YOUR ATTORNEY.

FOR ILLUSTRATION ONLY - Consult your attorney for legal advice ON CONTRACTS IN YOUR STATE
Reprinted with permission, California Association of Realtors®, Endorsement not implied

(72) Buyer Takes Over Existing First - Seller Obtains New Second - Buyer Makes Payments on First - Seller Makes Payments on Second (50/50 Ownership) - Duplex - Live Together

* WOW! Take a close look at this, A person owns a duplex and has equity in it, but can't afford to tap it because of the negative cash flow. So we bring a partner in for 50% ownership if he makes the 1st payment of $375.00 per month. Then we get a new 2nd for $20,000 cash and no negative cash flow. The equity partner has an easy payment on his half with no down payment. The possibilities are limitless!

REAL ESTATE PURCHASE CONTRACT AND RECEIPT FOR DEPOSIT

THIS IS MORE THAN A RECEIPT FOR MONEY. IT IS INTENDED TO BE A LEGALLY BINDING CONTRACT. READ IT CAREFULLY.

CALIFORNIA ASSOCIATION OF REALTORS* (CAR) STANDARD FORM

_______________, California. _______________, 19_______

Received from _______ David Del Dotto and/or assignee _______

herein called Buyer, the sum of _______ -One Hundred- _______ Dollars $_____ 100.00

evidenced by cash ☐, cashier's check ☐, or _Note in Escrow_ ☐, personal check ☐ payable to _____ Seller

_______________ , to be held uncashed until acceptance of this offer, as deposit on account of purchase price of

_____ -Seventy Four Thousand- _____ Dollars $_____ 74,000

for the purchase of property, situated in _______________ , County of _______________ , California,

described as follows: _____ 1503 Garver Avenue _____

1. Buyer will deposit in escrow with _______________ the balance of purchase price as follows:

    A. The buyer agrees to take over the existing 1st loan of $40,000 payable at 11% interest with payments of $375.00 per month.

    B. The seller will obtain a new equity 2nd loan of $20,000 from Beneficial Finance Corp. payable at 18% interest only for 5 years.

    C. The buyer and seller agree to enter into an equity sharing partnership for 4 years upon the following conditions:

        *1. The buyer will make all payments on the first loan including taxes and insurance of $375.00 per month.

        2. The seller will make all payments on the 2nd loan of $300.00 per month.

        3. Each party will live in one separate unit of the above-mentioned duplex and have 50% ownership of the entire property.

        4. Subject to parties signing an equity sharing agreement prepared by an attorney before close of escrow.

Set forth above any terms and conditions of a factual nature applicable to this sale, such as financing, prior sale of other property, the matter of structural pest control inspection, repairs and personal property to be included in the sale.

2. Deposit will ☐ will not ☐ be increased by $_______ to $_______ within_______ days of acceptance of this offer.

3. Buyer does ☐ does not ☐ intend to occupy subject property as his residence.

4. The following supplements are incorporated as part of this agreement:

☐ Structural Pest Control Certification Agreement   ☐ Occupancy Agreement   Other ☐ _______

☐ Special Studies Zone Disclosure   ☐ VA Amendment   ☐ _______

☐ Flood Insurance Disclosure   ☐ FHA Amendment   ☐ _______

5. Buyer and Seller shall deliver signed instructions to the escrow holder within _______ days from Seller's acceptance which shall provide for closing within_______ days from Seller's acceptance. Escrow fees to be paid as follows:

6. Buyer and Seller acknowledge receipt of a copy of this page, which constitutes Page 1 of_______ Pages.

Buyer_______________ Seller _______________

Buyer_______________ Seller _______________

A REAL ESTATE BROKER IS THE PERSON QUALIFIED TO ADVISE ON REAL ESTATE. IF YOU DESIRE LEGAL ADVICE CONSULT YOUR ATTORNEY.

FOR ILLUSTRATION ONLY - Consult your attorney for legal advice ON CONTRACTS IN YOUR STATE

Reprinted with permission, California Association of Realtors®, Endorsement not implied

(73) Buyer Assumes Existing First - Seller Lives Free

* This will work nicely for an elderly person who is being plagued by the rising cost of living, especially the cost of energy to heat and cool the home. Many senior citizens are on a fixed income and will need help in the future. So we can agree to make their house payments in exchange for a percentage of ownership in their house.

As the investor we would have a tax write-off for interest paid, depreciation on part of the building, and a huge equity build-up. Our monthly payments would be relatively low and we would be helping the elderly. This would work great for one of our relatives who needs help.

REAL ESTATE PURCHASE CONTRACT AND RECEIPT FOR DEPOSIT

THIS IS MORE THAN A RECEIPT FOR MONEY. IT IS INTENDED TO BE A LEGALLY BINDING CONTRACT. READ IT CAREFULLY.

CALIFORNIA ASSOCIATION OF REALTORS® (CAR) STANDARD FORM

_______________________________ , California. _______________ , 19______

Received from ________________ David Del Dotto and/or assignee ________________

herein called Buyer, the sum of __________ -One Hundred- __________ Dollars $ 100.00

evidenced by cash ☐, cashier's check ☐, or _Personal note in_ personal check ☐ payable to ________ A Reliable

___Title Company___ , to be held uncashed until acceptance of this offer, as deposit on account of purchase price of

___-Fifty Five Thousand-_______________________________________ Dollars $ 55,000

for the purchase of property, situated in________________________ , County of________________________ , California,

described as follows: ________ 1400 Carver Road

1.   Buyer will deposit in escrow with ____ the balance of purchase price as follows:

   A.   The buyer and seller agree to enter into an equity sharing
        agreement upon the following conditions:

      *1.   The buyer will assume the existing 1st loan of approx.
            $19,000 payable at 8% interest with monthly payments of
            $150.00 per month.

      2.   The seller will live in the house for free until death
           or until the property is sold by mutual agreement.

      3.   Each party will have 50% ownership.

      4.   A detailed equity sharing agreement will be signed by
           both parties before close of escrow.

Set forth above any terms and conditions of a factual nature applicable to this sale, such as financing, prior sale of other property, the matter of structural pest control inspection, repairs and personal property to be included in the sale.

2.   Deposit will ☐ will not ☐ be increased by $ ________ to $ ________ within ________ days of acceptance of this offer.

3.   Buyer does ☐ does not ☐ intend to occupy subject property as his residence.

4.   The following supplements are incorporated as part of this agreement:

Other

☐ Structural Pest Control Certification Agreement   ☐ Occupancy Agreement   ☐ ______________

☐ Special Studies Zone Disclosure   ☐ VA Amendment   ☐ ______________

☐ Flood Insurance Disclosure   ☐ FHA Amendment   ☐ ______________

5.   Buyer and Seller shall deliver signed instructions to the escrow holder within ________ days from Seller's acceptance which shall provide for closing within________ days from Seller's acceptance. Escrow fees to be paid as follows:

6.   Buyer and Seller acknowledge receipt of a copy of this page, which constitutes Page 1 of________ Pages.

Buyer_______________________________   Seller _______________________________

Buyer_______________________________   Seller _______________________________

A REAL ESTATE BROKER IS THE PERSON QUALIFIED TO ADVISE ON REAL ESTATE. IF YOU DESIRE LEGAL ADVICE CONSULT YOUR ATTORNEY.

(74) Seller Refinances Existing First - Seller Keeps 50% Ownership in Lieu of Note

* The seller has pulled $25,000 of the equity of his house out before entering into an equity share agreement. Instead of carrying a second note, he has agreed to keep 50% of all future appreciation in the home. He will have tax benefits and may gain more money by keeping 50% instead of selling at perhaps a lower price or a low note rate. The seller has made the property marketable and the buyer has gotten in with no down payment and a low monthly payment.

REAL ESTATE PURCHASE CONTRACT AND RECEIPT FOR DEPOSIT   in lieu
THIS IS MORE THAN A RECEIPT FOR MONEY. IT IS INTENDED TO BE A LEGALLY BINDING CONTRACT. READ IT CAREFULLY. of note
CALIFORNIA ASSOCIATION OF REALTORS® (CAR) STANDARD FORM

_________________________________ , California. _____________ , 19_______

Received from ______ David Del Dotto and/or assignee ______

herein called Buyer, the sum of ______ -One Hundred- ______ Dollars $ 100.00

evidenced by cash ☐, cashier's check ☐, or Personal note ☐, personal check ☐ payable to ______ Seller

_________________________ , to be held uncashed until acceptance of this offer, as deposit on account of purchase price of

______ -Fifty Thousand- ______ Dollars $ 50,000

for the purchase of property, situated in _____________________ , County of _____________________ , California,

described as follows: ______ 1127 Encina Avenue ______

1.   Buyer will deposit in escrow with _________________________________ the balance of purchase price as follows:

    A.   Subject to the seller obtaining a new 1st loan from
        Guarantee Savings for $25,000 payable at 12% interest
        with payments of 257.15 per month.

    B.   Seller then agrees to enter into an equity sharing
        agreement with the buyer under the following terms:

    *1.   Buyer will be granted a 50% ownership and will
        share 50% of all future appreciation over and
        above $50,000. Buyer will live in the house and
        will make all the principal, interest, taxes, and
        insurance payments on the house.

    2.   Seller will waive a second mortgage and keep a
        50% ownership in the property. All existing equity
        will be paid before any appreciation profits at the
        sale of the house or when buyer exercises his right
        to buy the seller out.

    3.   This agreement will be for 5 years and all details
        will be outlined in the equity sharing agreement to
        follow.

Set forth above any terms and conditions of a factual nature applicable to this sale, such as financing, prior sale of other property, the matter of structural pest control inspection, repairs and personal property to be included in the sale.

2.   Deposit will ☐ will not ☐ be increased by $ _____________ to $ _____________ within _____________ days of acceptance of this offer.

3.   Buyer does ☐ does not ☐ intend to occupy subject property as his residence.

4.   The following supplements are incorporated as part of this agreement:

Other

☐ Structural Pest Control Certification Agreement   ☐ Occupancy Agreement   ☐ _____________

☐ Special Studies Zone Disclosure   ☐ VA Amendment   ☐ _____________

☐ Flood Insurance Disclosure   ☐ FHA Amendment   ☐ _____________

5.   Buyer and Seller shall deliver signed instructions to the escrow holder within _____________ days from Seller's acceptance which shall provide for closing within _____________ days from Seller's acceptance. Escrow fees to be paid as follows:

6   Buyer and Seller acknowledge receipt of a copy of this page, which constitutes Page 1 of _______ Pages.

Buyer_________________________________   Seller _________________________________

Buyer_________________________________   Seller _________________________________

A REAL ESTATE BROKER IS THE PERSON QUALIFIED TO ADVISE ON REAL ESTATE. IF YOU DESIRE LEGAL ADVICE CONSULT YOUR ATTORNEY.

(75) Partnership Makes Down Payment - Occupant Owns 50% with no Down

* In this case a group of professional people have formed a partnership and are using their cash to make down payments for people. In turn, the occupant-partner will take care of the house and make all the payments, therefore eliminating management and negative cash flow problems for the partnership.

(75) Partnership makes down payment - occupant owns 50% with no down

REAL ESTATE PURCHASE CONTRACT AND RECEIPT FOR DEPOSIT

THIS IS MORE THAN A RECEIPT FOR MONEY. IT IS INTENDED TO BE A LEGALLY BINDING CONTRACT. READ IT CAREFULLY.

CALIFORNIA ASSOCIATION OF REALTORS® (CAR) STANDARD FORM

____, California, _______________, 19_______

Received from _______________ David Del Dotto and/or assignee _______________

herein called Buyer, the sum of _______________ -One Hundred- _______________ Dollars $___100.00___

evidenced by cash ☐, cashier's check ☐, or ___Note___ ☐, personal check ☐ payable to ___Seller___

___________________________, to be held uncashed until acceptance of this offer, as deposit on account of purchase price of

___-Seventy Four Thousand-___ Dollars $___74,000___

for the purchase of property, situated in _______________, County of _______________, California,

described as follows: _______________ 249 Cherry Lane _______________

1.   Buyer will deposit in escrow with _______________ the balance of purchase price as follows:

*A. The partnership L.B.D. Associates agrees to put $7,400
     cash down payment upon the following terms:

     1.   Subject to approval of the house by a partner occupant
          within 60 days of acceptance of this offer.

     2.   Buyers to obtain a new 90% loan from lender of
          buyer's choice at current interest rate and terms.

     3.   Buyers to enter into an equity share agreement with
          partner occupant to be detailed in a contract prepared
          by an attorney.

B.   Sale to include all appliances, carpets and drapes.

Set forth above any terms and conditions of a factual nature applicable to this sale, such as financing, prior sale of other property, the matter of structural pest control inspection, repairs and personal property to be included in the sale.

2.   Deposit will ☐ will not ☐ be increased by $_______________ to $_______________ within_______________ days of acceptance of this offer.

3.   Buyer does ☐ does not ☐ intend to occupy subject property as his residence.

4.   The following supplements are incorporated as part of this agreement:

☐ Structural Pest Control Certification Agreement   ☐ Occupancy Agreement   Other ☐ _______________
☐ Special Studies Zone Disclosure   ☐ VA Amendment   ☐ _______________
☐ Flood Insurance Disclosure   ☐ FHA Amendment   ☐ _______________

5.   Buyer and Seller shall deliver signed instructions to the escrow holder within _______________ days from Seller's acceptance which shall provide for closing within_______________ days from Seller's acceptance. Escrow fees to be paid as follows:

6.   Buyer and Seller acknowledge receipt of a copy of this page, which constitutes Page 1 of_______ Pages.

Buyer_______________________________________   Seller_______________________________________

Buyer_______________________________________   Seller_______________________________________

A REAL ESTATE BROKER IS THE PERSON QUALIFIED TO ADVISE ON REAL ESTATE. IF YOU DESIRE LEGAL ADVICE CONSULT YOUR ATTORNEY.

CREATIVE FINANCING - CONTRACT EXAMPLES

(76) Co-Mortgage Helps get New First for 25% Ownership

Just think about all the people who would like to buy a home but can't meet the income requirements of the lender. What if we co-mortgaged with the people for an interest of, say, 25% in the house? They couldn't get the loan without us, so they would think it's a good deal. And it *is* a good deal for both of us. It doesn't cost us anything to co-mortgage, while they get the house they want. When they are ready to buy us out, we get 25% of the *appreciated* value of the house!

REAL ESTATE PURCHASE CONTRACT AND RECEIPT FOR DEPOSIT

THIS IS MORE THAN A RECEIPT FOR MONEY. IT IS INTENDED TO BE A LEGALLY BINDING CONTRACT. READ IT CAREFULLY.

CALIFORNIA ASSOCIATION OF REALTORS* (CAR) STANDARD FORM

_______________________________________ , California, _______________ , 19_______

Received from ________ David Del Dotto and/or assignee _______________

herein called Buyer, the sum of ______ -One Hundred- _______________ Dollars $____ 100.00

evidenced by cash ☐, cashier's check ☐, or ___ Note in Escrow ☐, personal check ☐ payable to_____ Seller

_______________________________ , to be held uncashed until acceptance of this offer, as deposit on account of purchase price of

______ -Eighty Thousand- _______________________________ Dollars $____ 80,000

for the purchase of property, situated in _______________ , County of_______________ , California,

described as follows: ______ 5900 Mable Road _______________

1.   Buyer will deposit in escrow with _______________________ the balance of purchase price as follows:

A.   The above-named buyer agrees to co-mortgage with Mr. and
      Mrs. Young Couple to qualify for a new conventional 90%
      loan from a lender of the buyer's choice, upon the
      following conditions:

      1.   Mr. and Mrs. Young Couple will make the down payment
            of $8,000.

      2.   Mr. Del Dotto will have 25% of the ownership in the house.

      3.   An equity share agreement will be executed during the
            escrow period.

Set forth above any terms and conditions of a factual nature applicable to this sale, such as financing, prior sale of other property, the matter of structural pest control inspection, repairs and personal property to be included in the sale.

2.   Deposit will ☐ will not ☐ be increased by $____________ to $____________ within____________ days of acceptance of this offer.

3.   Buyer does ☐ does not ☐ intend to occupy subject property as his residence.

4.   The following supplements are incorporated as part of this agreement:

Other

☐ Structural Pest Control Certification Agreement   ☐ Occupancy Agreement   ☐ _______________

☐ Special Studies Zone Disclosure   ☐ VA Amendment   ☐ _______________

☐ Flood Insurance Disclosure   ☐ FHA Amendment   ☐ _______________

5.   Buyer and Seller shall deliver signed instructions to the escrow holder within ___________ days from Seller's acceptance which shall provide for closing within____________ days from Seller's acceptance. Escrow fees to be paid as follows:

6.   Buyer and Seller acknowledge receipt of a copy of this page, which constitutes Page 1 of_______ Pages.

Buyer_______________________   Seller _______________________

Buyer_______________________   Seller _______________________

A REAL ESTATE BROKER IS THE PERSON QUALIFIED TO ADVISE ON REAL ESTATE. IF YOU DESIRE LEGAL ADVICE CONSULT YOUR ATTORNEY.

FOR ILLUSTRATION ONLY - Consult your attorney for legal advice ON CONTRACTS IN YOUR STATE

Reprinted with permission, California Association of Realtors®, Endorsement not implied

(77) Private Lender Loans on Second for Lower Interest and 20% Ownership

* This offer is subject to the buyer finding an investor who will give him an 11% loan secured by a second mortgage. In exchange for this low interest rate loan he has agreed to give the investor a 20% equity share position which will help the investor's yield on the investment.

REAL ESTATE PURCHASE CONTRACT AND RECEIPT FOR DEPOSIT

THIS IS MORE THAN A RECEIPT FOR MONEY. IT IS INTENDED TO BE A LEGALLY BINDING CONTRACT. READ IT CAREFULLY.

CALIFORNIA ASSOCIATION OF REALTORS® (CAR) STANDARD FORM

_____________________________________ , California, _____________ , 19____

Received from _________ David Del Dotto and/or assignee _________

herein called Buyer, the sum of _________ -One Hundred- _________ Dollars $ 100.00

evidenced by cash ☐, cashier's check ☐, or _ Note in Escrow _ ☐, personal check ☐ payable to _____ A Reliable Title Company _____ , to be held uncashed until acceptance of this offer, as deposit on account of purchase price of

_____ -Fifty Nine Thousand- _____ Dollars $ 59,000

for the purchase of property, situated in _________________ , County of _________________ , California,

described as follows: _____ 1717 Maplewood Drive _____

1.   Buyer will deposit in escrow with _________________ the balance of purchase price as follows:

    A.   Buyer agrees to qualify for and take over existing 1st loan of approximately $20,000 payable at 9% interest with payments of $180.00 per month.

    *B.   Subject to the buyer obtaining a new second loan for $30,000 from a private lender payable at 11% interest with interest only payments of $275.00 per month for 10 years.

        1.   Buyer will give 20% of the equity in the house to the private lender to obtain this loan.

        2.   All equity sharing agreements will be written by an attorney and agreed upon by both parties.

    C.   Subject to the seller taking back a 3rd note secured by a mortgage for $9,000 payable at 10% interest with all principal and interest due in one balloon payment 10 years from close of escrow.

Set forth above any terms and conditions of a factual nature applicable to this sale, such as financing, prior sale of other property, the matter of structural pest control inspection, repairs and personal property to be included in the sale.

2.   Deposit will ☐ will not ☐ be increased by $ _____________ to $ _____________ within_____________ days of acceptance of this offer.

3.   Buyer does ☐ does not ☐ intend to occupy subject property as his residence.

4.   The following supplements are incorporated as part of this agreement:

Other

☐ Structural Pest Control Certification Agreement   ☐ Occupancy Agreement   ☐ _____________

☐ Special Studies Zone Disclosure   ☐ VA Amendment   ☐ _____________

☐ Flood Insurance Disclosure   ☐ FHA Amendment   ☐ _____________

5.   Buyer and Seller shall deliver signed instructions to the escrow holder within _____________ days from Seller's acceptance which shall provide for closing within_____________ days from Seller's acceptance. Escrow fees to be paid as follows:

6.   Buyer and Seller acknowledge receipt of a copy of this page, which constitutes Page 1 of ______ Pages.

Buyer _____________________________   Seller _____________________________

Buyer _____________________________   Seller _____________________________

A REAL ESTATE BROKER IS THE PERSON QUALIFIED TO ADVISE ON REAL ESTATE. IF YOU DESIRE LEGAL ADVICE CONSULT YOUR ATTORNEY.

(78) Trust Funds Provide Low Interest Loan and 20% down Payment for 33% Ownership

* In this case a partnership is not only providing the down payment but also a low interest rate loan for the partner, In turn, the partnership is taking 33% of the ownership. This program has been used to a limited degree in central California, although the syndications have had trouble raising enough cash from private investors. This would be a good use for pension money or retirement money funds and a great boost for the real estate business.

REAL ESTATE PURCHASE CONTRACT AND RECEIPT FOR DEPOSIT   33%

THIS IS MORE THAN A RECEIPT FOR MONEY. IT IS INTENDED TO BE A LEGALLY BINDING CONTRACT. READ IT CAREFULLY
Ownership
CALIFORNIA ASSOCIATION OF REALTORS® (CAR) STANDARD FORM

_______________________, California, _______________ , 19______

Received from _____________ David Del Dotto and/or assignee _________________

herein called Buyer, the sum of ___________ -Five Hundred- ___________ Dollars $___500.00___

evidenced by cash ☐, cashier's check ☐, or __Note in Escrow__ ☐, personal check ☐ payable to___A Reliable___

______Title Company_____ , to be held uncashed until acceptance of this offer, as deposit on account of purchase price of

______-Seventy Five Thousand-_________________________________ Dollars $_75,000_

for the purchase of property, situated in ___________________ , County of_______________ , California,

described as follows: ___________ 459 Hope Lane _____________________________

1.   Buyer will deposit in escrow with_______________________________ the balance of purchase price as follows:

*A.   This offer is subject to the buyer qualifying for an
equity sharing partnership with the H.E.L.P. partnership
syndication under the following terms:

1.   The partnership will provide a $15,000 cash down
payment on behalf of the buyer.

2.   The partnership will provide an 80% loan at 12%
interest for the term of the equity sharing agreement.

3.   The buyer will live in the house and make all the monthly
payments including principal, interest and taxes for 67%
of the ownership.

4.   All details of the equity sharing agreement will be
outlined in a contract and signed by both parties
before close of escrow.

Set forth above any terms and conditions of a factual nature applicable to this sale, such as financing, prior sale of other property, the matter of structural pest control inspection, repairs and personal property to be included in the sale.

2.   Deposit will ☐ will not ☐ be increased by $______________ to $____________ within_______________ days of acceptance of this offer.

3.   Buyer does ☐ does not ☐ intend to occupy subject property as his residence.

4.   The following supplements are incorporated as part of this agreement:

		Other
☐ Structural Pest Control Certification Agreement	☐ Occupancy Agreement	☐ ______________
☐ Special Studies Zone Disclosure	☐ VA Amendment	☐ ______________
☐ Flood Insurance Disclosure	☐ FHA Amendment	☐ ______________

5.   Buyer and Seller shall deliver signed instructions to the escrow holder within ___________ days from Seller's acceptance which shall provide for closing within______________ days from Seller's acceptance. Escrow fees to be paid as follows:

6.   Buyer and Seller acknowledge receipt of a copy of this page, which constitutes Page 1 of_______ Pages.

Buyer_____________________________   Seller _____________________________

Buyer_____________________________   Seller _____________________________

A REAL ESTATE BROKER IS THE PERSON QUALIFIED TO ADVISE ON REAL ESTATE. IF YOU DESIRE LEGAL ADVICE CONSULT YOUR ATTORNEY.

FOR ILLUSTRATION ONLY - Consult your attorney for legal advice ON CONTRACTS IN YOUR STATE
Reprinted with permission, California Association of Realtors®, Endorsement not implied

CREATIVE CONTRACTS:
LEASE - OPTIONS

* We are leasing the property for six months and then giving the tenants the option to buy. We can use this program on a house we hate and want to give away, usually after pulling some cash out of it. Or, it could be a property in a bad area we want to dump. By crediting all the monthly payment toward the purchase, we can get some of the renters out of the idea of always renting. And we can get rid of a negative cash flow and maybe make a few thousand on the deal.

REAL ESTATE PURCHASE CONTRACT AND RECEIPT FOR DEPOSIT
THIS IS MORE THAN A RECEIPT FOR MONEY. IT IS INTENDED TO BE A LEGALLY BINDING CONTRACT. READ IT CAREFULLY.
CALIFORNIA ASSOCIATION OF REALTORS® (CAR) STANDARD FORM

____ , California. _____________________ , 19_________

Received from ___________ Jack Jones ____

herein called Buyer, the sum of __________ -Five Hundred- _____________________ Dollars $ 500.00

evidenced by cash ☐, cashier's check ☒, or _____________________ ☐, personal check ☐ payable to Seller

_________________________________ , to be held uncashed until acceptance of this offer, as deposit on account of purchase price of

_____ -Fifty One Thousand- _______________________________ Dollars $ 51,000

for the purchase of property, situated in ___________________ , County of _____________________ , California,

described as follows: _______________ 521 Pine Street _______________________________

1. Buyer will deposit in escrow with _________________________________ the balance of purchase price as follows:

*A. The above buyer agrees to lease the house at the
     above stated address for six months with an option
     to buy under the following general terms:

     1. The lessee will pay $600.00 per month for six
         months, of which all the payments will apply
         to the purchase.

     2. At the end of six months the lessee will have the
         option to take title to the property subject to
         the existing financing which will be outlined in
         a detailed lease-option agreement and signed by each
         party prior to close of escrow.

     3. The lessee will pay a $2,000 option fee plus all
         closing costs to transfer the title at the end
         of six months.

Set forth above any terms and conditions of a factual nature applicable to this sale, such as financing, prior sale of other property, the matter of structural pest control inspection, repairs and personal property to be included in the sale.

2. Deposit will ☐ will not ☐ be increased by $ _______________ to $ _______________ within _______________ days of acceptance of this offer.

3. Buyer does ☐ does not ☐ intend to occupy subject property as his residence

4. The following supplements are incorporated as part of this agreement:

Other

☐ Structural Pest Control Certification Agreement   ☐ Occupancy Agreement   ☐ _______________

☐ Special Studies Zone Disclosure   ☐ VA Amendment   ☐ _______________

☐ Flood Insurance Disclosure   ☐ FHA Amendment   ☐ _______________

5. Buyer and Seller shall deliver signed instructions to the escrow holder within _______________ days from Seller's acceptance which shall provide for closing within _______________ days from Seller's acceptance. Escrow fees to be paid as follows:

6. Buyer and Seller acknowledge receipt of a copy of this page, which constitutes Page 1 of _______ Pages.

Buyer _____________________________   Seller _____________________________

Buyer _____________________________   Seller _____________________________

A REAL ESTATE BROKER IS THE PERSON QUALIFIED TO ADVISE ON REAL ESTATE. IF YOU DESIRE LEGAL ADVICE CONSULT YOUR ATTORNEY.

(80) One-Year Lease-Option - No Credit Back

* We are not going to give any credit back on the monthly payments on this particular house. We have locked in our price, which buyers like to see, making it attractive to the buyer. We added $5,000 to $7,000 to the price for which we bought it, anyway, so if they exercise their option it will mean money in our pocket. In the meantime we've had no negative cash flow for the year, and the property has appreciated at no cost to us, if the option is not exercised.

** Always make the buyer pay the closing costs if you can; every dollar saved will help.

(80)   One-year lease-option - No credit back

REAL ESTATE PURCHASE CONTRACT AND RECEIPT FOR DEPOSIT
THIS IS MORE THAN A RECEIPT FOR MONEY. IT IS INTENDED TO BE A LEGALLY BINDING CONTRACT. READ IT CAREFULLY.
CALIFORNIA ASSOCIATION OF REALTORS® (CAR) STANDARD FORM

_______________________ , California. _______________ , 19________

Received from ___________ Jack Jones _________________________

herein called Buyer, the sum of ___________ -Five Hundred- ___________ Dollars $___ 500.00

evidenced by cash ☐, cashier's check ☒, or _______________ ☐, personal check ☐ payable to___ A Reliable Title Company ___ , to be held uncashed until acceptance of this offer, as deposit on account of purchase price of

___ -Fifty Four Thousand- ___________________________ Dollars $ 54,000

for the purchase of property, situated in ________________ , County of________________ , California,

described as follows: ___ 451 Rumble Road ___________________________

1.   Buyer will deposit in escrow with _________________________ the balance of purchase price as follows:

   A.   The above buyer agrees to lease the house located at
         451 Rumble Road for one year with the option to
         purchase under the following general terms:

      1.   The lessee will pay $540.00 per month for one year
            and have the option to buy the house for $54,000 at
            the end of the year.

      2.   The lessee at the time of exercising his option will
            take over the existing 1st loan of $45,000 payable at
            12% interest with payments of $462.88 per month.

    *3.   The lessee will pay $9,000 cash to the seller for his equity.

      4.   All of the lease-option details will be outlined in the
            lease-option agreement and signed by all parties prior
            to the close of escrow.

   **5.   The lessee will pay all the closing costs at the time
            the option is exercised.

Set forth above any terms and conditions of a factual nature applicable to this sale, such as financing, prior sale of other property, the matter of structural pest control inspection, repairs and personal property to be included in the sale.

2.   Deposit will ☐ will not ☐ be increased by $ _____________ to $ _____________ within_____________ days of acceptance of this offer.

3.   Buyer does ☐ does not ☐ intend to occupy subject property as his residence

4.   The following supplements are incorporated as part of this agreement:

                                                          Other
☐ Structural Pest Control Certification Agreement   ☐ Occupancy Agreement   ☐ _______________
☐ Special Studies Zone Disclosure   ☐ VA Amendment   ☐ _______________
☐ Flood Insurance Disclosure   ☐ FHA Amendment   ☐ _______________

5.   Buyer and Seller shall deliver signed instructions to the escrow holder within __________ days from Seller's acceptance which shall provide for closing within_____________ days from Seller's acceptance. Escrow fees to be paid as follows:

6.   Buyer and Seller acknowledge receipt of a copy of this page, which constitutes Page 1 of______ Pages.

Buyer_______________________________   Seller _______________________________

Buyer_______________________________   Seller _______________________________

A REAL ESTATE BROKER IS THE PERSON QUALIFIED TO ADVISE ON REAL ESTATE. IF YOU DESIRE LEGAL ADVICE CONSULT YOUR ATTORNEY.

(81) Two-Year Lease Option - $200 Per Month Credit Back

* We're giving a lot of incentive to the future buyer by crediting $200 per month of his monthly payment towards the purchase. This lease-option plan works the best for me. The monthly payment isn't so much that they can't afford it, and I can still credit them $4,800 per year towards the purchase. I usually have no negative cash flow and frequently get the house back at the end of the two-year period. Then I just add appreciation to the price of the house and lease-option it for another couple of years.

REAL ESTATE PURCHASE CONTRACT AND RECEIPT FOR DEPOSIT
THIS IS MORE THAN A RECEIPT FOR MONEY. IT IS INTENDED TO BE A LEGALLY BINDING CONTRACT. READ IT CAREFULLY.
CALIFORNIA ASSOCIATION OF REALTORS· (CAR) STANDARD FORM

_______________________________________ , California _______________ , 19_______

Received from _______ Jack Jones _______

herein called Buyer, the sum of ____ -Five Hundred- ____________________ Dollars $__500.00

evidenced by cash ☐, cashier's check ☒, or _____________ ☐, personal check ☐ payable to ____ Seller

__________________________ , to be held uncashed until acceptance of this offer, as deposit on account of purchase price of

____ -Sixty Thousand- _____________________ Dollars $__60,000

for the purchase of property, situated in _______________________ , County of _______________ , California,

described as follows: _______ 1500 Amber Lane __________________

1.   Buyer will deposit in escrow with _______________________________ the balance of purchase price as follows:

    A.   The above buyer agrees to lease the house located at
          1500 Amber Lane for 2 years with an option to buy
          under the following general terms:

        1.   The lessee will pay $600.00 per month for 2 years
              of which $200.00 per month or a total of $4,800
              will be credited the lessor towards the purchase.

       *2.   At the end of 2 years, the lessee will have the option
              to pay off the seller his existing equity of $10,000
              less $4,800 credited to the lessor and take over the
              existing loans of $50,000.

        3.   All the existing financing and lease-option details
              will be outlined in an agreement and signed by all
              parties concerned before close of escrow.

        4.   Lessee agrees to take the house in "as is" condition
              and waives the pest report.

Set forth above any terms and conditions of a factual nature applicable to this sale, such as financing, prior sale of other property, the matter of structural pest control inspection, repairs and personal property to be included in the sale.

2.   Deposit will ☐ will not ☐ be increased by $_____________ to $_____________ within _____________ days of acceptance of this offer.

3.   Buyer does ☐ does not ☐ intend to occupy subject property as his residence.

4.   The following supplements are incorporated as part of this agreement:

☐ Structural Pest Control Certification Agreement   ☐ Occupancy Agreement   Other ☐ ___________

☐ Special Studies Zone Disclosure   ☐ VA Amendment   ☐ ___________

☐ Flood Insurance Disclosure   ☐ FHA Amendment   ☐ ___________

5.   Buyer and Seller shall deliver signed instructions to the escrow holder within _____________ days from Seller's acceptance which shall provide for closing within _____________ days from Seller's acceptance. Escrow fees to be paid as follows:

6.   Buyer and Seller acknowledge receipt of a copy of this page, which constitutes Page 1 of_______ Pages.

Buyer_______________________________   Seller_______________________________

Buyer_______________________________   Seller_______________________________

A REAL ESTATE BROKER IS THE PERSON QUALIFIED TO ADVISE ON REAL ESTATE. IF YOU DESIRE LEGAL ADVICE CONSULT YOUR ATTORNEY.

FOR ILLUSTRATION ONLY - Consult your attorney for legal advice ON CONTRACTS IN YOUR STATE
Reprinted with permission, California Association of Realtors®, Endorsement not implied

(82) One-Year Lease-Option - Buydown

* We're getting $2,400 up-front cash from the seller to provide lower monthly payments for him for the year. So, he's buying down the payment. We can adjust a person's monthly payment to anything he wants during our lease-option period: Few people realize they are actually giving us their money to use during the year; all they are looking for is lower monthly payments.

REAL ESTATE PURCHASE CONTRACT AND RECEIPT FOR DEPOSIT
THIS IS MORE THAN A RECEIPT FOR MONEY. IT IS INTENDED TO BE A LEGALLY BINDING CONTRACT. READ IT CAREFULLY.
CALIFORNIA ASSOCIATION OF REALTORS- (CAR) STANDARD FORM

_______________________ , California. _______________ , 19______

Received from _____________ Jack Jones _____________

herein called Buyer, the sum of _____________ -One Thousand- _____________ Dollars $ 1,000.00

evidenced by cash ☐, cashier's check ☐, or _____________ ☒, personal check ☐ payable to_____ Seller

_____________ , to be held uncashed until acceptance of this offer, as deposit on account of purchase price of

-Sixty Five Thousand- _____________ Dollars $ 65,000

for the purchase of property, situated in _____________ , County of _____________ , California,

described as follows: _____________ 1901 Royal Lane _____________

1.   Buyer will deposit in escrow with _____________ the balance of purchase price as follows:

A.   The above buyer agrees to lease the house located at
1901 Royal Lane for one year with the option to purchase
under the following general terms:

*1.   The lessee will pay $2,400 cash to the seller at the
beginning of the lease period and pay $400.00 per month
as a lease payment for one year.

2.   At the end of the one year period, the lessee will have
the option to purchase the property by paying the seller
his $10,000 equity and taking over the existing 1st loan
of $55,000 payable at $600.00 per month.

3.   The seller will credit the buyer $2,400 towards the purchase
at the end of the year if the option is exercised.

4.   The details as to this lease-option agreement will
be provided by an attorney and will be signed by all
parties concerned.

Set forth above any terms and conditions of a factual nature applicable to this sale, such as financing, prior sale of other property, the matter of structural pest control inspection, repairs and personal property to be included in the sale.

2.   Deposit will ☐ will not ☐ be increased by $ _____________ to $ _____________ within_____________ days of acceptance of this offer.

3.   Buyer does ☐ does not ☐ intend to occupy subject property as his residence.

4.   The following supplements are incorporated as part of this agreement:

Other

☐ Structural Pest Control Certification Agreement   ☐ Occupancy Agreement   ☐ _____________
☐ Special Studies Zone Disclosure   ☐ VA Amendment   ☐ _____________
☐ Flood Insurance Disclosure   ☐ FHA Amendment   ☐ _____________

5.   Buyer and Seller shall deliver signed instructions to the escrow holder within _____________ days from Seller's acceptance which shall provide for closing within_____________ days from Seller's acceptance. Escrow fees to be paid as follows:

6.   Buyer and Seller acknowledge receipt of a copy of this page, which constitutes Page 1 of _____ Pages.

Buyer _____________   Seller _____________

Buyer _____________   Seller _____________

A REAL ESTATE BROKER IS THE PERSON QUALIFIED TO ADVISE ON REAL ESTATE. IF YOU DESIRE LEGAL ADVICE CONSULT YOUR ATTORNEY.

(83) Two-Year Lease-Option - Equity Share

* Whenever we're lease-optioning a property we always get a cash down payment of some sort as a deposit. Also, collect first and last lease payments up front.

** We're going to have two good years of appreciation before we give half of the property to our lessee in an equity share agreement. Just think how nice it would be to buy properties with nothing down, lease option them with no negative cash flow, get two year's appreciation and then still own half from then on with no management. This program gives buyers an opportunity to get started in home ownership with no down. We also get the full tax write-off during the two year option period, and a 50% write- off after the equity sharing option has been exercised.

REAL ESTATE PURCHASE CONTRACT AND RECEIPT FOR DEPOSIT

THIS IS MORE THAN A RECEIPT FOR MONEY. IT IS INTENDED TO BE A LEGALLY BINDING CONTRACT. READ IT CAREFULLY.

CALIFORNIA ASSOCIATION OF REALTORS® (CAR) STANDARD FORM

_______________________, California, _______________, 19____

Received from _____ Jack Jones _____

herein called Buyer, the sum of _____ -One Thousand _____ Dollars $ __1,000.00__

evidenced by cash ☐, cashier's check ☒, or _________________ ☐, personal check ☐ payable to _____ Seller* _____

_________________, to be held uncashed until acceptance of this offer, as deposit on account of purchase price of

_____ -Sixty Two Thousand- _____ Dollars $ __62,000__

for the purchase of property, situated in _________________, County of _________________, California,

described as follows: _____ 1209 Ridgeview _____

1.   Buyer will deposit in escrow with _________________ the balance of purchase price as follows:

A.   The above buyer agrees to lease the house located at
      1209 Ridgeview under the following conditions:

**1.   The lessee will make monthly payments of $600.00
        per month for 2 years and then will have the option
        to have a 50% interest of ownership in an equity
        share agreement with the seller.

2.   If the equity share agreement is exercised by the
      lessor at the end of the 2 year period, the house
      will be appraised by a licensed appraiser and the
      lessor will be granted 50% ownership of the property
      with 50% of all future appreciation.

3.   The details of the lease-option and equity share
      agreements will be provided by an attorney and
      will be signed by all parties concerned.

Set forth above any terms and conditions of a factual nature applicable to this sale, such as financing, prior sale of other property, the matter of structural pest control inspection, repairs and personal property to be included in the sale.

2.   Deposit will ☐ will not ☐ be increased by $ _____________ to $ _____________ within _____________ days of acceptance of this offer.

3.   Buyer does ☐ does not ☐ intend to occupy subject property as his residence

4.   The following supplements are incorporated as part of this agreement:

Other

☐ Structural Pest Control Certification Agreement   ☐ Occupancy Agreement   ☐ _________________

☐ Special Studies Zone Disclosure   ☐ VA Amendment   ☐ _________________

☐ Flood Insurance Disclosure   ☐ FHA Amendment   ☐ _________________

5.   Buyer and Seller shall deliver signed instructions to the escrow holder within _____________ days from Seller's acceptance which shall provide for closing within _____________ days from Seller's acceptance. Escrow fees to be paid as follows:

____

6.   Buyer and Seller acknowledge receipt of a copy of this page, which constitutes Page 1 of _____ Pages.

Buyer_________________________   Seller_________________________

Buyer_________________________   Seller_________________________

A REAL ESTATE BROKER IS THE PERSON QUALIFIED TO ADVISE ON REAL ESTATE. IF YOU DESIRE LEGAL ADVICE CONSULT YOUR ATTORNEY.

FOR ILLUSTRATION ONLY - Consult your attorney for legal advice ON CONTRACTS IN YOUR STATE

Reprinted with permission, California Association of Realtors®, Endorsement not implied

(84) Seller held to Guaranties

In many real estate negotiations, the Seller makes representations about the property that are later found to be overstated or simply false. You may be able to sue for damages or rescind the purchase, but that is a legal hassle. You may desire to keep the property but simply want to pay a lower price.

* Build into the purchase a note for a substantial amount of the "down payment" which is tied to the guaranties the seller has made. If the guaranties are not met, you simply give notice of the failure, which must be cured by the seller within 10 days or the note is automatically void. Make sure the list of guaranties is clear and specific, so there will be no chance for the seller to claim he did not make such a representation.

(84) Seller held to guaranties

REAL ESTATE PURCHASE CONTRACT AND RECEIPT FOR DEPOSIT
THIS IS MORE THAN A RECEIPT FOR MONEY. IT IS INTENDED TO BE A LEGALLY BINDING CONTRACT. READ IT CAREFULLY.
CALIFORNIA ASSOCIATION OF REALTORS® (CAR) STANDARD FORM

_____________________________________ , California. _____________________ , 19_______

Received from ____

herein called Buyer, the sum of ___________ -Twenty Five Thousand- _______________ Dollars $ 25,000

evidenced by cash ☐, cashier's check ☐, or Note of buyer ☐, personal check ☐ payable to_____ Seller

___________________________ , to be held uncashed until acceptance of this offer, as deposit on account of purchase price of

________ -One Hundred Thousand- ___________________________ Dollars $ 100,000

for the purchase of property, situated in ___________________________ , County of ___________________________ , California,

described as follows: ____

1.   Buyer will deposit in escrow with ___________ Escrow Company ___________ the balance of purchase price as follows:

     *A.   Buyer's note for $25,000 shall be void if the property
         does not conform to the seller's representations set
         forth in exhibit A attached hereto. Notice of failure
         to conform shall be given in writing and the failure must
         be cured within 10 days or the note is automatically void.

     B.   (Other terms and escape clauses)

Set forth above any terms and conditions of a factual nature applicable to this sale, such as financing, prior sale of other property, the matter of structural pest control inspection, repairs and personal property to be included in the sale.

2.   Deposit will ☐ will not ☐ be increased by $ _____________ to $ _____________ within _____________ days of acceptance of this offer.

3.   Buyer does ☐ does not ☐ intend to occupy subject property as his residence.

4.   The following supplements are incorporated as part of this agreement:

                                            Other

☐ Structural Pest Control Certification Agreement   ☐ Occupancy Agreement   ☐ _______________

☐ Special Studies Zone Disclosure   ☐ VA Amendment   ☐ _______________

☐ Flood Insurance Disclosure   ☐ FHA Amendment   ☐ _______________

5.   Buyer and Seller shall deliver signed instructions to the escrow holder within _____________ days from Seller's acceptance which shall provide for closing within _____________ days from Seller's acceptance. Escrow fees to be paid as follows:

____

6.   Buyer and Seller acknowledge receipt of a copy of this page, which constitutes Page 1 of _______ Pages.

Buyer_______________________________ Seller _______________________________

Buyer_______________________________ Seller _______________________________

A REAL ESTATE BROKER IS THE PERSON QUALIFIED TO ADVISE ON REAL ESTATE. IF YOU DESIRE LEGAL ADVICE CONSULT YOUR ATTORNEY.

(85) Realtor held to Guaranties

In many real estate negotiations, the realtor (not the seller) is the one making all the representations about the property that are later found to be overstated or simply false. You may be able to sue for damages, but again, that is a legal hassle. You may really want to keep the property but simply penalize the realtor for the misrepresentations.

In this case, once you've written these provisions in your offer, the realtor and seller will have to negotiate between themselves how to handle the problem of a potential misrepresentation. It will probably make them come back to you during the negotiation of the sale and set the record straight about any overstatements or misrepresentations. You may never have to use this technique in your final purchase offer.

* Build into the purchase offer a note for the amount of the commission which is tied to the guaranties the realtor has made. If the guaranties are not met, you simply give notice of the failure, which must be cured within 10 days or the note is automatically void. Make sure the list of guaranties is clear and specific.

REAL ESTATE PURCHASE CONTRACT AND RECEIPT FOR DEPOSIT

THIS IS MORE THAN A RECEIPT FOR MONEY. IT IS INTENDED TO BE A LEGALLY BINDING CONTRACT. READ IT CAREFULLY.
CALIFORNIA ASSOCIATION OF REALTORS® (CAR) STANDARD FORM

____ , California, _______________________ , 19______

Received from ____

herein called Buyer, the sum of ____________________________ —Six Thousand— ________ Dollars $___ 6,000

evidenced by cash ☐, cashier's check ☐, or ____ Note ____________ ☐, personal check ☐ payable to____ Seller

____ , to be held uncashed until acceptance of this offer, as deposit on account of purchase price of

_______________—One Hundred Thousand—_____________________________________ Dollars $_______________

for the purchase of property, situated in __________________________________ , County of______________________ , California,

described as follows: ____

1.   Buyer will deposit in escrow with ________ Escrow Company ________________ the balance of purchase price as follows:

*A.   Buyer's note for $6,000 shall be void if the property
       does not meet the seller's guaranties made to buyer by
       the realtor as set forth in exhibit A attached hereto.
       Notice of failure to meet the guaranties shall be given
       in writing to seller and the failure must be cured
       within 10 days or the note is automatically void.

B.   (Other terms and escape clauses)

Set forth above any terms and conditions of a factual nature applicable to this sale, such as financing, prior sale of other property, the matter of structural pest control inspection, repairs and personal property to be included in the sale.

2.   Deposit will ☐ will not ☐ be increased by $________________ to $________________ within________________ days of acceptance of this offer.

3.   Buyer does ☐ does not ☐ intend to occupy subject property as his residence.

4.   The following supplements are incorporated as part of this agreement:

		Other
☐ Structural Pest Control Certification Agreement	☐ Occupancy Agreement	☐ _________
☐ Special Studies Zone Disclosure	☐ VA Amendment	☐ _________
☐ Flood Insurance Disclosure	☐ FHA Amendment	☐ _________

5.   Buyer and Seller shall deliver signed instructions to the escrow holder within _____________ days from Seller's acceptance which shall provide for closing within________________ days from Seller's acceptance. Escrow fees to be paid as follows:

6.   Buyer and Seller acknowledge receipt of a copy of this page, which constitutes Page 1 of _______ Pages.

Buyer ____   Seller ____

Buyer ____   Seller ____

A REAL ESTATE BROKER IS THE PERSON QUALIFIED TO ADVISE ON REAL ESTATE. IF YOU DESIRE LEGAL ADVICE CONSULT YOUR ATTORNEY.

(86) Buy - Lease Back

As part of the sale, you may need a guaranteed tenant to cover the loan payments each month, and the Seller may need a place to stay - at least until he is ready to move to a new location. Most banks will give you better consideration for a loan if the property is already rented and the rent covers the monthly payments.

* Use a standard lease or rental agreement you can find at most stationary stores which have the clauses applicable in your State.

REAL ESTATE PURCHASE CONTRACT AND RECEIPT FOR DEPOSIT

THIS IS MORE THAN A RECEIPT FOR MONEY. IT IS INTENDED TO BE A LEGALLY BINDING CONTRACT. READ IT CAREFULLY.
CALIFORNIA ASSOCIATION OF REALTORS® (CAR) STANDARD FORM

____ , California. _____________________________ , 19__________

Received from ____
herein called Buyer, the sum of ________ -One Thousand- _________________________ Dollars $ 1,000 _______
evidenced by cash ☐, cashier's check ☐, or _____________________ ☐, personal check ☒ payable to_________

_______________________________ , to be held uncashed until acceptance of this offer, as deposit on account of purchase price of
________ -One Hundred Thousand- __________________ Dollars $ 100,000 ______

for the purchase of property, situated in _____________________________ , County of_______________________ , California,
described as follows: ____

1.   Buyer will deposit in escrow with _________ Escrow Company __________ the balance of purchase price as follows:

    *A.   Seller agrees to lease the property for $900 per
          month on a standard rental agreement. (Copy
          attached hereto)

    B.   (Other terms and escape clauses)

Set forth above any terms and conditions of a factual nature applicable to this sale, such as financing, prior sale of other property,
the matter of structural pest control inspection, repairs and personal property to be included in the sale.

2.   Deposit will ☐ will not ☐ be increased by $______________ to $______________ within______________ days of
acceptance of this offer.

3.   Buyer does ☐ does not ☐ intend to occupy subject property as his residence.

4.   The following supplements are incorporated as part of this agreement:

                                                           Other

☐ Structural Pest Control Certification Agreement   ☐ Occupancy Agreement   ☐ _________________________
☐ Special Studies Zone Disclosure   ☐ VA Amendment   ☐ _________________________
☐ Flood Insurance Disclosure   ☐ FHA Amendment   ☐ _________________________

5.   Buyer and Seller shall deliver signed instructions to the escrow holder within ___________ days from Seller's acceptance which
shall provide for closing within_________________ days from Seller's acceptance. Escrow fees to be paid as follows:

____

6.   Buyer and Seller acknowledge receipt of a copy of this page, which constitutes Page 1 of_________ Pages.

Buyer_____________________________________ Seller _____________________________________

Buyer_____________________________________ Seller _____________________________________

A REAL ESTATE BROKER IS THE PERSON QUALIFIED TO ADVISE ON REAL ESTATE. IF YOU DESIRE LEGAL ADVICE CONSULT YOUR ATTORNEY.